D1523920

KNIGHTS OF MALTA

Introduction by D. LawDog
Edited by C.V. Walter

Raconteur Press

Shield of Malta

Copyright © 2022 by Chris French

The Siege

Copyright © 2022 by By Brennen Hankins

CONTENTS

LAWDOG'S INTRODUCTION

Behold me: Gobsmacked.

And more than a bit humbled.

I knew we had enough stories for *Ghosts of Malta*, but in this modern world of 15 minute attention spans I really thought folks would have wandered on to whatever the latest hotness was before we would start collating stories for *Knights of Malta*.

Boy, was I wrong.

That little island of my birth has filled not one, nor two, anthologies, but is well on the way to a third and possibly fourth collection.

Wow. Just ... wow.

If you are a new Reader -- welcome! In your hands you hold stories about an obscure little archipelago in the middle of the Mediterranean which holds temples which were ancient when the Egyptians started stacking rocks at Giza, has been the centrepiece of Machiavellian intrigue, watched empires rise and fall, stood more than once against odds no sane man would have taken -- and dared defiance; dared to hold; dared to win.

1

Smugglers Hideout. Corsair's Roost. Crusader Bastion. Kings have marvelled at its streets, and emperors have been humbled at its walls. Knights, spies, smugglers, soldiers, merchants, future queens, mercenaries, kings, prophets, and restless men have all called it home, if only for a brief period.

An incredible place, like none other; rich in history, secrets, and blood.

American authors, most of whom had never even heard of the place, have all gathered, inspired by the history and stories of Malta, to gift you their visions of this magical place.

I hope that once you are done reading this little collection of ours that you will feel some of the wonder and devotion I have for that magical little island.

As always: All that is good and stirring about these stories is of the authors. Any errors are solely on me.

With that -- enjoy!

LawDog,

North Texas, 2022

SQUIRE DE SAINT-JEAN

E.C. RATLIFF

Malta, Fifth January, anno Domini 1366

I was fifteen, and I watched as a Crusade died.

It was Twelfth Night, as those of the English *langue* counted it. Tomorrow would be the Epiphany, when it was said the wise kings of the East and their knights came to honour the Christ-child. At home, it was a night of feasting and laughter. In the little churches there would be candles lit, and in the cathedrals, the bells would be roaring their song to the midnight hour.

A black night to have a feast, I thought, looking at the man on the cot.

A great knight was dying. Sir Guillaime de Vincent, a cousin of the Aragonese princes in Spain. The brothers by his side muttered paternosters endlessly, hoping against hope that he who had walked through plague and fire in France might yet live. Ever since the sack of Alexandria and our shameful retreat he had sickened, growing worse until...this. His mighty frame was wasted, blackened with a terrible burn from pitch and burning sand thrown from Alexandria's walls.

The room was hot and close, filled with murmurs and fear. I was serving my knight, the man who had brought me along the long march from Blackburn Abbey, merely three years before. Milord Henry, surname de Winne. His son was a sailor, or so he told me, but my lord was not. *Sir* Henry was the last of the great *chevaliers d'amor*, men who took on errantry for their lady…often to get away from those same ladies' husbands.

Ah, me, I digress. Suffice it to say that my Sir Henry had loved a woman well…and wrongly. It ended with the death of a husband and a wife, both of them loved by myself and my lord. In his grief, he volunteered to take the Crusade, hoping that he might cleanse his sins. His penance would be service to the Order. In the great retinue of my lord the archbishop Peter Thomas we had travelled from Avignon, serving under Ser Guillaume…and ended here, in Malta, an outpost of the Knights of Saint John. From here, one of the mightiest fortresses in all Christendom, we were to watch as all the hopes of the Crusade turned to ash.

At midnight that same night, I am told, my lord Peter Thomas died. In Famagusta, his body was raised to the heavens by a holy light. Not so with my lord Guillaime. He died hard, coughing and choking as his injuries filled his chest with blood. He had stayed alive long enough to get us here, bereft of money, but safe from the collapse of the armies. Already we of the Order were to shoulder the blame for the loss of the city.

As if carved of stone, Sir Henry knelt before the older knight, hoping for one last miracle. I saw his shoulders shake with grief, shuddering with a cold I could not feel. All of the clerics who knew the man wept openly, but Sir Henry could not condescend to such. He rose, his lean frame shadowing the shrunken priests, and turned on a heel. His spurs rang louder than the church bells in the silence.

4

"Squire, attend," Sir Henry ordered. His green eyes flared in a cragged face, black hair and beard salted with silver, his red donat's cote shining like flame in the dark. His right fist clenched at his empty swordbelt, his left hand wiping tiredly at his face. He strode out the door, black cloak billowing.

My name is Richard Tayler. Diccon to my mates, but to all else I'm Richard, the squire.

>>>>> <<<<<

"Come on, Richard," Sir Henry growled. "We must find the Pellegrine."

"That...pirate, sir?" I worried at my belt, feeling the lack of a sword keenly. "Would it not be better to leave on our own?"

Sir Henry stopped, his wolf-lean body almost hidden in the dark of the hall. "We must because we have no ship, no gold, and if we do not leave soon, will be caught up in...politics." He spat.

"I have no wish to see our holy endeavour turned into court dagger-play. Come."

We rushed through walks of a strong, white stone. Since we had been quartered with Ser Guillaime in the Castellum Maris, our beds were in the garrison tower. The place was imposing in the daylight, and I was well and truly spooked in the dark. Flames from torchlight made shadows jump and dance with every step.

The courtyards of the castle echoed, the granite blocks immovable as sin and twice as heavy. We were going out of the soldier's quarters, down, and back up to the citadel. It seemed Sir Henry wished we were less noticeable, sticking largely to shadowed walkways and corners. Milord De Winne walked at a brisk, official pace to fend off questioning. I followed, trying to keep up with the long stride of my knight and succeeding only in half-running.

"So," I puffed, trying not to show how weary I was. "We arrived on this rock a fortnight ago and you expect enough trouble by now that we need to hire a ship to get out? My lord…"

Sir Henry held up a hand, facing me fully for the first time. He looked like blood-drenched Death, hooded in his chapon and cloaked in black. The bones of his face stood out stark, and the moonlight made his swarthy features pale.

"We leave because there is more here than there appears. Guillaume was already dying by the end of the sack, but I have seen siege-wounds like his, lad. No sword pierced him at Alexandria. He should no' have died of a suckin' chest wound." My lord's anger thickened his Cornish accent, roughening his already basso growl.

"My friend has been *murdered*."

⤖ ⬿

Up we went, till we came to the receiving rooms of the castle. The Count of Modica, Manfredi Chiaramante, ruled this isle by law. His law was the extension of the King of Sicily, a fief granted to him by relation to the Aragonese.

In point of fact, though, the entire place was the possession of Giacomo de Pellegrino, a "trader" from Messina. Pirate, more like. Not a lord or a

6

knight as far as anyone I knew could tell. He held himself lord of Malta, at any rate, and not one of Malta's barons and knights ever seemed game to challenge him on it. He ruled well, being fair with taxes, never shorting other merchants, and he kept the pirates down. Other pirates, anyroad.

The Pellegrine was sitting by a window, watching a storm roll in over the harbour. It was a commanding view in the daytime, made strange by the play of wintertime fog and moonlight, and he sat with a cup of wine, perturbed not a whit.

A blunt, scar-cut face wrinkled by long days at sea was framed by silver hair, drawn back by some servant into a queue. Deep-set grey eyes twinkled over a wide nose and a broad mouth well used to laughter. His grin was rascallish over white teeth, framed by a blond-silver beard and broad moustache. His cote was green, his belt silver, shirt of the best linen, and he wore silk garters and tall black boots. I had not ever *seen* such extravagance except from the Byzantines.

So, of course, I *said* so.

"Ye look like a Constantinople whore," I blurted. Someday that will be the death of me, I know it.

I blanched, horrified. Sir Henry clapped his hand over his eyes, and I prepared to be gutted on the floor. That is, provided Sir Henry let me live. I could *feel* him glaring at me.

"Mihal's *bodkin*, boy," my knight muttered. I went redder than my cote, and tried my best to melt through the floor.

Giacomo de Pellegrino merely raised an eyebrow and threw his head back in a laugh, relaxed. "Oh, Enrico," he chuckled, "it is a shame to let a lad like this be scolded so. If every man in my crews were so honest...well, there would be half the men to pay, amico. And I'd be rich!"

He rasped another laugh, this time setting his cup on a table. Giacomo's hands clasped behind his back, becoming the picture of the thoughtful merchant. His eyebrows raised ironically.

"But, come, come, amico. Surely there is a reason a knight of the Order comes to my door in the dead of night, and on a feast day at that." He became more serious. "Be your master well?"

A muscle flexed in Sir Henry's jaw. He swallowed.

"Ser Guillaume is dead, Maestro Pellegrino."

The Pellegrine's eyes narrowed, his head tilted. "That is...unfortunate, Ser Enrico. Very, very unfortunate."

He moved across to a table, holding another cup for Sir Henry, who took it. Sir Henry gave little away on his face, but I thought I saw a flick of curiosity at the response. Whatever he had expected, this wasn't it. At a flick of my knight's eyes, I started, grabbing the jar to pour. I bowed, stepping aside.

"Be seated," Giacomo said softly. It was an order, not a suggestion. Sir Henry took a seat across from the sea-lord, and I made best to become invisible. Seen, not heard. For once. Giacomo sipped, a thoughtful expression upon his face.

"It is well known," he said, "that I make close accounting of all the comings and goings of this island. I assume that is why you are here." Again a statement. Lord Giacomo knew his position in this dance.

"It is well known, Maestro," Sir Henry nodded, sighing.

"We of the Order have depended upon your information before. If anyone could know-"

"*Silenzio!*" De Pellegrino held up a hand, suddenly still. Both Sir Henry and I froze. Rising, my lord Giacomo looked at us quietly, raising a finger

8

to his lips and moving to the window. He took the small dagger at his belt to hand and leaned out, looking nothing so much as a fisherman after a net. He stabbed down, and I heard a muffled shriek. *Someone at the window!*

There was a thud somewhere below him, I heard guards raising alarms and shouting down in the yards. Calmly, Lord Giacomo wiped his dagger blade with a bit of linen. He muttered something deeply offensive in Italian that I couldn't quite catch, and resheathed.

"Unfortunately, gentlemen," the pirate said, "I fear our correspondence is discovered. If you will come with me."

He reached into a chest, withdrawing a pair of daggers and a sword. The sword he tossed to Sir Henry, who caught it one-handed. One dagger he gave to me, the other, an evil-looking rondel, he tied to his own belt.

"I shall not have my guests slain under my protection," De Pellegrino said. "This is an offence that you will help correct." Sir Henry paused at this, and then nodded firmly.

"I will do so, and gladly." He buckled the sword about him and loosened it at the sheath. He blinked in surprise at the colour of the steel. "This is a fine blade, *signore.*"

"I...procured it from a ship bound for Alexandria," the silk-clad sailor grinned. "It's Toledo make." Both Sir Henry and I sucked in our breath at that. Toledo blades were a fortune in steel.

"Take it, my lord. I have *ten* of the like. The dagger, too, esquire."

A Toledo blade for *me*? I felt the heft of the dagger. It was almost a sword in itself, a triangular fang of steel half again the length of my hand from wrist to longest finger. The edge was bright white steel, clean and well-cared-for. It was the most valuable thing I had ever held.

"Thank you, my lord," I stammered. "We shall be in your debt." Sir Henry bowed.

"Well spoken, squire," Giacomo laughed. "Remember courtesy and silence cost nothing. It has served me well these many years."

Walking down into the yard below the window, we walked into a growing commotion. Alarm bells had rung, and the garrison was out about the walls, searching for threats. We came upon a silvery image in the moonlight. A group of three men surrounded a limp pile of clothing, where blood stained the stones. A fine wool cloak covered a body. One, bent over, was examining the corpse.

"Umberto, Gianni, what happened here?" Lord Giacomo barked. Two of the men straightened at the merchant-lord's tone. One was tall, fairly thin and bony, the other of average height but broadly built, with the strong shoulders of a smith or a mason. The third, more lithe than either, came up more slowly, holding a bloodstained cloak. The iron smell of a dead body was light, but noticeable.

"My lord," the taller guardsman said. His face was drawn with signs of weariness. He'd obviously been taking the middle watch, long wakefulness on a winter night, never an enjoyable chore. But on a feast day it were a painful annoyance, let me tell you. The other was more alert, and his eyes searched for threats and hands flexed on his weapons. The shorter man rushed to reply.

"M'lord Giacomo," he gruffed, "This man come down from a wall and crashed in front o' me without a sound. All I heard was a scream above me and then he were *there* at me feet."

"Calm yourself, Gianni," Giacomo soothed, "I'll not be hanging you for this, never fear."

The man visibly relaxed, blowing out a breath. "Alright, milord, alright. I saw none of what happened, but Umberto says 'e did, and I b'lieve him."

Umberto, the taller man, stretched out a hand to point to the window we had all been standing at not a few minutes before. "I heard a noise, thought it were a bird or some other beast rustling about, happens sometime. Dogs and the like, usually. But dogs don't be climbin' walls with a knife in their teeth."

At this, the guard presented a small blade, maybe half a hand long, wickedly pointed and obviously not some workaday tool. He handed it to Giacomo, who examined it carefully, and then tucked it into a sleeve. With far more than expert practice, I thought. Pirate.

"It's been fire-blackened," Sir Henry murmured to me. "Good for a night attack."

I nodded. I had not seen the like in my time as a squire, but Sir Henry had been a fighting man since the years before the Jacquerie, an era of such madness. Someone was out for killing Lord Giacomo. Sir Henry was convinced that Sir Guilliame had been murdered as well. Now the attempted assassin was dead.

Giacomo patted his guard on the back. "Indeed, Umberto. This dog was meant to rip his fang into me tonight. I gulled him from the window above."

The two guards looked up sharply, though the third figure only snorted softly, nodding as if to confirm a suspicion. I had yet to hear the third speak, and was extremely surprised to hear the voice of a lady. I had thought her a guard herself because of her mail coat, trews, and boots. Tall, for all that, near as tall as Umberto.

But.

"...a *girl*. In an *arming cote.*" I blurted.

The girl smiled, lips curling. "Not a girl, *boy*, a woman. Though you seemingly caught that I was clothed." She applauded ironically with fine gloved hands. Her eyes were a blazing, brilliant green, and they sparkled with mischief. Her hair was dark, black so deep it reflected blue in the moonlight, and suddenly her bearing was entirely different. Tall, assured...*noble*. I gulped, knowing I'd insulted someone for the second time that night.

"My squire is often impertinent," Sir Henry breezed between us. He bowed a courtesy, and in his best Norman French, excused me. "Such is the way of all young men before a beautiful lady. Especially one with no name." I blushed, thanking God and all the saints above for the darkness to hide it.

A full-throated laugh escaped the lady's throat. "Ah, the boldness of English knights," she answered in the same courtly French. "M'sieur, rest assured I have a name. No guest of Sieur de Pellegrino does not."

"Ah?" Sir Henry's manner changed as well, more animated and smooth. "Then may I have it?" He smiled in a way I had not seen in a long time, either. This was the courtly knight, not a serious donat of the Crusade. What was he playing at?

"M'sieur is charming," she replied, waving a hand, "but no, you may not."

"Ah, milady cuts my heart. *Le Belle Dame sans Nom* has no ring to it."

"Nonetheless, milord, such I must be for now." Her playful manner was cooling, but she *liked* the game. Her features were colder in this light, pale as the statues in old Rome, but I could almost see redness at her cheeks and a softening of those green eyes.

12

"For now?' An ease had settled into my lord's voice. "Then not forever."

"Nay, milord, not forever," She grew more serious, drawing herself more dignity. Her back straightened, and her face closed about the warmth she had let show just moments before. "I have business with my lord Giacomo. *Private* business," she said with finality.

"Private business that involves a sword and disguises," rumbled Sir Henry. Suddenly his manner was as forbidding as the rocks out in the harbour.

"Indeed, madame, that I can see." His arm swept toward Giacomo. "Do not permit me to bar your way, dear lady." Frustration made his voice a growl. The lady set her teeth and walked off, drawing Lord Giacomo away from us. Her posture was a dismissal. We were not welcome.

I was mystified; how these two could be playing at courtly love one moment and be so cold the next. Giacomo, for his part, seemed apologetic to us but drew off to speak to the lady. Sir Henry beckoned to me, moving toward the body.

"Look at him, Diccon," he said. "What d'ye see?"

"The body, sir, or Lord Giacomo?"

My lord raised a corrective hand, and I cringed. "All right, all right, Sir Henry."

I examined the body. Not a tall man, lean and hard muscled. Looked almost like one of the sailors I'd been talking to the day before. Death had twisted the sun-bronzed face into a rictus, crooked teeth open in a scream. A gory wound at the neck, still weeping some blood. Around his neck, soaked in the blood, there was a curious necklace...a copper bull's head, roughly made.

"Blood on his right hand, milord," I murmured. "Tried to stanch the bleed and fell from the wall, I expect." The two guards, who had kept silent during the exchange between nobles, came and looked, too.

"I'd say you're right, lad," said Gianni. The taller fellow, Umberto, looked back toward the wall, squinting. "Get a little light on that window with this torch," he said.

"There!" he pointed.

A bloody smear tracked to the ground, the top of which had five points like... "A handprint. Well, that settles that," I said. I felt satisfied. Problem solved.

"It settles nothing," said Sir Henry quietly.

Chapter Two

"Why shouldn't it, sir?"

I asked the question at almost a dead run, Sir Henry's cloak billowing past me with the fury of a winter wind. "Man gets a stab to his gizzard, he tries to save himself, falls and dies anyway," I puffed. "Could you slow down for *once*, y'great bloody Welsh racehorse!"

My lord stopped at a little alley, turning back with an eyebrow raised.

"A squire should attempt to be seen and not heard, save in battle, young Diccon." I ran to his side. Unbeknownst to me, he threw a foot out *just* so.

I tripped barefaced to the cobblestones, eyes streaming from the lack of air. "Next time, watch your feet, lad." He helped me to my feet, dusting me off none too gently. "And, I'm from *Cernew*. Cornwall to a john-come-lately *Norman*." He grinned. "Not that it matters much to Londoners. Ye couldn't tell a Gascon from a gallowglass. Those are Irish, by the by. Pirates mostly."

"I'm sorry, m'lord, I..."

"Ah, it is harsh I have been to you tonight, young Diccon. I need you to ask yourself a question. Why?"

"Why...what, my lord," I asked, shivering slightly. It was warmer than London would have been this time of year, but the air was still cool, it being January. It had felt like hours since we'd left Sir Giullaume's cot and the weeping priests with their warm candles. Though, looking at the climb of the moon, it truly had not been long at all.

"Why, on the same night that I discover one of the lords of the Crusade has been murdered, someone *else* tries to kill Giacomo de Pellegrino, a man who might as well rule Malta. 'Tis not as if Sicily nor the Spanish princes truly want it. It is too far away, the trade no real help to anyone's coffers. There are more pirates here than even the Genoese or the Venetians could put down, if they ever stopped killing each other long enough to care. Even the Order only uses this place as a safe port on the way to Rhodes or Cyprus."

"Put it that way, it makes no sense at all, milord."

"*Exactly*," Sir Henry hissed. "That is why we must find out."

"Weren't we trying to get out of Malta, sir?"

"Only because I thought I had no other choice," Sir Henry replied, "and that we were the target."

I studied my lord's face. "You don't think so any more, I take it." I sighed. This kind of thing never ended well. Avignon, that monastery in the Duchy of Milan, the brothel on the cheap side of London... "We're not going home at all," I accused.

"Nay, lad, that we're not."

The moon was well up and heading toward the wee hours of the morning, black shadows and white light mixing in ghostly dances punctuated by bright firelight from torches and windows. We were going to be skulking about in this murk all night, I could feel it. Thunder and blazes, had not we done enough this year?

"Murder has been done, assassination has been prevented," Sir Henry stated. "But I fear it will not end there. Giacomo de Pellegrino may be a pirate, but he keeps the sea-road safe for far more than just himself. If he is now in danger merely for helping us, it is our duty as Christian men and knights to aid."

" So, we stay close to the Pellegrine, then."

"Aye. We stay close to the Pellegrine."

We walked back to Lord Giacomo's side, who had not moved from his quieter conversation with the lady. Her hood was back up, her cloak hiding both mail and sword belt, and she almost looked something proper. I could finally see why my master had been so effortlessly courteous. Lord Giacomo, no shrinking cretin, was almost muffled in the natural poise of the lady, her bearing far more high court and telling than anything she spoke. She demanded nothing.

She merely commanded, and men obeyed.

She finished her conversation, it seemed, and snapped her fingers. Giacomo nodded, and the two guards, Umberto and Gianni, and several more, simply appearing from the shadows of the street, followed her through a covered walkway out of our little courtyard into the night.

"You will meet her again," Lord Giacomo spoke, turning to me. "That lady is not done with any of us yet." He snorted. His piratical nature was too much a part of him to be hidden very long. "Come, I must take you to where it is safe for all of us."

We took little notice of the folk at their revelry, the taverns and suchlike starting to quiet with the late hour, but the likelihood of our being noticed was lessened. More people in for a drink was less to see us about. I caught myself remembering Venice. Now *that* was a party. No worry about a knife in my gullet even if I was getting chased by five men with stout clubs. Ahh, Venice.

Sir Henry, on the other hand, seemed ready for a good war. He had tied his sword close and loosed it a finger at the scabbard, well prepared for a fight. I should have known better. Expecting no fights at the side of Sir Henry De Winne is expecting the sun not to rise.

We kept going into the castle, and down. *Very* far down.

"My lord," I joked, lamely, "If you wished to throw me in a dungeon for my remarks earlier this evening, you might as well have said."

Giacomo laughed. "Nay, young Ricardo, it is no dungeon. I always knew I would need a place myself and my men to bolt if the Sicilians came calling. They *do* own the island, after all, and in the end I find I am less inclined to keep it, should they insist." He gestured grandly.

"Then, I found this place."

The room opened widely, the ceiling suddenly far above us. An open space like a great chapel, it even had steps and a broad area where an altar would be in a church. But the shape was all wrong. Rougher, less formed. There was no cross-piece, no candles, no giltwork...but there was a statue of a woman. Tall as a small tree, she stood behind the altar, winged, crowned

17

with a bull's horns. In her right hand she held a sword. In her left, there was a sheaf like arrows...no, not arrows.

"Wheat." Sir Henry said. "She's carrying a kingsheaf o' wheat. I tied enough at harvest to know."

"Is she some Roman work, my lord?"

Sir Henry considered, looking back at Giacomo, who shrugged. "I am no educated man," Giacomo replied, "But I have been to Rome, and none of her many statues look so roughly done. I have seen the Demeter who carries a staff of grain, sometimes a sickle, but never have I seen a sword."

"She is some older goddess, then," Sir Henry stated. "There are men in the little villages and towns all over England that tie reeds together in a shape much like her. I took no hand in it." I blinked at my master curiously.

"It never... felt right." He sounded defensive, which was not like him. A curious revelation.

I looked back at the altar, which seemed darker than before. Something drew me to the face of the statue. I felt I was being looked at...examined, more like. The eyes were the deep blankness of old stone, but if I could just see past the shadows...Only to be snapped out of my reverie as Sir Henry spoke.

"Whoever... whatever she was, let her be forgotten, *gentilhommes*. Something about her is...hungry."

"Turn away, lad." His voice was suddenly sharp, the shape of his face strained with a superstitious awe. He gripped his sword hilt, making a cross over himself. "We know not of her, and must not try to know."

I looked back. I just wanted one more look. The stone lady seemed to be smiling, a quiet, welcoming look that a matron might give her son. Surely that could not be any sin. I heard a laugh, and felt one in my own throat. I could sit at her feet, I thought. It'd be safe here.

"Oh, look at her, my lord. She's harmless."

"Then why does she carry a sword, boy?" A different voice broke through. I fell, quite literally, out of my spell, striking my head on the floor. I needed to consult an astrologer. It must have been fated for me to fall on my face this night...not to mention see stars. The room spun, but I recognized the voice.

It was the voice of the lady in the street!

"Your master is right, young man," she declared. "Astarte is no goddess for Christian men to love." Her palm came up as if to ward off a blow, and I saw a spark like starlight between her fingers. I must have hit my head harder than I had thought. The light hurt, though, and that bell sound...

The lady's voice rose in a song that sounded like a hymn, but not church Latin nor Greek like the men of Constantinople use, and sudden light flared like noonday, enough to make me shield my eyes. I had sense enough to try to draw my dagger, but it too reflected the light in a thunderbolt, blinding me painfully. I heard another woman scream, cursing in some language I had never heard before, and Sir Henry roar a battle cry to Saint Michael. I felt, more than saw, his sword strike stone. Stone shattered, a wall fell, and I knew nothing more.

Up...up. I must get up, I thought. "UP!" a voice commanded. I figured that if I could remember who it was attached to I would. Could not seem to move, though, and I was tired, so tired. I had not gone to the weaver's yet, I thought sleepily. Father would be angry.

"Comin', father. I'm comin'." I murmured. Then I blinked. My father had been dead ten years that last autumn.

"What in God's name-" I roared. I could feel hands on me, and I tried hard to shake them off. I came awake with a snarl, dagger in my fist.

"Slowly, slowly, Diccon." There stood the lady, covered in dust from head to foot, green eyes framed by that same sable hair, her skin a near perfect white. Her lips were redder than last I had seen, and there was a light about her, like starlight.

"You are very weak, my boy," she said. "Do not allow yourself to stumble again in future."

"Stumble? What, I don't-" a hand was on my shoulder and I whirled. Sir Henry pulled me into an embrace, crushingly strong. If anything, I was even more shocked by this. I saw tears in his eyes as he looked at me. He was covered in dust, his hair almost white with it, and bleeding from a cut above his brow. His new sword, the Toledo blade, was still in his hand, but now it had a dint in its true-edge. I was going to be expected to fix that, I thought crossly.

"I thought I had lost you, boy," he croaked hoarsely. He kissed my head, embracing me again, and I sputtered.

"What in blue blazes–," I coughed, choking. It was the dust, surely. Just the dust. I was not cursing my lord to his face. I would never.

"My lord, this is unseemly," I tried again. It was the best I could do to summon back some of my dignity.

"What just happened?"

Sir Henry took a breath, wiping his eyes. "You nearly died, for one thing, lad. I lost you for an hour. It is nearly dawn." The lady walked serenely over to us both, laying a soft hand upon Sir Henry's shoulder.

"It was not merely his life that was in danger, *Henri*," she said. Making familiar with my lord's name. That was odd, but I was becoming used to consternation tonight.

"*Richard*," she pronounced my Christian name in the French manner, I noted, "Tonight your soul was at peril. You wandered paths men are forbidden, and had I not been here...well, it is best not to talk of it in darkness."

I wanted to object, but I heard the laughter again...and in my mind I saw eyes with the blankness of night in a face more beautiful than the sea, lips dripping blood and tongue lolling. The statue. That...thing in the altar. I shuddered, but I could not tell if it was horror...or a desire to see it again. "I just wanted to see..." and felt myself weeping. I wiped my eyes angrily.

Something softened in the lady's eyes. "Yes, young one. *Her* touch, above all, inspires such things. Even Blessed Solomon the King could not stay her blandishment, and it led to much mourning for all his house. Come, on your feet."

I rose, feeling the world turn about me, and tried to walk a step. My knees buckled, but I caught myself, with the lady's aid. She touched the back of my neck with a hand and I felt cold, *blessed* cold, shock me awake.

"God's *bones*," I shuddered. "What was *that*?"

The lady smiled secretly, putting up her hood once again. Her chuckle was music as she walked ahead.

"That, too, will need to wait for another time," I heard Sir Henry suddenly beside me. "For now I know what we are here for."

Lord Giacomo was at the furthest end of the chapel...no, I thought. A temple. A pagan temple, at that. His face and clothes were as battered as we, and his rondel was stained with something dark and dripping. Whatever had gotten on the other end of that tonight, they had gone away either bleeding or dead, I was almost certain.

"One day, dear lady," he said, ignoring the rest of us, "I will know what business it is you are in." He held up a hand. "Do not think of telling me now. I have never before seen such a night, and I will not speak of it ever again save in the light of day."

"That, I think, is for the best, my lord," said Sir Henry. "My master was well bound in our lady's business, and it ended in his death." He bowed to the lady. "But it was not her fault. I can see it now."

At this Lord Giacomo raised an eyebrow. "Enrico!," he chided. "Sir Guillaume, a cousin to the princes of Aragon, is murdered, and you suspected an unknown lady you had just met that night? Why not myself? I have no love for the Spanish lordlings, and they, no love for me."

"With respect, my lord," said Sir Henry, "No. Sir Guillaume was as reliant upon your sources of information as any of us in the Order. He chose this place because it was a fortress, well away from the *routiers* and the politics of the Crusader lords at our home at Rhodes. We were here to hide, and you were to hide us. But we were also here for another reason." Sir Henry nodded to the lady.

"It is not my place to speak that."

The lady removed her hood, suddenly as clean and collected as if she had just stepped from a bath, not done...well, anything that had happened this night.

"Lord Giacomo, myself and the Sisters must keep our business secret most *especially* in days of war, and when in contact with merchants, one never knows what might slip out. Ser Guillaume was sworn to me, and to keep us from harm. It was his preparation that saw us safe from Alexandria months ago, and I thank you, as well."

"I, lady?" replied Giacomo, idly cleaning his dagger. "You are welcome to all you desire from me, but you have yet to ask."

"Your hospitality alone, Giacomo," said the lady, "that was more than enough. Fleeing a city soon to be sacked was taxing upon even the stoutest hearts, and many of my folk are frail."

"But," sighed Giacomo, "my hospitality did not prevent that goodly knight from being murdered on his deathbed." His face grew more stern and deadly.

"And I myself have escaped the Reaper more than twice this night. You will explain." he commanded.

"*Si, maestro,*" she replied in Italian, "I owe Sir Henry such as well. I am a Sister of Solomon, of the chapterhouse of Alexandria and the Library. We are...nuns, after a sort, though I myself have not taken holy orders. I, like Sir Henry, am a *donat*. We were instructed by His Excellency Bishop Peter Thomas to flee our ancient home, and Ser Guillaume and his retinue were to be our surety."

"But then my master took his injury at the west gate, nearly dying," filled in Sir Henry. He grew thoughtful. "You were well out of the city. He spent himself to get here, to ensure his mission. Still nameless."

"Yes, Sir Henry," sighed the lady...the sister, I suppose now I should say. "Though not nameless. Ye have seen my power, the least I can do is give that." She straightened, gathering up a stillness about herself. "I am Catherine, once Baroness D'Hiverne, but I am more of the Order now than I am of that family."

"But," I could not help but blurt, "*what* are you? That light, that noise, the statue...and what does this have to do with our captain?"

I was tired, confused, and my head was still swimming like after a cup of strong wine. I wanted *something* to make sense, and not a thing was. I was still half convinced I was dreaming.

"I cannot answer all of your questions at once, young squire, but as to what I am, that is simple. I am an enchantress."

Lord Giacomo nodded, as if confirming something. Sir Henry seemed startled, but more at me than at the lady. Lady Catherine, now. I was having none of it.

"A witch," I snorted. "There's no such thing. I knew a witch in England. She were a toothless old grandmother with bad eyes and a worse temper. Nothing more."

"Witch, I agree," Lady Catherine allowed, "Is an ill term to describe it. I am, certes, no withered hag," she stated, preening slightly.

"So, what? Some peddler selling love potions and scrying at crystal balls?"

The lady laughed. "Assuredly not, young sir. Crystals are useless stone. Pretty, but useless."

She thought to herself, weighing her words. "What was it the Greeks called it...ah, *magos*. Magi, after the great Solomon and the Three Kings. We are not hedge peddlers selling smoke bundles and muttering at bones, as the pagans do. Still less am I that worse kind."

"Worse kind?" I asked. "Sir Henry, what is she talking about?"

"A worse kind, indeed, boy." said Sir Henry. "I would sooner leap into fire wearing cloth draped in oil than face that again. You were not with

24

me yet." Something dark passed behind his eyes. "Fool that I was," he muttered.

"There is a worse kind, yes." said Lady Catherine solemnly. "These make covenants. Some with old, forgotten, gods like Astarte." *That wicked smile again.*

"Others," she said, with her voice hollow, "with the Fallen Star himself." She crossed herself, and that same silver light followed her hands as she signed it. "*Vade retro condemnator, vade retro interfector, vade retro qui decipetur, Satanus.*"

"*Amen*" replied both Sir Henry and Lord Giacomo. I crossed myself, unthinkingly.

"Ser Guillaume came to me in August of this previous year, hoping to find lodging places for you and your...sisters," Giacomo said. "He and I had known each other for many years, often as a neutral go-between for myself and the Aragonese. And the Kingdom of Sicily, for that matter. A knight-captain of the Order of Saint John is a useful friend for any man," he grinned.

"I can only assume he was killed due to...*that*."

We all looked away from the shattered pile of stone at our feet. Lady Catherine, I was surprised to see, had tears in her eyes. "Guillaume was killed to keep me from discovering this place. A deity of slaughter and fertility is exactly what our enemies would seek to raise during a Crusade."

Sir Henry paced. He was thinking furiously, I could tell, trying to find a connecting thread in all of this. I had long since given up. A crusader lord, witches, a lost god I had never even heard of, and a murder. It made less sense than the mummer's plays I saw on the hangman's square in London. He suddenly stopped, stricken like a thunderbolt.

25

"*Famagusta.*" He swore, loudly and violently. "The Lord Bishop Thomas was going to *Famagusta!* He is there *now!*"

Lady Catherine seemed just as stricken, pale with fear. "He knew. That is why he sent us here."

"Not only did he know," Sir Henry growled, counting off points with his fingers, "he intended that Guillaume be here to support you, for Lord Giacomo, no friend to the Cypriotes but no enemy either, to house you, and for the Order itself to assist you. But with Guillaume dead and unable to give me his orders..." he let the thread hang. He sat down on a carved step, taking up his sword, shaving away his frustrations with every pass of the whetstone. His voice grew calmer, more venomous.

"This debacle of a Crusade has already been a three-day wonder to all of Christendom. A band of *routier* and greedy barons riding Peter de Lusignan's trail, hoping for loot. Half the men I led at the West Gate had no idea there were Christians in the city itself, not that they cared. I killed more men wearing St. George's cross the second night than I did *ghulami*, and I hated them worse."

I remembered. Fire, the screams of women, and shrieks of men disembowelled, a sword in my fist for the first time. A blade coming down, my shield up, pushing forward into a Flemish knight's face. Sir Henry's poleaxe tore the head from his shoulders, and I tasted iron. Blood, blood like...*like was on the lips of the goddess*. I recoiled.

"They," I felt my gorge rising. "They wanted...*that*?" I coughed, which became a wretch. A thousand images of blood and flame washed over me like a rolling tide. I could *taste* the horror of Alexandria's sack, the smell of the soot, hearing Sir Giullaume's scream as the burning sand mixed with pitch was thrown from the wall before the assault on the gate...

"We were...we were supposed to be fighting for God! For Christ and the church!" I shouted, looking desperately at my master's face, searching for some sign of a lie.

"I was going to be a *knight*," I fell to my knees. Unashamedly, my master embraced me. He cradled me like a small child.

"Oh, lad, no," his sorrow was plain as stone, "No, this was not your doing, no, shhh."

He stood me before him, looking me in the eye. "Listen to me, Richard." He gripped my shoulders like iron.

"Diccon, listen to me," he said fiercely. "The things we did, that we had to do to *save* lives, were not your fault. *Alexandria* was not your fault. The madness was... was demonic. Men driven by greed and lust, and foolish, petty pride. It did not make them knights. It was not what will make you a knight."

I started. Sir Henry smiled.

"What will *make* you a knight," he repeated. "Is understanding that what they were doing was *wrong*. It was evil, unworthy, and born of wicked desires. We are men of arms, certainly," he held up a hand to still my objection.

"We are not men of *blood*. Nor is knighthood born of the flesh. Bishop Peter and I discussed this often, and Sir Guillaume, too. What makes a knight different from the bandit on the road? Why is he something more than a common killer?"

"Master, I do not *know*," I wailed.

"A knight is sworn to defend that which the men of blood seek to possess, young squire." Lady Catherine's cool, low voice broke in, surprising us both. "As Blessed Michael struck the great Dragon to the Earth in the time before Adam, so knights strike at the same devourers and liars, the murderers, thieves and worse, who have taken up Satan's cause even if they do not bow to his throne."

"This war was not fought for God, boy," Sir Henry declared. "It was fought so that Famagusta could enrich itself beyond the reach of Great Alexandria, free from competition. It was Mammon, not Christ, who marched before the men of the West Gate." He sighed.

"King Peter is a goodly knight, the very best of us. But his barons wanted none of the costs of a war and all of its rewards." He nodded to the lady. "I think you know what I mean, Lady Catherine."

"Aye, Sir Henry," continued Lady Catherine. "There were Christians enough to shame Our Lord at Alexandria, and God will curse them, but...there was a reason we were ordered to leave. Some of those brought along were no Christian men at all."

"Nor did they even aspire to the nobler old gods of the Danes or the Greeks. They wanted power, gold, and prowess in battle. After that, fine sons to make them look strong. Fine women." Her hands traced more of that fearful light, making shapes in the air.

"Astarte is such a power. Her followers are gifted with might like bulls." Men wearing bull's horns danced in circles about ghostly, beautiful women, who had cruel faces and jaded eyes.

"Women, too, are gifted. Beauty beyond earthly charms, bodies ripe, golden as the sheafs in harvest."

"No man who swears to Astarte will not be slaked by the women in her thrall, and their bedding will make sons, always sons. The daughters..."

"The daughters are fed to Astarte's sacred flames." Lady Catherine spat. "Or worse, her consort, the Saturn of Bulls."

The light coalesced to a blurrily drawn shape like a bull, but also like a man...and with the most obscene traits of both.

"Do not dwell too long on the face of that one," she cautioned, "A wickeder demon there is not in Hell." The shapes twisted and melted with a snap of Lady Catherine's finger, disappearing.

"But what does this have to to do with the murder? Who killed Sir Guillaume?" I asked.

Lady Catherine sighed. "I do not know, but without him, my folk are in danger. It was our duty to find and snuff out this cult that had so infiltrated the Crusade."

"Rest assured," Sir Henry replied, "I believe it my duty in my lord's absence to protect you and your folk, Lady Catherine. As to the murder..." Sir Henry motioned Lord Giacomo to his side. "Lord Giacomo, I came to you earlier this evening for information, when we were rudely interrupted."

"Indeed." The pirate smiled, "And I think you will find it most illuminating to note that I have discovered the murderer's weapon."

Sir Henry and I looked at him curiously. Giacomo silently withdrew the same slim dagger he had taken from the corpse of his own would-be assassin. "*Perfetto.* Your description to me of the wound you discovered matches this weapon perfectly. I have seen this style in Italy, especially Genoa. A small knife, easily hidden in a sleeve...or a robe. One of your brothers is not so fraternal, eh?"

"The monks!" I exclaimed. "One of the attendant monks killed a lord of the Crusade?"

"Not a monk, no," Lord Giacomo stated, dropping an item into Lady Catherine's hand. "I think this is what you were looking for, my lady."

In her hand, the lady held the necklace with the brazen copper bull's head. Astarte's bull, the Saturn of Bulls, she had called it. Lady Catherine nodded, her eyes flashing rage.

"Men shall die for this."

⇶ ⥽

That, sirs, was my introduction to Sister Catherine of the Order of Saint Solomon. Woe betide the man who wakes the flame in those eyes. I knew not what adventures awaited me in her train from that night on, and that was merely the beginning, but I would take what God set before me. I am Richard Tayler, and I write this chronicle in the hope that our sacrifices and deeds be not forgotten as that statue once was. I sign this Richard, squire de Saint-Jean. *Given to the hand of Fra. Joseph de Venne, knight brother of the Hospitallers of the Order of Saint John of Jerusalem, Rhodes, and Malta.*

NYCTOPHOBIA

TUVELA THOMAS

Nyctophobia: fear of the dark

Cleithrophobia: fear of being trapped

Mazeophobia: fear of being lost

Monophobia: fear of being alone

I love caves, always have. My parents took me to Carlsbad Caverns and ever since, I can't get enough. It's the best when I get to explore newly discovered passages. Maybe I'm the first one to see a stalactite or set foot in a passage. Okay, it's not always quite that neat. I might be getting that feeling of exploring uncharted territory only to trip over a Bud Light can. And then, I have to laugh at myself.   Anyway, it's an adventure, even if someone's been there before.

Lots of people get spooked by the dark, the echoes, or the thought of millions of tons of rock hanging over their heads. But none of that has ever bothered me. It's a little odd that I'm feeling nervous about this cave in Malta. It's awesome that I get to travel. And I'm getting paid for it! The family matriarch died and all the grandkids went over to the family house to start splitting up the estate. They found a door that no one in the family had known was there. Lo and behold: a cave is on the other side of the door. The Cardona family wants to make a little attraction out of it. They're talking about a bed and breakfast with cave tours. Chris and I are going to survey the tunnels and see if it's safe for tourists.

You hear about this in other places with Karst topography, of course. When tons of caves are around people incorporate them into their root cellars (or whatever). And why not? They're the same temperature all year round. Plus, it's square footage you didn't have to build.

The Maltese islands are giant chunks of limestone plunked down in the Mediterranean. The wind, waves, and rain have had their fun and made caves all through the place. Imagine an island made out of swiss cheese and you've just about got the idea. Then, mankind got in on the action and added tunnels and shafts. So, this has been a thing for the locals to use the caves for God-knows-what for centuries.

The family contacted my friend (and former professor), Chris Erikkson, who has been studying and writing papers on the caves of the Mediterranean for years. He asked me to come along and help with the survey. I couldn't say no. We're going to be worming our way through a cave that hasn't been visited in ages. And there's no telling what we'll find either. There could be anything down there (or nothing but dead ends and damp). Maybe the old broad used the cave for a trash chute. There's a cave in Missouri that was used as a crypt for the family farm dogs for seventy years. Yeah, don't worry, that one's not open to the public. But I was able to sweet talk them into accepting a fee so I could visit for scientific purposes. For an additional fee, they gave me dog biscuits to leave at the markers. That was fun to write into the grant proposal, let me tell you.

I am really excited about this trip. But wouldn't you know it? I'm just the least bit worried. This is the kind of cave that makes me nervous. It's not the cave itself; we'll take it easy and be careful. The thing that gives me the heebie jeebies is the unknown of who else might be down there. It's not like there's some organizational grid for the tunnels to follow. For all we know it's open to other passages to other homes and hidey holes. But, hey, the money is decent and I get a new stamp in my passport.

⋙⋙ ⋘⋘

I scooped up my backpack at the oversized luggage in baggage claim. I know it makes me look like a hostel-stooping college student, but I love my pack. I can shove so much stuff in there. Chris was waiting for me as I left the customs hall. He's six foot and lean with blonde curly hair and dimples when he smiles. He has that tan and slightly weathered look of a man who works and plays a lot outdoors. Chris grinned when he saw me and I knew that the little crush I'd had on him in my school days was still intact. "That pack is bigger than you are." he teased. He pulled me close for a hug.

"It's been too long," I say. "It's been over a year since the conference."

"What have you been up to since then," I ask.

We chatted comfortably for several minutes as we walked out into the parking lot where a car waited. It was a short and narrow Euro CarThing. It would be comical in America, but appropriate given that the old streets here were originally meant for horse-drawn vehicles. "Oh hey, you found a car that's my size," I quipped. One of the reasons people like to go spelunking with me is because I'm petite. I'm a five foot tall skinny blonde. If I say the squeeze is too tight, you damn well better believe me.

"Maggie, this is Elias Cardona."

I smiled at the man standing next to the car, "Hi Elias, nice to meet you." We shared a firm handshake. The driver is a man of middling height and dark hair, dark eyes. "Nice to meet you," he said in a lightly accented English.

"Elias has agreed to show us around and take us to his family home where we will be staying."

We all pile into the car with only one hang up. Chris offered to let me ride shotgun, so I hopped into the right front seat. I found myself looking at the steering wheel instead of the dashboard. I looked at it, blinking a moment, and then laughed at myself. Elias grinned and held out the keys, "Do you want to drive?" I laughed again and clambered over to the left side.

"I forgot you drive on the left side of the road here."

"That's alright," Elias reassures me. "You can drive when you're not jet-lagged."

"Where are we headed?" I ask

"We'll go to the house in Birkirkara. It was my grandmother's until she passed last month. But it has been in our family for over two hundred years."

"I'm sorry about your grandmother," I said.

"She was a good woman and loved by all." Elias downshifted and continued, "While we were cleaning the house, my cousins found a doorway in the basement. You will see. Many of the children wanted to play inside. My aunt Maria got the idea that we should use it as income for the maintenance of the house."

"And so you contacted Chris," I said.

"Aunt Maria has big plans to open our home to tourists. Not everyone in the family approves of this."

"Well, why not," I asked.

He thought that over for a minute before answering, "Families are complicated."

"Don't I know it," Chris replied.

I settled in for the rest of the ride. Most of the buildings were made of limestone, the color of warm sand. The streetscape had a feeling of confinement I nearly found repressive. Steep walls met flat roads with sharp unforgiving edges. Life revealed itself in the bright colors of the doorways: cobalt, fire engine red, teal, and cheerful jade green. An abundance of plants on window ledges and peeping out of pots by the doors further relieved the monotony. As we made our way across the island, I began to see beauty and soul in the architecture.

We were welcomed warmly by Aunt Maria and Elias's mother, Roberta. I fell into the single bed that night with a full tummy and a buzz. I was asleep the instant my head touched the pillow. And then I woke up a few hours later. Grumbling about the time change, I got up groggily and searched for a bathroom. After the necessities, I filled my water bottle and washed down a couple of antihistamines. I crawled back into the bed, pulled the covers over my head, and prayed to any power listening that I would be able to get back to sleep.

Apparently, someone upstairs was listening, because it was several hours before I woke up again. I pushed myself up. Sunshine was streaming through the cracks in the eyelet lace curtains. I took a long pull from my water bottle to chase off the dehydration of air travel and drinking. My room was small but comfortably furnished with a desk and an ancient office chair with brass casters. Someone had thrown a woven blanket over the seat to hide the springs that were attempting to poke through the worn green leather. The bed creaked as I got up and got dressed. I could smell coffee downstairs.

Chris grinned from the heavy wooden kitchen table where we had all shared dinner last night. Elias's mother handed me a large plate of scrambled eggs and poured a mug of coffee for me. I mixed in sugar and milk and drank deeply. The eggs were wonderfully fluffy and buttery. They disappeared with a rapidity that bordered on the embarrassing. "So," Chris said, "Are you feeling human yet?"

"Almost." One more cup of coffee and we were ready to start. Chris and I went down a couple of sets of narrow stairs into a storage space. A large wooden hope chest sat to one side of a half height door.

"There were blankets and baskets stored on top of the chest. Once they started sorting things out down here, they found the door," Chris explained.

"Was it sealed," I asked.

"Yes and no. It was painted shut. It took a palette knife and a little elbow grease to get it open."

We opened the door and peered in. There was an old wooden step just inside and a tunnel carrying off to the left. With my flashlight, I could just make out a turning 30 feet away. The height of the passage would let me walk upright; Chris would have to crouch. Chris spoke up at my elbow, "Don't trust that first step, it's rotten. I'll ask Elias to remove it. I think

36

it was a natural tunnel that's been widened. I only went as far as that first turn yesterday. Let's get our kit and see how far we can get. Elias is bringing a fan to help with the circulation."

Chris and I met again at the half door about a half hour later. Elias smiled warmly when he saw me in my overalls and carrying my helmet. He was arranging a fan near the entrance. "I tried to move the step, but it fell apart in my hands. It is swept to the side for now," he explained.

I pat him on the arm as I maneuver my way through the small door and down into the tunnel.

"Thanks, Elias."

"How long will you be," he asked.

"Two hours," Chris answered. "More or less."

Elias nodded and looked at his watch to mark the time.

And we were off. I had a thrill of exhilaration. By all indications, no one had been down here in decades. My heart beat a little faster as we crouched and walked to the first turn. We flipped on our headlamps and flashlights. The tunnel zigged and zagged and we came to a chamber. I stopped and played my lights around. It was roughly ten feet by twenty with a fifteen foot ceiling. There were indications that the space was largely natural, though the floor had been smoothed. We examined the floors and saw long rectangular discolorations. Chris pointed at them, "It looks like this may have been used as storage at some time."

"That would make sense," I agreed.

After the floors, we walked the perimeter looking for branching tunnels. I was praying that this wouldn't be the end. There had to be an outlet, didn't there?

We found two branches. One quite narrow trending down and then one near the ceiling of the storage chamber. We took measurements and noted them in our field book. Down the narrow tunnel it twisted and turned for what seemed a long time. We had to take off our packs and slide through sideways for parts. Finally, we came to a chamber the size of a small closet. I struck a match from my pack and held it in front of me. The flame burned brightly. I smiled at Chris, "We should turn around soon; we told Elias we'd be a couple of hours." We drank our water and discussed the tour possibilities.

"You know that narrow part could be quite fun for people wanting an adventure."

"Yeah! It's a good, easy start," I answered.

"We should turn around now and double check for branches as we go," Chris asked.

"Sure, we need to ask the family about getting a ladder down here, so we can check out that higher tunnel in the Storage Chamber."

"Good idea," Chris said from ahead of me. He was having a harder time fitting through this narrow bit than I was, so he was setting the pace. "So, are you seeing anyone?"

I mulled that for a moment, "I've been dating an EMT off and on for a few months. It's not serious."

Chris looked back and grinned, "Scheduling issues?"

"His hours don't help. And his sense of humor is... darker than this cave."

Chris laughed, "I hear that comes with the job."

"What about you? Are you seeing anyone," I asked nonchalantly. At least, I hoped it sounded nonchalant.

"No one special."

I bit my lip to keep myself from grinning like an idiot. We walked on in silence until we got back into the storage chamber. We checked the height of the other tunnel we wanted to check out. "A ten foot ladder should do the trick"

"Three meters," said Chris, "for our Maltese friends."

"Oh, yes. Right hand drive and the metric system. We aren't in Kansas anymore."

"Here. Climb up on my shoulders," he stated, "you can get a better look".

"Let's do that next trip if they can't get us a ladder right away. We've been a little longer than we said."

"Alright." Chris sounded disappointed, but I shrugged it off. I didn't want to worry our hosts and have them start to think that this whole tour thing was a bad idea. I was enjoying my work and I didn't want to get sent home early.

We left our kit in the basement and headed up to the kitchen. Aunt Maria was bustling around making soup. I was sure it was big enough to feed an army. The smells of onion and herbs made my stomach rumble.

"How was it," she asked.

"It's going well. We'd like to borrow a ladder for our next trip down."

"Of course. ELIAS!" she bellowed.

He came tramping down the stairs into the kitchen. He looked at us, his watch, and nodded. "You are well? Do you need something?"

Chris answered, "We'll need a ladder when we go back down in a couple of hours. Maybe about 3 meters?"

"I can find something. You should eat. Aunt is the best cook in the family, but don't tell my mother I said that."

Maria was already pouring piping hot soup into bowls for them. They sat at the rough hewn table. She brought over a tray of bread and softened butter, "*Kul, kul*. Eat. You must keep up your strength."

While they were eating a large orange tom cat sauntered into the dining area from the kitchen. His amber eyes took in the scene and he uttered a "mrrt". I smiled and put my hand down where he could see it.

"Careful," Chris warned, "he bit me yesterday."

I brought my hand back up and continued eating. "Mrrt" is the only warning I got before 17 pounds of cat landed in my lap, settling immediately and anchoring himself with claws. I 'oofed' a bit and looked down. He returned my gaze and blinked slowly. "I think I've been claimed," I laughed nervously.

"He seems to like *you*," said Chris.

"Maybe he just doesn't like men."

Aunt Maria came in at just that moment and took in the scene. "Bah, cats! Elias, come get your mongrel!"

"Oh, it's okay, I don't mind. He's cozy," I assured her. Aunt rolled her eyes and said something in Maltese and returned to her domain in the kitchen. Chris and I shared a laugh.

"Do you suppose this is chicken in the soup," I asked.

"It might be. Or, it might be rabbit."

"I'll just pretend it's chicken," I said. The cat was still in my lap, overflowing the edges, twenty minutes later. Elias reappeared from the door to the basement.

"I've got your ladder," he said.

"Great," I said, "Uh, can you get this cat off my lap. He's sort of... attached."

Elias' eyebrows perked upward and he smiled to see the tom lounging across my legs. "The nice lady has work to do; you need to let her get up now." The tom looked Elias dead in the eye and hissed. "Yes, I see. You like the lady. But, Maggie needs to go explore the caves now." Elias came up close and gently unhooked the claws from my coveralls. The cat hissed again and then jumped up onto the table and began lapping up what was left of my chicken (I hope it was chicken) soup. Elias spoke to the cat, "You'll get in trouble for being on the table." He moved the bowl to the floor. "There now. I'll be the one to get in trouble with Aunt."

We made sure to visit the bathroom before we went back down. While I waited my turn Elias tapped my arm and asked, "How is it you know the air is safe?"

"Good question. We use matches or lighters to make sure there's enough oxygen.

"Ah, well in that case," he said. He pulled a lighter out of his pocket. It was a chrome Zippo with a brass figure on the side.

"Thanks," I said, "I've been using matches. Who is this on the side?"

"He is St. Benedict. He lived in a cave; He will protect you."

"Wow. Thank you," I said. I tucked the lighter into a zipper pocket on my coveralls. I wasn't sure what else to say. No one has given me a saint-bearing zippo before. "I'll make sure to get him back to you when we're done."

Elias smiled and his eyes seemed to spark. I wondered if there was more than helpfulness on his mind. I wasn't even sure how old he was. There was a touch of grey sprinkled in his black hair at the temples, but no wrinkles other than a slight crease across his olive forehead.

The three of us went down the stairs in good spirits. A worn wooden ladder had already been placed there by Elias. Chris checked it over.

"I will help you take it to where you want it," Elias offered.

Chris shook his head, "We can get it. It's not far."

About twenty minutes later we were placing the ladder under the hole we wanted to check out in the 'Storage Chamber'. "You know," I said, "We'll have to come up with a better name for this for tourists."

"I suppose we'll think of something."

Chris held the ladder while I climbed up. I shined my lights through and found that it didn't go very far. "Sorry Chris. Nothing here. Just a dead end. There are some cracks in the ceiling, but nothing exciting."

"Oh well," he shrugged. I slithered down the ladder and we played our lights around again to make sure we hadn't missed anything. "It looks like just the one outlet here."

We retraced our steps back through the narrow serpentine and began covering new ground. It trended downward and branched. We took the right way which had us quite nearly crawling. Then it opened out into a chamber in a teardrop shape. We stopped and I struck another match to check. It burned brightly for us. Chris took out the pad and pencil and sketched out our path. I measured out the length and height with a laser rangefinder.

The left fork turned out to be longer but dead-ended into a tight sideways squeeze that even I couldn't fit. Chris called me back and we ended there that day. We'd been longer than I thought and I was very glad for a good meal, even if it might be rabbit.

I turned in early that night since Chris was talking about making a long day of it tomorrow. And we went back into the cave right after breakfast. We only saw Elias's mom; she gave us breakfast and a bag of sandwiches and fruit for lunch.

The left turning of the first fork was our plan for the day. After many twists and turns we took a branch that went nowhere and then back to the main tunnel. This went on a ways in which we could walk comfortably. At last, there was a round chamber about ten feet in diameter that split into a few different directions with tunnels looking a lot like the one we came through. I marked the one we'd come through with chalk.

We took a stop for lunch sitting on the ground.

Chris was grinning ear to ear, "I thought we were coming to the end, but look, it just keeps going as far as I can shine my light."

I smiled back. "It's great. Hey, you know, I think I feel a draft."

I turned around to face the wall I'd been leaning against and shined my flashlight through a gap that we'd missed seeing in the dark. "It looks like a tight fit," I told Chris. "I think it opens up about ten feet in."

"Can we make it," he asked excitedly.

"I don't know. I'll take off my pack and see how far I can get."

"Okay."

I began to slide through on my belly. I got a few feet in easily and the gap narrowed. I had to turn my head to the side. Even so, my helmet was bumping and scraping along the ceiling and floor

"How's it going," Chris asked.

"Oof. I should've eaten after."

"Can you see anything?"

"There's definitely another chamber up ahead. Ugh." I panted with the effort of squeezing myself through. I finally fitted myself through and was able to roll up to a sitting position.

I played my light around and gasped.

"What is it?" Chris demanded.

"It's a room! Definitely man-made. There are alcoves around the walls and some kind of altar in the middle. Chris! I think it's a temple."

"Are you sure?"

I laughed at him as I looked up at the ceiling, "Yeah, there are some glyphs like they have in the Hypogeum: the red swirl things. Oh my stars."

"Are there any artifacts?"

"Uh, yes! There's a box in one of the niches," I told him.

"I want to see it, can you bring it out?"

I frowned at the request, "Are we allowed to do that?"

My voice echoed in the temple while I thought it over. We would probably have to involve the Antiquities people or whoever handled archeological finds, now.

Chris sounded very disappointed when he said, "No, I suppose not. Can you take pictures?"

"Sure." I pulled my phone out and used it to take some pictures of the niche with the box.

There was a doorway to my right. "Hey, Chris! There's another way in here. It must connect to something on your side."

"Good, I'm not going to be able to get in there the way you did," he answered. "Okay. Let's try this. Turn off your lights for a few minutes and then I'll shine my light through the doorway I found here. Maybe you'll see my light from where you are."

"Good idea, Maggs," he said.

I set a timer on my phone and walked around and took more pictures. Then, I sat on a block that had fallen from the ceiling. When my phone started beeping, I got up and went through the carved doorway outlined in red. "Okay, Chris," I called. I flicked on the flashlight and hoped.

"I see it," Chris answered. I kept shining my light down the passage and Chris soon appeared carrying my pack and his.

He handed me a bottle of water, "I thought you might be needing that. This is amazing, Maggie! Can you imagine the kind of publicity we could get?" "Thanks." I took a long drink of my water, "I hadn't thought of that yet. I'm shocked we found anything this cool."

Chris wandered around joyfully exclaiming over the workmanship of the carved altar. He found the bronze box in the niche I had told him about. I chugged down the last of the water in that bottle while I walked over to him. He ran his fingers across the edge, removing a layer of dust.

"Maybe we shouldn't touch it," I said.

He sneered, "It's just a layer of dust. What animal is that on top?"

I looked at it closer, "I can't really tell. It's some kind of bird, I suppose."

"Yes," he said dreamily. He blew forcefully on the lid and more dust went flying. I coughed a bit and stepped back. Glints of the metal shone through a heavy patina.

"I wonder how old it is."

Chris just shook his head, "I wonder how much it's worth."

Realizing I was still hungry, I turned to get an apple from my pack. I tripped over my own feet and only just caught myself on the altar. I held onto the edge and felt like the world was tilting. "Chris, did you feel that?"

"Feel what?"

45

I grabbed on tighter as the room started to spin. I felt drunk. "Chris! Bad air!" Then, I was on the ground looking up at him. "Chris, help." He scooped me up in his arms and threw me over his shoulder.

I woke up sore and thirsty. Hungover? I blinked a few times and couldn't see any difference between my eyes being open and closed. I began feeling around for my bedside lamp and my fingers touched rock. Then, I remembered: cave, bad air, and Chris scooping me up. "Chris," I say and sit up sharply. Pain lances through my head and ribs. I nearly fainted again with the intensity of it. I breathed in slowly and shouted his name again. I listened intently for an answer or the sound of breathing. But I hear nothing except my own echoes.

I really needed light. I pulled off my helmet to see what was wrong with the head lamp. There was a large dent in the helmet on the right side that I could feel with my fingers. I guess that's partly why my head hurts. But the head lamp was missing. Okay, no problem, I thought. I've got other sources of light.

I felt in my pocket where I usually keep my phone. It was gone and the zipper left open. Maybe it fell out while Chris was carrying me. That would have made sense, except I'm usually meticulous about zipping that pocket closed. Things were fuzzy, but I was sure I closed it after I took those once-in-a-lifetime photos. I drew my knees up to my chest and laid my aching head on them. I remembered fainting. I remembered Chris picking me up just before. Maybe I'd been too much of a burden and he laid me down somewhere so he could get help.

Then he should have left some basic gear nearby for me, in case I woke up. I felt around with my hands in a circle. And then I felt around in a wider circle. Coming up empty, I sat back and pressed my hands against my thighs. I felt the lighter through my pant leg. I said a silent prayer of thanks. I looked around carefully first, for any source of light. I thought there might be something in a vaguely up direction. I waved my hand between my eyes and that slightly-less-dark patch. I could just perceive the movement. Or my mind was playing tricks on me.

I flicked on the lighter. The only sights were rock and dirt. No colorful backpack. No water bottle, no flashlight. No Chris. Nothing. The chamber here is about twenty or thirty feet deep and narrow. I walked the perimeter, checking for exits. The only exit I can find is the one that is up. It's a steep slope. I wouldn't have hesitated climbing it with ropes. I could climb it without those, if I had decent light. I flicked off the lighter and sat. I was desperately thirsty. My gear and partner were gone. I called for him again, pitching my voice towards that hole up above and got no answer. I had to have rolled down that slope and lost the lamp on the way. It sure felt like it. As the fog cleared from my mind, pain was registering from all over my body. *He left me.* I tried to laugh it off, but laughing hurt. *He wanted the box but I wouldn't take it. He found a hole to shove me through and left me to die.* I made a sound that was between a gasp and a sob. Without my supplies, phone, or watch I was as good as dead. A deep fear swept in like an icy wave. I was lost in the dark. The lighter's fuel wouldn't last forever and if I hadn't found my way by then, I was doomed.

It doesn't matter what happened or how I got here. I have to get out. I tried to take a steadying breath, but that hurt. First thing: water. I listened hard and thought I heard a drip, drip. I turned that way and lit the lighter again. There was a little rivulet of water dripping down the wall. I turned my helmet upside down and held it under the dripping. I waited patiently in the dark. I drank from the helmet. The water tasted like minerals and sweat. I repeated the experiment several times, until I felt better.

I opened the top of my overalls and stripped off the long-sleeve shirt underneath, leaving just my sports bra and shorts under the overalls. Kneeling down, I began tearing that shirt into long strips. I tried to remember what the material was... a polyester or polypropylene. Plastic, basically. It was going to make for a yucky, bitter smoke but that couldn't be helped. I stuffed the strips into a pocket of my overalls and started feeling around for rocks. They had to be heavy enough to weigh down one end of a strip, but not so much that they'd add a lot of weight. I figured that I had one shot at this, maybe two.

I went back for more water and peed off to one side. I was as sparing as I could be with the lighter. I tried to remember if Elias had said anything about refilling the Zippo. "St. Benedict, I hope you can help me get out of here. If you do, I'll light a candle or whatever it is people do to honor you." I took the first strip, weighed it down with a rock, and lit the tail end of it with the lighter. A yellow flame with a trace of blue started it's march up the strip. Before I could overthink what I was about to do, I pocketed St. Benny and started my scramble up to that opening.

As the first burning strip faded, I pulled another strip out and plonked it down with it's weight as high up as I could reach. It wasn't directly in my path, but close enough to light the way. I tried to never look directly at the flame to preserve my night vision, but it's hard not to look. A lot of this climbing I was doing was by feel. My hands were growing raw as I lit the third strip. I panted there for a moment and I picked out my next holds. As I shifted to make my move, my left foot slipped followed by my right. I clung tightly with my hands and scrambled my feet to find purchase. It was

48

a horrible moment as I hung there in near darkness. I found a solid place to put my right foot and forced myself to keep going, pushing through the terror. *Be scared later.*

I was glad I had peed just before I started.

I'll never know how long that climb took. I measured time in strips of burnt fabric. Climb, climb, climb, find a good stable spot. Place my strip and rock, rest a moment. Light. Keep going. I couldn't see how far I'd climbed, a tender mercy in my little world of struggle and pain. I could finally make out my goal. Sweat dripped off my nose onto the rough rock next to my hand. A few more feet to go.

I cannot explain the feeling of reaching the top. It must be something like what a woman feels when she has, at last, birthed her baby. Exhaustion, fear, and joy were all rolled into one. I laughed and cried as I crawled out of the abyss into a tunnel trending down and right, up and left. With a splitting headache and aching ribs, I stood up slowly, bracing myself on the walls.

There is a sudden bright light in my eyes. "I thought I heard something," Chris says in a low growling voice I barely recognize. It's too bright, I can't see. But I can hear his rushing steps. I try to run the other way, trip, and sprawl against the wall of the tunnel. He grabs my coveralls and spins me around. Chris slams my back against the tunnel and knocks the wind out of me. I blink furiously against the light of his headlamp. He says nothing as his hands slide up towards my neck. *I'm going to die now. And after all that work! It isn't fair!* His hands encircle my throat and he starts to squeeze.

The lighter is still in my pocket. I grab that faithful Zippo and hold it up under his chin and light it. Reflexively, he loosens his grip on me and tilts his head back. I take the opportunity to put my knee into his groin as hard as I can. I try to punch him in the nose as he leans forward, but it lands awkwardly. I rip the headlamp off his helmet. Chris growls and grabs my coveralls again. Vaguely, I realize that I hear rapidly approaching steps, maybe I've been hearing them for some moments. Someone else, a man comes tearing up the tunnel and throws himself on Chris. Chris's helmet goes rolling off into the darkness. I manage to separate myself from them and crawl away coughing and sputtering for air.

The stranger is battering Chris in the face and head with a flashlight. The light traces a vertical line up and down the cave wall again and again. Chris tries to fight back by putting his arms up, but after a couple of hits with the heavy-duty flashlight, his arms go limp and the sounds of the blows go from crunchy to smooshy.

Elias stops. I am backing away from the scene along the wall. I take in Chris lying there dead with a panting Elias straddling his body. The Maltese man slowly meets my gaze. "Do you need the hospital," he asks me.

My voice was raspy and weak, "I don't know".

Elias grimaced and then stood up and walked over and knelt down beside me. *When did I sit down?* He placed a gentle hand on my throat. It felt warm and the place he touched felt immediately better.

"Thanks. Thank you for- He was going to kill me."

Elias nodded, "I know."

"And thank you for the lighter," I say as I hold it out to him.

Instead of taking it back, he closes my fingers around it, "Keep it. Where are you hurt? Can you still walk," he asks.

And I groaned at the thought. We weren't done. We still had to get out of the blasted thrice-forsaken cave, "I can walk."

He handed me a bottle of water from the little rucksack that he was wearing, "Rest for a few minutes. I'm going to see if his pack is close."

I nearly emptied the bottle in one long draft. I sat there marveling at the thought of having light and breathing. But thinking of that, reminded me where I got that headlamp from and the fact that a very dead body was not but a few feet away.

When Elias came back, I was trembling all over. He sat with his back to the wall and pulled me into his arms and stroked the back of my head. He spoke softly in the sort of voice you use to comfort a hurt child. Crooning words that I didn't understand. As my tremoring calmed, he spoke again in English.

"I found the supplies. We'll get what we need and leave by the way I came. It's not too difficult a way."

He said it so plainly, it sounded like a plan for a picnic. We'll just drive down to the beach and spread a blanket. His voice was calming and I wanted him to keep talking. "How did you find me," I asked.

Elias's chest expanded with a deep breath, "Would you believe me if I said I put a little enchantment on the lighter I gave you?"

"You mean, like magic?"

"Yes," he said.

I thought over the things I could remember of the day: Finding an ancient temple, being nearly strangled, and fighting for my life. Maybe this was all a nightmare, but I didn't see how a dream could possibly hurt so much.

"I could believe anything."

"Well, then, that is how I found you. I could... feel... that you were in trouble. And then I knew to come looking."

"Why did you give it to me," I asked.

"I didn't trust Erikkson. There was something about him. He was too eager to be down here," Elias answered.

"And all over a box."

"Yes, the box. I saw it in the bag. Did you open it?"

"No. What is it?"

"It's a- you might call it a family heirloom. We'll need to put it back."

"Did you know about it?"

"I knew of it, not its exact location."

We got up slowly and Elias led me to Chris's backpack. Elias took out the metallic box and laid it aside reverently. I devoured the candy-coated chocolate candies we found immediately. There was jerky, water, and nuts, too. My cell phone, extra batteries, a t-shirt of polyester, a pen flashlight with batteries and some warm socks helped to round out the load. Elias encouraged me to put on the t-shirt and change socks. We were almost done when a pill bottle rolled out. Elias picked it up as I was still putting my Wellies back on. "What is it," I asked.

"Rohypnol," he said grimly.

"Oh, the water," I said as horrible new possibilities occurred to me. I looked up at Elias, "Well, that's the only part of me that doesn't hurt."

"If he had, I'd have to resurrect him and kill him again. Slowly. More than once."

"You could do that?!"

"That's not really my line, but it could be done."

The thought made my head ache more profoundly. I just nodded like this was a normal conversation. Yes, of course, enchanted lighters and necromantic vigilantism were commonplace, right?

Reprovisioned, we started walking. Elias led the way with his flashlight and I followed behind with Chris's headlamp on my helmet. He insisted on taking the bulk of the load, but I had a few snacks and extras in my pockets. I was reluctant to be entirely separated from supplies again.

We arrived back at the temple. I hadn't recognized the way, because it was the way Chris had gone earlier. I stumbled along next to Elias and showed him the niche it had come from.

"What is that box," I asked him, "What's so special about it?"

He looked at me and smiled. "I could tell you-"

"But then you'd have to kill me," I said, finishing the line.

"Noooo, nothing so dire. It's a family secret that not even all of the family knows. If I told you, you'd have to join the family."

"But how would I become family? Oh!" my brain slowly caught up to his gist. If I married him, he might tell me what the hell had happened today. He'd already told me flat out that he was using magic. The room chose that moment to start spinning again. "I don't think I can handle any more revelations today."

Elias held me up, "I'm sorry. It's too much to take in and you probably have a concussion." He scooped up my pack, which was still laying there on the ground. As we left the temple he stopped at the doorway. He held up his hands and spoke softly. Where an opening had been, it now appeared that there was a solid wall. Elias tenderly took my hand and drew me away.

It seemed hours later that we were headed back up to the storage chamber. A search party was getting ready to set out. They took one look at me and wrapped me up in a blanket that looked like tin foil. I giggled at the thought of being wrapped up like a burrito. I wondered if I was going nuts.

Chaos, noise, and light swirled around as we were ushered up the stairs. I heard Elias talking animatedly, trying to direct the chaos. A paramedic shined a light in my eyes and asked me questions. Yes, I knew my name and where I was. I was a little fuzzy on when, because I didn't know how long I'd been in the cave. I refused to go to the hospital. I didn't want the noise and light. I just wanted to sleep.

Insisting that I have peace and quiet, he took me to a room that was dimly lit and sat me in a chair. "The Inspector wants a blood sample for a toxicology screen," he said. I nodded and he proceeded to draw a vial of blood and left. I laid my head in my hands and tried not to cry again.

The door swung open and a man with sparse hair and wearing a suit and tie entered. He sat down in the chair next to me. I realized this was a police officer. He set down a hot tea on the table in front of me. He took out a notepad and smiled, "I am Inspector Aiden de Monte. You've had a hard day."

"You have no idea."

"Can you tell me about it," he asked.

I know, even in this state that I mustn't say anything about the Temple or the box. "It's really fuzzy."

"You're an American, I believe," he said.

"Yes, my name is Margaret Deer. I'm a speleologist: a cave scientist."

"I see."

"I- We- Dr. Chris Erikkson and I were exploring and charting like the Cardonas asked us to. But we got into a pocket of dead air- at least, that's what I thought at the time. I know now that he probably drugged my water. I passed out. I remember him throwing me over his shoulder like a sack of potatoes. And when I woke up, I was alone in the dark. My supplies were gone. All I had was a lighter and my helmet."

"Go on."

"It was a part of the cave I didn't recognize. I managed to climb out and then he must have heard me. He attacked me."

"Who attacked you?"

"Chris- Dr. Erikkson"

"He," I choked on a sob. "I don't know what he was thinking. He tried to strangle me and I- I burned him and then we- I- Elias...." By this point, tears streamed openly down my face and my nose was running.

"Who did you burn: Chris or Elias?"

"Chris, he had me pinned against the wall. He was choking me. I had a lighter and I used it to burn him. His chin, I think."

"Ah, clever."

"Elias, he saved me. He saved my life. He came running up and, and-" I collapsed into sobs.

The policeman patted me on the arm. "I have his statement already. He said you were late in returning from the cavern and he went to find you.

"It seems that Dr. Erikkson had ill plans for you, my dear. If you think of anything else to tell me, you can call at any time. I will have to ask you to remain in the country until we get all the answers we need." He held out a cream colored business card and I took it.

He started to slip out the door, when I asked, "Inspector, what does 'ma-buba' mean?"

He repeated it back to me, "*Mahbuba*?"

"Yes, that's it," I said.

He looked down, smiled faintly and answered, "It means that Elias likes you very much."

Roberta helped me shower. She clucked over the bruises which covered my body like polk-a-dots. She tossed a much-too-large flannel nightgown with a lacy collar over my head and pulled the blankets up to my chin. As I drifted down into sleep, Elias's giant orange cat thumped onto the bed and laid down by my hip. He was purring so hard, I could feel the bed vibrate.

I stayed an additional couple of weeks to heal up and in case the police wanted to talk to me again. I went in to give a full statement of what I could remember. The family decided against cave tours after what had happened. I can't say I'm sorry about that.

Elias took me out to dinner one night. My bruises had faded to the point I could wear a dress and not have people stare. The Italian bistro was off the tourist scene, which I appreciated. Noise and lights still bothered me. We were seated in a corner for some privacy.

"I don't understand why he didn't just take it and leave. He had all our notes."

Elias swirled his wine glass absentmindedly, "I think he was lost. That part of the cave you had not explored fully. And the box has some powers of its own. I don't think it meant for him to find his way out."

"Oh. So it's cursed."

Elias smiled, "You might say that. It's cursed for those who should not handle it."

"You handled it," I point out.

"So, I did."

"And I don't see anything bad happening to you," I continued.

"True." He put down his glass and picked up my hand. "Maggie, dear, I really shouldn't say anything more."

"Unless I marry you," I smiled.

Elias blinked heavily, "I didn't know if you'd remember what I'd said. Maggie, I'd be lying if I said I wasn't interested. I know you're tough-minded, smart, and cute. You'd fit right in here. For me, it's enough. But for you? If we could find you a job, would you stay?"

Who am I to say no to a Maltese would-be necromancer with a cursed box in his basement?

THREE SIPS OF ESPRESSO

Robert McDonald

The note was short and to the point:

Roger,

Long time, no see. I'll be at Gleneagles at 7PM. Come buy me a drink.

Sincerely,

Bob Parker

P.S. Show up or your application to the Malta Permanent Residence Program might hit a snag.

I crumpled the note that had been waiting for me at the front desk of the Water's Edge Hotel on Pretty Bay Beach when I arrived back from a day spent eyeballing the Eastern European and Near Eastern beauties frolicking in the waves.

I had been on Malta for three weeks getting a feel for the island nation, its people, and the pace of life. It had been a productive trip. I had fulfilled the most immediate requirements to obtain my Permanent Resident status, and with it, a Malta passport good for travel into any EU nation. All that was left was to decide which apartment lease I wanted to sign, and then a six month stay to establish my residency.

Now this.

I tossed the note into a trash can on my way to the elevators. While I waited for an elevator to arrive, I once again cursed the day I had allowed myself to come under the thumb of the Central Intelligence Agency.

>>>⟩ ⟨⟨⟨⟨

Gleneagles bar is on the island of Gozo near the spot the Malta ferry disembarks. It was an hour drive, give or take a few minutes for traffic, plus the ferry ride, from my hotel. I knew of the bar even though I had not yet to made my way to Gozo for a visit.

When I arrived, I found Bob Parker and his 1980s mustache sitting at one of the outdoor tables drinking Cisk beer from a bottle. I made eye contact, gave him the finger, and went into the bar. I walked up to the bar, ignored the group of tourists speaking loud French at one table, and got a dismissive glance from the lone man sitting at the bar. He looked like a local fisherman who would just as soon use the tourists polluting the atmosphere as bait.

The bartender made eye contact with raised eyebrows, and I ordered a Laphroaig, neat. He snagged the bottle from behind the bar, poured the Scotch into a rocks glass, and sat it in front of me. I paid from a wad of Euros, then took the glass and went back outside.

"You really like that piss?" I asked as I sat in a chair directly across from Parker.

"Beer is beer." He lifted the glass and took a large swallow.

"Why am I here, Bob?"

He smiled, teeth flashing behind his walrus mustache. "I thought you might like to join me for a drink at the favored watering hole of A.J. Quinnell. He's the guy that wrote the book *Man on Fire*. He lived on Gozo and drank here."

I sipped my Scotch. "His name was Philip Nicholson. Quinnell was a pen name. Why am I here?"

Parker drained his beer and set the glass aside, leaned back in his chair, and folded his arms over his stomach. His smile was gone.

"I need you to do a job."

I shook my head. "No, no fucking way. I did that job for you in Mexico. We're even."

I started to get up, already going through a mental checklist of items I needed to handle before I could leave Malta. Leaving would mean flushing my plans for a back door out of the US if things went bad at home, but there were other places to escape to and live a comfortable life in the sun. Giving up on Malta would be worth it to get away from Parker and whatever it was the CIA wanted done here.

"Sit down."

The tone caused me to snap my eyes back to Parker, and I glared through narrow slits. "Fuck you."

He took a deep breath and blew it out. "Sit down or before you make it ten steps the IRS will freeze all of your accounts. Ten seconds after that they'll freeze the accounts of everyone you know, from that blonde bartender you were entertaining in Key West, to your gun dealer buddy Danny Fletcher in Birmingham. By tomorrow your personal assistant will be under arrest for tax fraud, ol' Danny Boy will be getting a colonoscopy from the BATFE, his wife will have her nursing license revoked, and that Jew you let play bartender will be facing charges for that run in he had with the bikers in Vegas. So, sit down."

I sat.

Every fiber in my soul wanted to shoot him in the face and go on the run, but that wouldn't do a thing to help my friends. Parker's compatriots would ruin their lives and use the power of the US government to do it. I couldn't let that happen to my friends.

"Thank you," he said. "That was the stick. I was hoping to lead with the carrot, but you know how you are."

"Go on."

"Do us this little favor and you and your friends will not be put under the scrutiny of the entire United States government. You will be forgiven for handing that hard drive over to Project Libertad after you promised me you had given me the last copy. You really pissed off a lot of people with that stunt. Lucky for you the average citizen believes it when FOX, CNN, and MSNBC all say hundreds of videos showing government employees and elected officials flagrante delicto, with what appeared to be minors, was all just an elaborate deep fake by the Russians to distract everyone from their Ukraine ambitions. The spook killing that Congressman in Memphis helped."

All that risk, and the fucking media had just taken their marching orders from DC and run with the deep fake story. Then they had capitalized on the tragedy of the "black man brain washed by the Alt-Right" who, in the belief that his daughter had been raped by a congressman, had beat the distinguished member of the House of Representatives to death with a baseball bat outside a Memphis health club. Pundits on both sides of the aisle expressed outrage, Big Tech vowed to scrub the internet of the "fake" videos, and it all went away.

"If everyone buys the deep fake story then how do you figure I owe you anything?"

He snorted. "Just because the average citizen believes it doesn't mean the conspiritards do. Not a day goes by without some asshole on the internet bringing it up. The cost of increased security alone is enough to make a sizable number of people want me to just shoot you. But I'm convinced you can be useful, and the internet cranks make sure those pieces of shit keep their heads down and that they act in the best interests of national security."

"You mean they act in the interests of the Deep State," I said. "Every one of those people should be impaled on a stake in front of the Washington Monument."

He rolled his eyes. "Those people are much more valuable alive. A dead asset is no asset at all. Better to keep them alive and use them the best we can. You should be thankful we think that way, otherwise..."

He made a gun with the fingers of one hand, pointed it at me, and mimed dropping a trigger.

I took a deep breath and reminded myself that no matter how satisfying it might be, killing him would not solve my problem. "What do you want me to do?"

He smiled. "That's the spirit! I need you to visit a Rwandan expat, Jean-Bosco Kambanda, that owns a coffee import business near Freeport. It's close to your hotel, so it won't be too out of your way, not that anything is around here. He's an old school Hutu génocidaire, one of the ones the government in Rwanda never managed to convict after the civil war. He spent some time in the refugee camps in Zaire before he was able to go home and rebuild his coffee plantation. The Rwandans started making noises a few years ago about putting him on trial and he bugged out for France. Then he ended up here. Recently, he revealed he has some photos of the then junior Congressman from Connecticut in a compromising position with a young refugee while he was touring the camps with a UN inspection mission. Kambanda has offered the photos for sale on the Darknet, and we need to make sure we get them. We want you to convince him to give you the photos and the negatives, and then we want you to put a bullet in his head. I figured you wouldn't have a problem with that, considering his past sins, and getting us the photos and negatives will go a long way toward showing your contrition for past misdeeds."

"Who's the Congressman?"

"Former Congressman now." He said a name.

"Isn't he the Deputy Secretary of State now?"

Parker grinned. "With the photos our Rwandan friend has we'll be able to ensure there are no more uranium deals with Russia, no pallets of cash going to Iran, and that China gets serious about patent enforcement."

"And a child rapist gets a pass?"

"Freedom isn't free, my friend," he said. "And we'll make sure he doesn't do more than sniff a few kids at public appearances."

The last thing I wanted was to help Parker. The fact that he and others within the federal establishment were willing to use whatever dirt, up to and including evidence of sexual abuse of children, to further their idea of national security instead of working to punish the guilty was nauseating.

It was also something I couldn't change. I could do what I was told, or I could see my life and the lives of the people I cared about the most destroyed by men and women who would pat themselves on the back as saviors of truth, justice, and the American way.

"Fine," I said. "I'll do it."

⤜⤚⤙ ⤐⤑⤒

The dossier Parker provided me was short on details. There was a redacted report, written in French, that had a photo of Kambanda with the words "présumé génocidaire," which the magic elf box in my pocket told me meant "suspected génocidaire." I didn't bother to attempt to translate the rest of the report since it didn't really matter what it said. It wouldn't change what was about to happen to him.

The rest of the dossier contained more recent photos and a brief biography, which is where I learned he was married to a Maltese woman, and that they had one child, a daughter. They lived in a three-story building constructed from the ubiquitous Maltese limestone on Triq Tal-Gurgier. The first floor was taken up by the business, and the next two made up the soon to be unhappy family's home.

I spent three days observing the place from the outdoor seating area of a small café just up the street, and I was able to positively identify Kambanda the first morning. The rest of time was spent getting to know the family's habits.

The wife was a nurse, and she left for work early every morning. Kambanda then took their daughter to school and came back home. The wife brought the daughter home after work. Then they usually had dinner on one of the balconies that protruded from the building over the sidewalk and street.

On the fourth day I drove past the address just after ten in the morning. I parked in an empty space just out of sight of the front of the building, walked back to it, and went through the business entrance. The first thing I noticed inside was the strong aroma of coffee. The second was Kambanda smiling at me as he watered some plants in the small entry foyer.

"May I help you?"

The voice was deep and had what to my ear was the distinct flavor of Africa. This close, I could see he was a bit older than the photos in the dossier revealed and that he had a small scar on his forehead, but there was no doubt it was the same man whose photo was attached to the French report.

I smiled. "Yes, my name is Jim Crumley. I'm looking for the owner of Kivu Coffee Importers."

"I am the owner, Jean-Bosco Kambanda," he said, holding out a hand to shake.

"Excellent," I said, taking the hand and giving it a firm shake before releasing it. "I own a small chain of coffee shops in the United States. I'm in Malta on vacation and I absolutely fell in love with the espresso being served at this delightful coffee house near my hotel on Pretty Bay. The owner informed me the coffee beans were from Rwanda and that he had purchased them from a local importer. Which brings me here. Would you be open to importing some of your coffee to the US?"

The uncomfortable smile on his face told me that he had not expected to be faced with a gushing American intent on buying his coffee beans as soon as he opened for business.

"I do sell to a few of the local coffee houses," he said. "Most of the coffee goes to the continent. Since Malta is an EU country this presents no problem. Importing agricultural products into the United States is no small matter. I do not believe the amount of coffee you would require for a small chain would be a cost-effective endeavor. However, if you would like to purchase a small amount for your own personal use that can be arranged."

I gave him a wide smile. "Forgive me my modesty. When I said small, I meant in comparison to Starbucks or Dunkin'. I own over three hundred locations across thirteen states, mostly in the South. I do believe we could make the effort worth your while."

His face showed surprise, but he returned my smile.

"In that case, Mr. Crumley, please join me in my office and let's discuss this proposal in more detail."

꒜꒜ ꒜꒜

I followed Kambanda through double doors into a small warehouse space. The odor of coffee was more intense here, and the space was crammed with pallets holding bags of coffee beans. He led me along a winding, narrow path to the back of the building where a low wall topped with glass enclosed a large office.

We entered the office and he gestured towards a wingback chair sitting in front of a library table he was using as a desk. He went behind the desk and pointed at a narrow table behind it that held a safe on one end and a coffee bar on the other.

"Since you enjoy espresso may I offer you a cup?" he asked. "I have not had my usual cup this morning and I would be pleased if you would join me."

"Of course," I said.

I watched as he prepared the coffee. He started by turning on a hot plate. He then went about preparing an Italian Moka pot, first filling the bottom half with water, then filling the funnel with ground coffee from a plastic storage container and finishing by screwing on the top of the pot. He placed the pot on the hot plate but left the lid up.

He stood, half facing me as he talked and worked. "I learned to make Cuban style coffee from an American journalist while in a refugee camp in Zaire during the Rwandan Civil War. It was hard to come by sugar in the camp, but he had a source of it from a UN aid worker who kept him supplied with anything he needed. He would trade whatever he could spare for interviews with the refugees."

He filled a small bowl with a couple tablespoons of sugar.

"The key is to use the first few drops of the coffee to make the sugar foam," he said. He removed the now brewing pot from the hot plate and poured a little coffee into the bowl before replacing it and turning the hot plate off. "Once it starts to brew you can take it off the heat, it will have enough."

He picked up the bowl and began to whisk the sugar and coffee mixture vigorously. After a minute of this, he nodded and set the bowl down. The coffee had finished brewing and he poured two small, white espresso cups almost full, then mixed a teaspoon of the sugar foam into each cup so that the surface of the coffee formed the perfect thin coat of light foam.

He picked up both cups, leaned over his desk to place one in front of me then sat down facing me. "Please, tell me what you think."

I took a small sip and let the flavor roll over my tongue. It was bold and bitter, but the sweetness of the sugar foam cut the bitter down so that a pleasant after taste was left on the palate. "Delicious," I said.

He smiled in satisfaction. "So, Mr. Crumley, how many kilograms of this can I interest you in?"

I smiled, took another larger sip of the coffee, set the cup on his desk, reached into my jacket, and took out a Star BM 9mm pistol and pointed it at his face.

His smile morphed into a frown, and with an audible huff of anger he sat back in his chair and raised his hands. "Are you going to kill me? If so, do it and leave. I don't have any cash here, and I won't leave with you to get it from a bank."

I felt my eyebrows go up, and I lowered the gun so it was pointing at his chest. "You can put your hands down, just make sure I can see them. I take it this isn't your first experience looking at the muzzle of a gun?"

He snorted. "I'm from Africa. We are more than familiar with men with guns where I am from."

The contempt in his voice was the exact opposite of the fear I had been expecting. A man who is afraid can be unpredictable, but he is usually easy to control if you give him the hope that he can avoid that which he fears. A contemptuous man is one who first must be broken before you can control him. I didn't have time to break this man.

"Look, I'll keep this simple. I need the photos and the negatives you're trying to sell. Give those to me and this will be painless."

He shook his head. "I give you what you want, and what? You shoot me in the head? That's not a very good bargain."

"It's better than the alternative," I snapped. "You cooperate and you die quick. You don't, I start cutting pieces off until you do."

"Not very civilized, cutting off pieces of people."

"You would know," I said. "How many did you hack apart with a machete?"

He glared at me, and his eyes communicated a cold, contemptuous hate. It did not feel like the hatred of a guilty man, but instead like that of a man who knew, with absolute certainty, that he was a better man than you.

"You're proud of what you did, aren't you?" I accused.

He sneered, and disgust rolled off his words. "Proud? No. I take no pride in what I did, but I know I had no choice. I knew what I was doing, and why. Do you?"

The audacity of the genocidal bastard amazed me. I couldn't help but smile. "I'm protecting a child rapist by killing a genocidal piece of shit. I'm not proud of it, but it's the only way I can keep people I care about safe from evil men more powerful than I am."

The expression of contempt on his face slipped away and was replaced by a raised eyebrow and the hint of a smile. "I think you and I have more in common than you think, Mr. Crumley. Is that really your name? I seem to recall an American writer named Crumley."

His words caught me off guard. "It's Devereux, actually. I borrowed Crumley from the author. James Crumley. How did you hear of him?"

He smiled and rolled his eyes. "I like reading crime fiction. Not every African is a hut dwelling illiterate looking for the next skull to bury his machete in, Mr. Devereux. Some of us can read."

"You can read and murder, how delightful," I said.

"Ah, but we share those traits, don't we? I would be willing to wager I have murdered less than you. Can you guess how many I have killed?"

I didn't know what his game was, and I knew I shouldn't be playing it, but I found myself somewhat charmed by the old génocidaire who liked Cuban coffee and American crime novels. "How many?"

Voice full of regret, he said, "Just one."

His large, dark eyes were full of sorrow now, and a part of me wanted to believe it was just an act. Another part of me, the part that knew what it felt like to look out from eyes like the ones focused on mine, knew it wasn't.

"If I am to die today, I most certainly deserve it," he said. "What I did haunts my dreams, and I am willing to face whatever punishment God has in store for me. I will give you what you want, and you may do what you must. I won't give you any trouble. I just want to ask you for two things."

A professional assassin would have never let the conversation go on for so long. A professional would have already tied him to a chair and been well on his way to getting the photos and negatives by any means necessary so that he could put a bullet in the génocidaire's head and be done with it. I was a professional, but I was only an assassin because I had no other way to protect my friends.

I let curiosity dictate my actions. "Ask."

"Let me tell you how I came to be here, with you pointing that gun at me. It won't take long, I promise."

"And?"

When he spoke, his voice was pleading. "Don't harm my wife and daughter. They know nothing that would be a threat to anyone."

I hadn't even considered the wife and daughter beyond finding a time when they were away to do what I had to do. Now, thinking on it, I felt two emotions at once: shame, that I had put myself in a position where a man could see me as a threat to an innocent woman and child; admiration, for a man who when all was said and done had accepted his own fate and worried only for that of his family.

"I'm not going to hurt your family," I said. "And I'll listen to whatever you need to say."

"Thank you."

⟫⟫⟫⟩ ⟨⟪⟪⟪

I let him pour us each a glass of Jack Daniel's from a bottle he kept behind the desk. He showed no concern for the gun I kept pointed at him, but he also moved in a way that always kept his hands visible. I rested the weight of the pistol on top of my crossed legs as the muzzle tracked him back behind his desk.

When he was seated again he took a large swallow of the whiskey, and then he began his story.

"When the genocide began it was like the entire country was caught up in a fever. The anger had been there for so long, simmering under the surface, and once the first killings began it was like a signal that now it is time to let that anger boil over. Men were using farm tools to hack apart the neighbors who had lived next to them in the same village their entire lives. Militias traveled through the villages and found any who hesitated. They put a machete in their hands and a gun to their heads and made them choose.

"I had a farm near Kiyumba where I grew and roasted coffee beans. When the killing started I offered to shelter two Tutsi families from the nearby town. I had done business with them, and I did not want anything bad to happen to them. For the first few days everything was fine. I had sent all of my workers home when the trouble began so it was just me and those two families. Then one of the young women, worried about a boy, ran away to try and visit him. When her parents realized she was gone they wanted to go into the town to find her. I convinced them to let me go instead.

"I found her walking along the road before she made it to town. I convinced her to return to the farm with me by promising that I would go into the town and check on her friend once she was safe. She agreed and we started back. I didn't realize until it was too late that we had been seen. A group of militia members followed us back to the farm. They surrounded us before we could get out of my car, and they checked our identity papers. When they saw she was Tutsi, they were angry. They wanted to know why she was with me, why hadn't I killed her, and were there others.

"She was afraid, so afraid, and I was afraid they would search the farm and find the others. I told them that she worked for me, and that everyone else had run away. They searched the house, and when they found no one, I breathed a sigh of relief. They searched the warehouse where one of the families had been staying, but again they found no one. The others must have run into the fields when they saw the truck coming behind my car onto the farm.

"I was so relieved, because I knew that if those people had been found I would have been killed with everyone else. I hoped that just maybe they would let this one Tutsi girl go unharmed, that they might think she was one I was employing to warm my bed. But I was wrong."

He stopped speaking long enough to take another swallow of whiskey and I could see tears standing unshed in his eyes.

"When they finished searching the farm, the leader of the men threw a machete at my feet. It still had blood and bits of skin stuck to the blade. He pointed a pistol at my head and said, 'Kill her.' I hesitated and he hit me in the head with the pistol."

He rubbed the scar on his forehead.

"He yelled at me to pick up the machete and kill her. She tried to run but one of the men, laughing, hit her in the head with the butt of his rifle. She fell on the ground and then sat there. The blood dripped down her face and on her clothing. She just sat there, looking at nothing."

The tears that had been standing in his eyes began to fall, making long, dark trails down his face as he looked into my eyes. I wanted to look away from those eyes, wanted to be anywhere but in that office. I couldn't look away no matter how much I wanted to pull my eyes from his, and I couldn't stop listening no matter how badly I didn't not want to hear any more of his story.

"I did not want to hurt her, but I also did not want to die. I told myself if she had not left the farm, none of this would have happened. I told myself it was *her* fault. I picked up the machete and I walked over to where she was sitting, staring off at nothing, with the blood dripping down from her head. She did not look up at me. She just sat there.

"When I hit her in the head the first time I was trying to strike hard so it would kill her quick and she would not suffer, but I was so weak from fear the blow did not land with enough force to kill. She started screaming then, but she still didn't move, didn't try to get up, or to protect herself. The screaming was terrible! I just wanted it to stop! I needed it to stop! I hit her again, and again, and again. Then it stopped.

"I fell to my knees and looked at what I had done, and I wept. The militia men laughed at me, got back into their truck, and left. When I had the strength, I buried her. Her family and the other never came back while I was there. I still don't know if they escaped or were found and killed. I am ashamed to say I am glad I never saw them again. I don't know how I could have faced them after what I had done."

He took a deep breath, let it out, and drank more of the Jack Daniel's. He set the glass back on the desk and wiped the tears from his eyes, and then he looked into mine again. This time I did look away. He wasn't a génocidaire. He was one of their victims. But because he had crossed someone powerful, I had been sent to kill him, and to rob his wife and daughter of his presence in their lives. I wanted to vomit.

"Not long after, the Rwandan Patriotic Front pushed into the area," he said. "They were a rebel group of Tutsi refugees who had been fighting the Hutu government, and they eventually pushed the government and the génocidaires out of Rwanda and into Zaire. I was afraid I would be killed for a being a Hutu, so I fled as well. I spent a year in the refugee camps in Zaire. That's where I met the journalist who taught me about Cuban coffee. That is where I got the photos that you were sent to retrieve."

He picked up his glass of whiskey and looked at it. There wasn't much left in the glass, just enough to swirl it around the bottom. He brought it to his mouth and turned the glass up, then sat it down hard on the table. I flinched at the unexpected noise, but he didn't seem to notice.

"The camps were set up under the UN High Commissioner for Refugees," he said, and laughed bitterly. "In reality, the army and government of the displaced Hutu regime controlled the camps. They wanted time and resources to strike back into Rwanda, so they played up the plight of the poor, starving refugees for the cameras by day, and by night they offered up anything and everything that the UN people and visiting *dignitaries* could ask for, including our children."

His voice was now filled with the same contempt it had held when I first pulled the gun on him, but it also held an extra layer of loathing for the people who had preyed on the refugees.

"I had heard rumors about what was happening to some of the children," he continued. "I told my journalist friend, Patrick, about them on one of his visits. Patrick told me he would look into it. I didn't see him again for a week and when I did, he was looking over his shoulder every few seconds as if someone was after him. He tried to pretend everything was all right, but I didn't believe it. I pressed him to talk to me, to tell me what had happened. He finally just said they were going to kill him. I asked him who was going to kill him, but he would not tell me. He gave me a roll of film and told me to keep it safe. He said if anything happened to him I should send it to his employer. Before I could ask who that was two soldiers came walking toward us. He ran as soon as they saw him and they began shouting for him to stop. When he didn't, one of them raised his rifle and shot him in the back.

"When they shot him everyone started screaming and running in all directions. I took the opportunity to slip away before the soldiers could question me about why I was talking to him. I found out later that the government in exile claimed he was a spy for the RPF. The UN condemned the killing and demanded justice, but nothing was done. Why would it be?"

He shook his head in disgust.

"I took the film and went home. I thought my chances with the RPF were better than the with the Hutu génocidaires who would be looking for the journalist's friend in the camp.

"My farm had been burned sometime after I fled, so there was a lot to do. I forgot about the film as I rebuilt. By this time the trials of the génocidaires had started, and I was worried that any day I would be picked up by the authorities, but I was never accused. After a while, I stopped worrying. I worked my farm and saved as much hard currency as I could get into my hands.

"When I felt like I had enough, I sold the farm to a neighbor and emigrated to France. I took the film with me. I always kept it close, even as I tried not to think about it. I worked in a coffee house in Marseille, and that is when things changed."

He smiled now as he looked over my head, lost in memory.

"Six years ago, a beautiful woman from Malta was visiting Marseille. She visited the coffee shop every morning, and she was full of questions. Where was I from, what had I done there, what did I want to do now. She never asked about the genocide, though I am sure she knew of it and that I must have been there when it happened.

"One day she asked me to dinner, and it was love from there on. Before we married, I told her everything. I didn't think she would still want me, but I couldn't marry her with that secret between us. She told me the past was the past, and that I should leave it there.

"We decided to live in Malta to be close to her family. After my daughter was born, I decided I needed to do something more than just work for someone else. My wife is a nurse, and she does well, but I wanted to be a provider. I wanted her to work because she wanted to, not because she had no choice. I contacted the man who owned my old farm and arranged my first shipment of coffee. I didn't have any trouble selling the beans to local coffee houses, and I even sell to my old employer in Marseille. Life was going well."

The smile was gone now, and he rubbed one hand over his head.

"One night, about three months ago, I had a nightmare about killing the girl during the genocide. It happens from time to time. It frightens my wife. She says I need to let go of the past, and that I should start by throwing away the film from the refugee camp."

He shook his head and looked down at his feet.

"I should have listened to her, but instead I developed the film. The horror in those photos made it hard for me to eat for days. I recognized the man committing the horrors from TV, I knew he was an American politician. I knew I could not forget what I had seen, and that I must try to bring his acts to light. I sent one photo to the US Embassy along with a letter offering to provide more and any other assistance I could. That was a week ago. You were the response."

I met the rekindled contempt in his eyes and made up my mind. "Where are the photos and negatives?"

He shook his head in disgust. "They're in the safe behind me."

"Take them out and place them on the desk. Then face the wall and I'll disappear. When your wife and daughter get home, leave. Find some place to hide for a while. Maybe once the photos are gone, you'll be safe."

His left eyebrow went straight up. "You would let me go?"

"Yes," I said.

"What if my story was all a lie?"

"Then it was a convincing lie," I said. "I'd rather believe it's true. Even if you tried to sell the photos instead of just turning them over to the US government, I don't think your daughter deserves to grow up without a father."

"Thank you," he said, and gestured behind him. "May I get the photos now?"

I nodded. He stood up and turned his back to me to open the safe. I listened to the clicking of the dial as he spun it back and forth, and then he operated the lever and opened the door. He body blocked my view of the interior as he reached inside. When he took his hand out of the safe and turned back toward me I saw the small black pistol he held.

I threw myself to the side out of my chair just as he fired, and he missed. My shoulder hit the ground and I grunted in pain as I kept a two-handed grip on the Star and pressed the trigger three times. All three shots hit him in the chest, and he dropped his gun and staggered back against the table holding the safe.

I climbed to my feet, keeping my pistol trained on him as he slid down to a sitting position on the floor. I stepped around the desk and kicked the dropped pistol away.

"Why?" I asked. "I was going to let you go!"

"Couldn't take the risk," he gasped.

And then he died.

I went to the safe. A quick search revealed a small manila envelope holding photos that made my bile rise, as well as the negatives. I slipped the envelope into a pocket and searched the floor of the office until I found the three spent pieces of brass ejected from my Star BM.

I saw the cup of espresso he had made for me, and I thought the jolt of caffeine would help settle my nerves. I took my third sip. It was bitter and cold. I poured what was left in the trash, knocked back the glass of Jack Daniel's to wash away the bitter taste, then took both glass and coffee cup with me out of the office.

I left the building and used a burner cell phone to make a call to the local police. I told them I had heard what sounded like gunshots coming from inside the Kivu Coffee Importer building then hung up. I didn't want his wife or daughter finding him.

I powered off the phone then tossed it, the coffee cup, and the whiskey glass into a trash bin on my way back to my car. I could still taste the bitterness of the cold espresso.

ANCESTORS

ART WELLING

The island of Malta, in the fall of 1941. The United States had yet to enter in the war with Germany, but most of the military expected it to happen soon enough. The various military intelligence services were all scrambling for any information they could find so the United States wouldn't be caught flat footed when Congress finally declared war.

Petty Officer Charles Marshall is on a mission for United States Naval Intelligence. This sunny morning finds him hiking the rocky hills and pastures above a small Maltese port city in search of a girl. He thinks she may be the key to his finishing the mission. Marshall was sent to Malta to track down a rumor passed to Navy Intelligence by their peers in Great Britain, who knew the US navy had a man in the area. The rumor was almost certainly nothing of real importance, but his superiors wanted to know for certain, and now the Brits owed them one.

It helped that it was a beautiful day, and the hills reminded him of his family home in Kentucky. His by-the-regs uniform may have been a bit warm for the job, but he was on good duty and not complaining. His brown hair was buzzed short, and his Navy tan seemed to soak up the afternoon sun as he slowly tracked his target

The story begins....

"Merde! Son of a Sterva! Gamo!"

Eliza might have appeared to be 17 or maybe even 18 years old, but she cursed like a collection of sailors in a dockside bar. The rock she was digging at didn't seem to notice much.

The man watching her certainly did. He moved out of the trees he was using as cover and took a step toward the girl. Without turning around, she spoke to him "Far enough. Close enough. You finally worked up the nerve to show yourself, big man. Well done!" With that she turned, holding the shovel in her left hand, while her right rested on the butt of a holstered pistol that looked huge on her slight frame.

He stared at the pistol, figuring out that it was a US Colt .45 automatic. The holster looked like a reworked military piece, with no flap left and slots cut to let it ride on her belt. Maybe it looked too big for the girl, but she didn't seem to notice or care. In fact, he damn near shivered with the cold stare she aimed at him. Caution seemed to be reasonable at this point.

"You knew I was there?" he said quietly. It was a still day, and his words carried as far as the pretty child, but probably no further. "I thought I was careful".

"Big man, I knew you were coming before you did," the girl said, clearly holding back a scornful laugh. It was galling, but her hand did not leave the pistol. He was close enough to see it was carried fully cocked, and almost certainly had a round in the chamber. That left nothing but her draw and maybe four pounds of pressure on the trigger to make his day turn FUBAR (Fouled up beyond all repair).

For some reason, he never even questioned her ability to shoot him without hesitation.

"I'm not sure what that means, but I've been sent here to talk with you. You are Eliza Magri, are you not? If you wish, I will sit down here and throw my ID to you" said the man who gave off an air of deference all out of proportion to Eliza's physical stature. Colt .45's had a way of encouraging that.

He looked at the girl and realized she might be on the high end of his age estimate. Her hair was dark brown and pulled into a tight ponytail that hung just past her shoulders. She was dressed in dark and worn working clothes that set her lightly tanned skin in contrast. What struck him most were her eyes. They were a light blue that seemed almost icy in comparison to her wholesome peasant girl appearance.

Eliza continued the cold stare for another few heartbeats and then nodded acceptance. Still, her hand remained on the pistol as she let the shovel fall to the ground. He was not surprised to see the handle hit the ground behind her where it was as far from him as possible. The girl didn't seem to believe in good human nature at all.

Moving slowly, he sat down with his legs splayed apart, clearly unable to get back up quickly. He was doing everything he could to allay her concerns, but she obviously was not giving him an inch. He slowly reached into his outside jacket pocket and removed his leather ID wallet. Judging the distance, he tossed it at her feet so close she only had to bend her knees and her left hand grabbed it.

He watched as Eliza brought the id into her line of sight without ever once taking her eyes off him. One-handed, she opened the leather wallet and glanced quickly at the identification card displayed. As close as he could count, her eyes were off him for no more than two seconds at a time.

Even if he'd wanted to move on her he wouldn't have made it two feet before being shot. He was impressed.

"Charles Marshall, US Navy. Even if this is real, am I supposed to be impressed?" she said with one eyebrow lifted. "Why would a US soldier be here, and what do you want from me?"

"Sailor, not soldier," he said.

"What? What's the difference?" said Eliza.

"Soldiers play in the mud. Sailors are professionals who work on the sea. Soldiers stand around waiting for us to take them places. They don't get to play in the mud if we don't haul their carcasses to the war" explained Charles, with a bit of a smile. The rivalry was real, but maybe now was not the time. "Also, it's Petty Officer Charles Marshal". He tacked on a smile that was real and hoped it would make him look likable.

She looked at him while considering this. He was indeed a big American man as only they seemed to breed. She'd known that before he stepped out of hiding as she'd seen him walking up the hill behind them. He walked with the easy arrogance of an American, who seemed to innocently own the world when they bumbled around. A little over six feet tall, and well-muscled for someone obviously not a farmer. His skin was too pale, but the brown hair and grey eyes gave him a more serious appearance when she took the time to really look.

Eliza tossed his ID back to him, and then backed away about 50 feet. "You are wasting my time Big Man. There is work to do. If you want to talk, then you must work. Pick up the shovel and dig up that rock. You work, we talk".

Marshall was amused, insulted, and impressed all at the same time. Here was a whisp of a girl and he had little choice. He could follow her orders, get shot, or walk away. His mission demanded he swallowed his pride and pick up the shovel. He began digging at the rock with the shovel as he talked.

"Yes, it's real. My name is Charles Marshall. I'm a Petty Officer in the United States Navy, and I'm here under orders from the Office of Naval Intelligence. My orders are to find you and investigate some stories that have come from this Island". He'd almost dug under the edge of the rock, and he jammed the shovel into the gap as he prepared to lever the rock up.

"NO!" she yelled at him. "You idiot! That will break the shovel. That tool is valuable, you fool. Have you never used a shovel before?". He was taken back enough to drop the shovel and take a step away from her.

"Not much digging to be done on a ship ma'am. All I really know about rocks is how to avoid hitting them. Bad for an officer's career to go around hitting rocks with his ship ma'am".

He really did know how to run a shovel because his family had a farm. He grew up working hard, and he certainly knew how to dig rocks. They damn near grew as a crop where he was from. Her anger at taking a chance with the shovel surprised him, but he passed it off as being poor. Shovels honestly did cost money, and money was probably scarce on Malta.

Eliza gave him a look that spoke of disdain, but with a hint of a smile. "There's no ship here and no water. What good is a big bad sailor man without a ship and water?"

"I'm here because the Germans are here. Up there, in the sky" he said as he pointed towards the sun. She didn't fall for it he noticed, and his respect moved up one more notch. "They are determined to take this island or destroy it and they don't care which. The Brits fight them, and so do we.

Anything that helps that, anything at all... that's my job. You might be able to help".

"Me? A poor stupid shepherd child? Do you take me for a fool?" Her smile had fled, and her eyes were cold again. Cold enough that he felt the chill despite the sun shining on him.

"Maybe. Maybe not. I hope to find out. It's why I'm here. Can we talk? At your home, if you wish. I have no secrets from your family" Charles asked. "I'll answer any questions you have if you will answer mine, is it a deal?"

"Maybe we have secrets from you, American, but yes. If you are fool enough to walk into our home on your own, then we will listen to what you have to say. Maybe you will even walk out again" she said in a cold voice that belied her age. He wondered if the war had made her this hard or if it was a Maltese thing. He decided then and there to skip any games and just be straight with these people. They weren't going to swing at a bum pitch, no matter how good it looked.

"I will take you to my father. You can explain yourself to him" she said. The look on her face made it clear she didn't expect much.

Taking the shovel in her off-hand, he noticed she kept her other on the pistol's grip. His position was crystal clear. The little girl with cold eyes had the means to end him and looked willing to use the shovel to dig his unmarked grave. A chill went down his back, but the mission required he shut up and deal with it right now.

She used the shovel and pointed towards the edge of the tree line, "Go that way. I will tell you when to turn".

They didn't speak as they walked, and she never got close enough for him to even hope of being tricky. For a brat, she certainly had skills in enough abundance to equal her lack of trust.

If it hadn't been for the burning itch between his shoulder blades, it would have been a beautiful day for a walk. The land reminded him of home, with grassy fields interrupted by copses of stunted trees and shrubs. All of it appeared well grazed to his eye, and as they crested the hill he saw why. A herd of long-haired goats, tended by a young boy, was feeding on the grass and shrubs.

His own experience ran towards horses and chickens, but he liked the looks of the goats anyway. As they walked, he wondered how they'd thrive back home on his parents' farm.

He waved to the boy, who stared at him. The goats shied away, and the boy was quickly busy guiding the herd in the opposite direction. When Eliza came into view the goats calmed, and the boy went back to staring. She moved her hands in some sort of code, and the boy simply nodded and went back to his goats.

Their trek was only about a mile, with her guiding him along from behind. He had enough time to wonder if he was being herded much like the goats were, and unhappily concluded that he was in exactly that position.

Eliza's home was a stone cottage that couldn't have been more than three or four rooms. Built untold generations ago, it looked like part of the landscape till the wooden goat shed and pens were taken into account, along with the smoke drifting from the short chimney.

A new cottage was being built alongside the original, and along the same lines. As they moved closer, he understood why the girl had been prying up the rock. Hundreds like it lay next to the building under construction, and an older man was finishing laying up a fresh rank of them into the new cottage wall.

"Far enough," she said. "Sit if you wish. This will take a moment" and the girl skirted far around him before moving to speak with the stone layer. They both gestured toward him as they spoke, and Eliza's lack of trust was quite evident. The elder man sighed and walked slowly towards PO Marshall.

"I am Eliza's father," the gentleman said in slightly halting English. "You are an American officer?"

"Petty Officer Charles Marshall, sir, of the United States Navy".

"There are no United States ships here. I expect you have a story young man. Does your family honor the rules of host and guest?"

"We understand the guest does no harm or refuses help to the host, and the host is obligated to provide safety, food, and rest for a short time. That's how my Daddy taught us anyway".

The old man considered this as he looked at Charles. "Good enough. Merhba lill-mistieden. Come into our home and we will speak", and he turned towards the older cottage.

Made a guest in their home by the old man, Charles was offered a seat at the table and a cup of tea was placed before him. Eliza set another for the father as he eased into his chair. Nothing was said till they had both sipped their tea. "My name is Henry Magri. I am the father to Eliza, and Peter who you saw with our goats. Are you hungry young friend?" he asked.

Knowing the offer was genuine, but also aware food was tight, Charles said "My thanks, but I have eaten well today. I came only to speak with you, but your hospitality honors me". Charles didn't think of it as a game. In his home in the rolling hills of Kentucky, such things were taken seriously. People there had little wealth, but much pride.

"Then, Petty Officer Charles Marshall, it is time to say what you came here to say," said the old man as he laid his gnarled hands on the table.

It didn't escape his notice that Eliza had not set herself a place at the table and stayed as close to the door as she could without being rude. It was also clear she'd kept a clear line of fire on him that didn't endanger her father.

"Thank you, Sir. Rumor has reached the ears of Naval Intelligence that something special seems to be happening here. A decision was made to investigate it by the PDB" Charles said.

"PDB?" questioned the old man.

"Powers That Be," said Charles with a slight smile. "I must remember not everyone knows our terms of endearment. In any case, the job got passed down the line till it hit my boss. He decided it fit me to do the investigating. That's why I'm here".

"Why you, if I may ask" asked Henry.

Laughing, Charles said "Because it wasn't important enough to send a real live officer, and I was the first person he saw after he had his coffee that day".

The old man thought about this, and a small smile came to his face. "As it ever is, my young friend. And this rumor that brings an American to my table?".

"We have heard that bad things happen to German forces when they get near this area. Not in wholesale lots, but in an awful picky way. Planes crash. Spies disappear. Even... bombs going off in midair without explanation" Charles said as he watched the old man's face, which was set in stone.

"Why do you bring such a crazy rumor to my door?"

"I came to Malta and listened to people talking. Brits are a superstitious bunch, so the gossip wasn't hard to find. They don't know anything for sure, except it involves this area. This is where the rumor brought me. I was raised to hunt, and this is where the dog pointed" said the Petty Officer.

"I can't see how we can help you, young man. I think you may be better seeking a priest than a poor shepherd family" said the old man, who then slowly got to his feet. It was obvious the interview was over, and Charles chose not to push the issue. He certainly wasn't giving up, but his mission was going in a different direction than he planned. He too rose, and with a nod moved to the door while Eliza stepped sideways keeping her hand on her pistol.

"Thank you, Sir. I appreciate you allowing me to speak. If Eliza can point the way, I'll head back towards my quarters now. With luck, I'll be there in time for dinner".

Charles knew something was off. Henry, the father, didn't laugh at the tale he told. Eliza was just too good at fieldcraft for a young girl. Things were not adding up in his experience, and suddenly he realized why his boss sent him instead of the other town-raised men in his command.

A moment later, they stood at the gate of the goat yard as Eliza gave him directions back to the small port village where he was staying. "One question Eliza, if I may?" Charles said. She just looked at him with a face that mirrored her father's.

"Where did you come across an American Colt .45 automatic?" He said, with an innocent glance at it.

Eliza stared at him coldly and turned to walk back inside the house with her father, not saying a word. Charles smiled and began the miles-long trek back to the portside village.

❧❦

That evening, seated at the dinner table, Henry told stories of the past to his children. They'd heard the stories before of course, but respect had them quietly listening. Eliza burned with curiosity about the big American who'd come calling, but her father seemed to be taking the long way around getting to it.

"My father, we must speak of that man. He came here with a purpose, not to buy a goat. He is dangerous to us".

"Child, even in this we are guided by our ancestors. You know this is true. There Is nothing to fear in this man. He would not have been allowed near us if it were otherwise". The elder man said. With that, they both

90

looked down at the table for a moment, seeming to be in another place for a moment. Their eyes lost focus for a moment, and they seemed to be listening to something, or someone. Peter took the opportunity to snatch another sausage for himself and was innocently eating when Eliza and Henry snapped back to the table.

"Enough for now. You heard... it is time to go. Ready yourself, and I will see to your rifle".

Eliza said nothing as she rose from the table and went to her room. There she changed from her white shirt and brightly colored skirt into typical peasant goat herder clothes. Well-worn but clean, a pair of old pants that may have once been dark green, and a baggy shirt that began life as a gray tunic. Together, the clothes made her appear to fade into the background. She pulled her hair up and tied it with a scrap of cloth before she added a floppy goat herders' hat which had several sad bits hanging loose. Altogether, she looked exactly like how everyone imagined a poor shepherd kid would look.

Back to the main room, she met her father at the door where he handed her an oddly shaped old feed sack. Along with it a satchel with a strap that she threw over her head and shoulder. That let the bag rest under her left hand, while she carried the sack in her right.

Standing back her father looked at her by the light of the lanterns in the room. "That will do Eliza. You are ready. Go with God my daughter. Listen to your heart and choose well".

She slipped out the door while it was open just enough and closed it quietly behind her. Moving as only a child raised to it could, she disappeared into the evening gloom as she walked away. Not even the goats noticed her pass by their pen as she moved like a whisper in the breeze.

One mile and then two went past as she simply walked the paths towards the seaside village nearest them on the island. She'd seldom been in the town itself, but a lifelong acquaintance with it made it seem like an extension of their own land. With a goat's sureness of foot, she made her way to a hill overlooking the port village. In the light from the gibbous moon, she could see waves hitting breakwater, and the boats rocking in the small bay.

The British used the area as a base of sorts for their smaller ships. A few destroyers floated at the pier and located between her and the port she could see their small airfield. The night air was quiet and carried the sounds of men being called from their beds. No lights were lit where she could see them, but the shadows of people running in the moonlight were visible to eyes well-adjusted by her long walk.

Moving to a rocky outcropping, Eliza settled herself down into a shallow grassy area. In front of her were a few rocks seemingly piled at random. It was on these rocks that Eliza unwrapped her odd sack, revealing an old rifle. The rifle didn't reflect much light, as it was a full-stocked military model. The wood was smooth but wrapped here and there with scraps of stained rags.

She ever so slowly slid the rifle over the rocks as a rest, with the muzzle coming even with a spot that strangely had no loose dust or dirt to blow around from the muzzle blast. To an onlooker, it would have become clear the position had been prepared long in advance. Years perhaps.

As she quietly waited, Eliza stared out from under her hat at the sea. Her duty lay in that direction, and that's where her focus was as well. Her concentration was deep enough that she never noticed as a man walked up the hill and sat down just on the other side of her rock mound. Neither did he notice her as she mimicked a shadow in the moonlight on the rocks.

They both sat there without a sound, unaware of each other for another 20 minutes or so. Then, a droning sound in the night from out to sea. Soon it was joined by another, and another as the sound multiplied and became the growl of a bomber flight. It was time for Eliza to perform her family's sacred role in the history of Malta, which is how she looked at it.

She lifted the bolt of her rifle, and quietly stroked a round into the chamber. 'Click click, Click click'. The sound carried far enough that the hidden man heard it, but he passed it off as insects in the night. Reaching up to the rear sight, she slid the adjuster forward to an unseen notch her fingers told her was correct. Once again, she wished she had the newer model of the rifle with a better sight but this one was what the ancestors provided.

Round in the chamber, she looked through the sights as the droning became shadows, and then the shadows formed into aircraft. What she was aiming at was unclear, but the rifle was steadily pointing at a place far in front of the first bomber, tracking its progress from at least half a mile away. As the plane came closer, her breathing stilled and listened for the word.

In her mind, the voice whispered "Now" and she squeezed the trigger. The rifle bucked as it sent the .30 caliber bullet from the muzzle at 2300 feet per second. She didn't move except to absorb the recoil and run the bolt to chamber another round. Before the first bullet hit, she fired a second on the same dark path.

She could see the first airplane in the flight jink to the right, and then turn nose down as it plunged into the bay. She took aim again, and when the voice spoke the word, she quickly fired three times. Without looking, she ejected the fifth empty casing and pulled a stripper clip of five more rounds from her pouch. In seconds she had smoothly reloaded the rifle and taken aim again.

She was just in time to see the second plane duplicate the actions of the first, diving straight into the waters of the bay and vanishing from sight. By now, she could hear the two lone fighters at the airbase struggling to take off and chase what was left of the bombers as they turned away without dropping their bombs. The German pilots had heard of the 'Ghost of Malta' and many had watched their fellow airmen fall from the sky without a reason they could see. Watching their two lead planes go straight in without spotting flak or fighter, they were willing to face their commander before they chanced the Ghosts.

Eliza heard rocks falling from the side of her mound, and a man's voice saying, "Son of A Bitch!". She ducked and tried to crawl away before he could come around to her side but didn't quite make it. Pointing her rifle at the man stumbling around the rocks, she held her fire as the man's hands shot straight up in the air. "Whoa girl, it's me. Petty Officer Marshal. I'm no threat!"

They stood there looking at each other in the moonlight. Neither moved while Charles prayed, and Eliza came to her decision. She lowered her rifle towards the ground, and in a loud whisper told him to get moving. "Move!

We must leave here now!" With her left hand she pointed up the path, and he started picking his way over the rocks.

⟫⟫⟫ ⟪⟪⟪

Once again, he found himself walking in front of the young girl while she had a gun on him. This was getting to be a very bad habit, but it had him chuckling to himself. All in all, he thought it was only slightly less dangerous on Malta than being on a British destroyer observing their hunting of German subs, his previous assignment. Even the food was pretty much the same. Poor quality and not enough of it.

"I'll go where you say, but now you must be straight and tell me the truth or kill me. I just watched you shoot two German bombers right out the air with that pop gun. I can't unsee that".

Eliza was cursing to herself under her breath, thinking furiously about what she could do. She'd been performing missions like this for two years, and never once had she been caught. She'd always trusted the ancestors to guide her, and this had never happened.

"Shut up and walk" she growled. The rifle was getting heavy in her hands, but she kept it ready as they walked the path back to her home. She'd always varied the way she came home just in case she was followed, no matter what the ancestors had to say. Her father had drilled her on it since she was a little girl. Tonight, she took the most direct way home. The situation she was in now was far outside her young experience and she decided she needed her father. Only he had the wisdom to deal with this. "Just keep walking. You know where we are going".

The drill as they approached the cottage was the same as before. She had him stop some distance away while she finished the walk to the door on her own. Eliza's eyes never left him as she tapped the door, and when it cracked open, she whispered a few words.

Henry Magri stepped out the door and settled with his arms crossed as he stared at Charles.

"Your family does not treat guest responsibilities as ours does. Do you have more words to speak this time?" said the old man, all sense of friendliness gone.

"Sir, I am no threat to you or your family. I didn't know Eliza was in those rocks when I came up the hill over the port. I heard the raid warning and went looking for a good place to observe it from. That was the closest I found. The first I knew about Eliza was when she downed those bombers with her trick shooting, and then she captured me and marched me back. Please ask her if I speak the truth" Charles said.

Henry and Eliza had a whispered conversation in Maltese, at the end of which she nodded while looking down.

"Come into the house, boy, and we will talk," the old man said.

The door was held open for him, and Marshal made his way inside. Henry waved him to his previous chair at the table while Eliza vanished, only to return in moments dressed as she had been for dinner. Her rifle had been left leaning against the table by her father. Charles had noted the safety was not on anymore.

"Eliza, tea for all of us please," said Henry. "Petty Officer Charles Marshall, can you forget what you saw tonight?'

"Sir, I will not lie to you. Even if it wasn't my duty to report what I've seen I could never forget that. If she hadn't done it twice in a row, I would have sworn it was dumb luck. Now I know what she did was on purpose. I just can't see how she did it." said Charles.

The old man sighed and seemed to cave into himself a little. He stared at the table for a few moments, and Marshall noticed Eliza doing the same thing. Then they both looked at him at the same time.

Henri Magri spoke in a quiet voice "What I am telling you is a secret this family has kept for generations. I'm telling you about this so you will understand when I say it will do you no good. What Eliza can do, and what I did, and my mother before me... we do because the ancestors gave us this duty to Malta."

"Of course, I'll listen Sir, but what happens after that I can't say yet." Said Charles.

"In that too, we shall trust in the ghosts of our ancestors". The old man went on "Malta has been at war for ten times longer than your nation has ever existed. Romans, Phoenicians, Turks, Italians, British, and now Germans. It's Malta against the world, and all because of where our home lies. We are every pirate's gate to the sea and every conqueror's stumbling block. They have all tried, and eventually, all failed. You see.... The land remembers. Kill enough of her sons and daughters, and the land rises against the invaders. It's the blood I think, soaking into the soil and rocks".

"Sir... I...." Charles stammered. He was lost in trying to understand the point.

"Shush child. Let an old man speak" Henry said as he accepted tea from Eliza.

"The island remembers, and in it turn reaches out. To us, and our family. The ghosts make it clear when our duty appears and makes what we do possible. Long ago we shot stones from slings. Then it was arrows, and knights faced our crossbow bolts. After that, it was musket balls, and now bullets. Our ancestors know when the invaders come, and when our little efforts can make it change. We are no army with cannons and ships and tanks. We are just a peasant family of goat herders, as this land has been sheltered for a thousand years. But sometimes just one bullet can change everything. We trust the ancestors to know when and where, and we do our best to follow their trust in us".

Henry could see PO Marshall was trying to understand, which was better than dismissing him for a crazy old shepherd. "Boy, you come from a young land. Here, we LIVE in history. We breathe it in with the very air itself. Through us, the land lives as we live with the land. It's not religion. It just is what it is". Marshal heard the old man say those words, but the voice could have been his own grandfather's. "It just is what it is" was something Charles had heard from Gramps almost daily most of his childhood.

"Sir, how can Eliza shoot the pilot of a plane in the air at half a mile? That's not possible on purpose" asked Charles.

"The spirits know. They know everything, as best we can tell. What happens on the rock of Malta, in the skies above her, in the seas near her; They know. They know the very movement of every breeze. You say it's not possible.... But you said if you'd seen it done just once you'd have called it luck. You know it's possible, you just don't believe in it not being luck" said the old man quietly, almost reverently.

"Why does that change my Duty?" said Charles. "I must still report what I know".

"If it's something that cannot be done outside our family, and away from Malta, what use is that to others? If by reporting you destroy what we do, have you not aided your enemy, the Germans?" the old man asked with pleading in his eyes.

Charles sat thinking a while, sipping his cold tea. He saw Henry glance at Eliza and understood the message that passed. "I know you can kill me and have your secret safe, and I know you are trying not to. I thank you for that. I think my family would understand and thank you too. What I don't know is if I can believe what you are telling me".

"If you don't believe, then what have you to report but the ramblings of a crazy old shepherd? But no, I think it best if you do believe. You shall accompany Eliza on her next calling, and witness for yourself the truth in what I say" said the old man with iron in his voice. "Till then, you should be our guest here. We only get as much warning as is necessary, and if you are not here when they call you cannot witness the truth".

Charles agreed to the offer, as there was nothing else he could really do. If they wanted him dead, he'd already be dead. The only way he'd learn what he had to was to be there, as the father suggested.

Charles had time to think on the hike to the port village to gather his clothes and gear. It was even longer on his way back with his duffle hanging off his shoulders, but the sweat helped him clear his mind. He'd heard lots of stories growing up in Kentucky, where his people had been since before it was a state. He supposed Malta had seen its people's blood spilled enough that anything might be possible here too. His own grandmother had a habit of talking to spirits, and nobody there was man enough to call HER crazy. Family tradition said she'd planted more revenuers than any ten Shiners in the county combined. If granny could talk to 'The Ancestors', then why not these people?

Back at the cottage, he was shown a room to use. It had been Peter's, but he'd happily moved to the small barn to make room (and just happen to be out from under his sister's thumb).

Charles took a chance on speaking with Eliza before she left him to his bed. "Your rifle is an old Springfield, like our Marines use now. Another American weapon like your Colt. Why American guns?"

Eliza studied him with a calculating gaze. "Americans make good weapons. I think your people understand war. I wonder if America also makes good men?"

Charles shivered as he tried to look away from her eyes. He was being judged, and not just by Eliza and her father.

>>>>>> <<<<<

Charles surprised himself by falling quickly into the routine with the Magri family. He went out daily with Eliza and her brother to bring the goats to the pasture. Typically, he and the girl took turns digging up rocks while Peter watched over the goats. By lunchtime, he and the girl carried rocks back to the cottage and helped Henry with the new cottage, and Peter followed near dark with the goats.

Charles decided he hated rocks. Not just rocks he could hit with a ship as a navy man, but all rocks right down the pocket-sized ones he carried back. To him, rocks took an evil position right up there with Nazis.

This went on for three days, all mostly comprised of goats, rocks, moderate amounts of food, and stories from Eliza's father after dinner. He learned quickly that sharing a glass of whiskey from his duffel bag made the stories a lot longer. Depending on the rocks he'd carried, this was not always a good thing.

On the fourth day, something changed at dinner. With the sun going down and the meal only half eaten both Henry and Eliza became quiet and stared into the distance. As one, they rose from the table.

"Change your clothes Eliza, and I'll get things ready," said the old man. He looked at Marshall. "It's time. Change your shirt. Take this old one of mine. It will do" said Henry as he tossed the PO a shoddy but clean old shirt.

"If I'm out of uniform I can be shot as a spy," said Charles, standing in shock.

"By who? The Germans? The British hold this island you fool" the old man said sharply. "Do as you are told. Change now!". Henry worked on loading the bag while Charles quickly changed out of his uniform shirt and into the ancient peasant tunic shirt.

Moments later Eliza was standing at the door putting on her satchel and taking the sack-wrapped rifle from her father. "You understand?" He spoke. "Yes Father, I have it. I know where to go".

"Eliza do not risk yourself for him" was his quiet response. Turning to Charles, "No offense my friend, but she is my daughter. Come back without her, and you never leave again".

The old man was not smiling, and Charles believed him with all his heart. "Aye Sir, return her or die trying. You have my word". Not even a wisp of a smile by the father. "I'll hold you to that".

➤➤➤ ⫷⫷⫷

Eliza walked past the goat pen, through the gate, and chose a path Charles hadn't been on yet. It led over the hills and made a line North as straight as any goat path ever could. She moved like a ghost herself, and it took an effort on his part to both keep up and stay silent. His childhood in the Kentucky hills was coming back to him, but it could have come quicker to his thinking. He'd spent plenty of time as a boy hunting small game and deer for the family, but Eliza had been trained to this since she could walk. She wasn't even breathing hard, despite refusing to let him touch her burden, let alone carry it for her.

Charles was having a hard time dealing with being led by a young girl. It just went against the grain for a Navy Petty Officer to take a back seat to a youngling, even though he was less than ten years older than the girl. Advancement came fast in a wartime Navy, and Marshall had proven himself under fire. His current assignment to Naval Intelligence as an aid to Captain Morgan had stretched his horizons, but he still operated under the old PO code. As far as he was concerned nobody was tougher than a US Navy Petty Officer, and being challenged by the competence of a mere girl was getting under his skin. Not being able to growl, yell, and give orders left him nothing but silently enduring. It just wasn't cute anymore, no matter how pretty the girl was.

He'd learned early in his Navy career that true respect had to be earned, and he was being forced to grudgingly respect a child for her field skills. He didn't like it one little bit, but he recognized it. Maybe he could find someone to yell at later and feel better.

As he followed Eliza around the hills on the paths he could barely see, he was thinking furiously of the coastal maps he'd memorized. Malta is an island, and the parts that mattered were mostly all where land met the sea. The shore was riddled with inlets and small ports, each home to fishing boats and in most cases smugglers. Quite often the two were superimposed and interchangeable. The island was also infamous for its caves, seemingly like a big chunk of Swiss cheese plunked down in the Mediterranean.

As best he could navigate with only glimpses at his compass by moonlight, they were headed towards a small bay that barely qualified for the name. Not quite a quarter-mile wide by less than that deep, it was just a blip in the coastline without a name on the map.

After two hours of walking, Eliza stopped by some trees and allowed him to catch up. "Here we rest for a short while. You are breathing too loud, like a mule. Try to control yourself big man" she whispered. "From here on we must be silent. The British seldom patrol here, but smugglers may. I prefer no one know we were here".

Whispering in return Charles replied, "Can you tell me where we are going? Do you even know, or do your spirits guide you?".

She stared at him in the gloomy moonlight coming through the trees. His eyes were acclimated nicely, and he could see as well as feel the heat of her stare. "My father thinks you must understand and believe. I do not. Your belief means nothing to me, only whether you are a danger to us".

Once again, Marshall felt the chill of fear he'd never admit to anyone. In the daylight, this girl was pretty and competent, if a bit distant to him. On a mission, she was nothing but frigidly efficient and emotionless. He had no doubts she could leave his body buried in a shallow ditch without shedding a tear.

To be honest with himself, he was finding her both frightening and attractive, and that was distracting him from his job. He smiled a little, and when he saw her eyes widen when she noticed, he smiled even more. If this went on, he'd be laughing like an idiot, so he looked away and shut his mouth.

Without another word, Eliza stepped away from the shelter and shadow of the trees and moved back to the path. Setting off at a quicker pace than before she was forcing him to match her or fall behind. She didn't look back, but he was aware she could hear his breathing which was soon 'As loud as Mule' again, and he resented it. Petty Officers didn't do a lot of hiking around moonlit goat paths, and that was yet another thing that rankled him. 'Join the Navy and see the world' he thought. There was a recruiter who certainly needed a dose of reality. He spent the next few minutes fantasizing about having his recruiter alone in the rope locker for a discussion on Naval lifestyles.

Eliza knew where they were going, but she would never admit it to the American she didn't know why yet. She was surprised he'd managed to keep up with her, and to be honest with herself he really wasn't that bad at being quiet on the trail at night. That was another thing she'd never admit to him. Damn his arrogance!

She knew where she was going, but the mission itself would be a mystery till there. That was always the way it happened. It didn't seem the ancestors were keeping secrets so much as they only saw so far into what would be. Sometimes she'd walk for hours, just to be told to go home. Other times her destination changed on the way. She'd learned to trust in the voice of Malta, as her father had always told her to.

This American; How could he understand? His land was new. Barely a few hundred years old. Her home cottage was older than that, let alone the spirit of Malta. Big arrogant Navy man.

⇒⇒⇒ ⇐⇐⇐

She was indeed leading them to an inlet North of Marsascala bay. She wasn't sure what she'd find there, but the picture of where she needed to be was firmly in her mind. It was a rocky prominence that overlooked the upper part of the inlet, and she'd been there enough to know the path and the layout. It was a good observation spot, but with little cover.

The inlet was home to a few fishing families. They sailed from there, made their catch and sold it down the coast, and came home in the evening. That was about all she knew. It barely qualified as a village, let alone a town. More like a collection of homes around a pathway to the sea. Even the smugglers didn't have much use for the bay, outside hiding from storms.

Henry had packed her satchel heavily, and she almost considered letting the American carry it. It was loaded with food and a canteen of water, since both Eliza and her father had gotten the message, she'd be away for a time. That usually meant she'd be laying low during the day while observing the area between naps. She also carried a rain poncho that was lovingly well patched but had seen better days. She'd use this as cover when needed, curled up under it among the rocks of whatever outlook she was sent to. The patchwork of grey weathered canvas was at least as good camouflage as anything the soldiers had.

It was almost dawn as they arrived where she needed to be; Near the top of a rocky outcrop that looked over the upper part of the inlet. Not the actual very top, but about fifty feet down the side where a natural cleft made a spot hidden from view to anyone at the half dozen or so homes. She could see the inlet and the area around the upper part of it well, while her position would be difficult for anyone not airborne to notice.

Creeping up to the edge of the rocks on her knees, she settled in to observe the bay. Charles mimicked her actions, also crawling on aching knees to lay on the rocks beside her. The crawl hurt as sharp edges dug into his hands and knees and legs, but he'd be damned if he would complain in front of the girl.

Eliza smiled faintly as he finished his crawl into place. She knew it was agonizing to someone who hadn't sewn padding into their clothes at knees and elbows, but somehow had forgotten to mention that part to Charles.

They looked out across the inlet from their position and were surprised to see two Submarines floating near the deepest part in the middle. There was a small Navy vessel tending them and flying a British flag. The fishing boats were all tied to their home docks, and aside from a few people doing repairs and mending nets, it was a bucolic scene except for the jarring sight of the military craft.

"I know why they are here," whispered Charles. "I was given a short brief on British operation in the area. Nothing secret, just the general outlines.

The Brits have been tearing up enemy shipping in the med using subs based in part out of Malta. The Italian and German bombers are hitting back to even the score. I'll bet the British are spreading out any submarines they have here to make them harder targets".

"That makes sense," said Eliza. "Perhaps these subs will be targeted, but I think we'll be here all through the coming day to observe. Whatever is coming is not till it gets dark again".

"My guess is those boats will submerge soon and spend the day on the bottom of the inlet. Bombers can't hit them if they can't see them" Charles said while looking through a small pair of shaded binoculars he'd pulled from under his shirt. She hadn't been aware they were there. "You can see them casting off lines from the tender now. They'll spread apart before submerging. Once they lay on the bottom no one will see a thing".

"We must sleep while we can and take turns to keep watch. What happens, happens tonight and we must be ready. It will be a long walk home afterward." said Eliza. "I am tired, so you take first watch. Wake me at noon." Once again Charles bristled at taking orders from a young girl, but it was her operation. He was just an observer for now. Eliza settled down in a depression on the rock, using her satchel as a pillow. Her arms were wrapped around her rifle like it was her lifeline, and he suspected she even slept that way at home. In moments she appeared to be asleep, as the morning sun was peeking over the rocks and warming them.

Sleeping and eating when the chance presented itself was a sailor's skill, in Charles's experience. One never could count on either being possible, so a chance to eat or sleep wasn't passed up. While he was tired himself, he was too keyed up to really sleep. Him taking the watch made sense, not that he'd tell her that. Now he had hours to just lay there and watch the inlet area, while silently cursing the rocks he was surrounded by.

Within minutes his prediction for the submarines came to pass. They drifted about a hundred yards apart and then slowly submerged. Once they were under, not even a ripple showed their presence.

Charles had no envy at all for the Limey submariners. He'd happily sail through anything the enemy could throw at him while on a Navy ship, but the thought of diving underwater in a glorified coffin gave him the heeby jeebies. They would be laying on the bottom running off batteries for lights and air circulation, while it got stuffy and cold. He knew most of the men would try to sleep as much as possible, but the watch had to be kept too.

Trying to avoid looking at the pretty girl sleeping only a few feet from him, Marshall kept a regular sweep of the area with his binoculars. Every few minutes he did it with naked eyes as well, so he wouldn't miss the bigger picture. The tender stayed in the inlet at anchor near where the subs had gone under. Now past dawn, the houses came to life, and soon after the fishing boats headed out. The weather was clear, and a light breeze kept the sun from being too warm. All in all, it was a very pleasant day to lay back and take it easy.

Charles wished that was all he had to worry about. This whole thing had passed strange and was on its way to just plain nuts, but he had no choice but to roll with it. Petty Officers got things done, period, and he wasn't going to do anything less.

At 10 am by his watch Charles had just finished another visual sweep of the inlet and had also done another of the trail up the outcropping. He wasn't going to have anyone sneaking up on them if he could help it. Laying back to rest his eyes, he glanced at Eliza who was still curled up a few feet away.

This time, he saw her eyes were open and she was quietly watching him.

"Hey", he said softly. "It's 10 am, and everything is quiet. The subs are on the bottom, or they snuck away underwater. The fishing fleet is out. That Brit boat tending the subs is still anchored in the middle of the bay".

She just watched him, not answering.

PO Marshall was on to her game and wasn't going to get rattled by a stare-down. He turned back to his watch and scanned the small bay once again. Nothing had changed in the last five minutes, but he watched anyway. The weight of her gaze was on him, and he could deal with that as long he needed to.

"I am awake and can take the watch. You may sleep now if you wish" Eliza quietly said. She rolled over to where she could see the area herself, just happening to move closer to him doing it. He was acutely aware of this but showed no sign he noticed.

"To be honest, I'd like to talk if you are willing. At least you could listen if you don't feel like talking back" He spoke. In return, Eliza just made a small sound without taking her eyes off the fisherman's houses. Charles took this as permission.

"I'm trying to understand what your father told me, about your family and the Island. There's no way it's not crazy, but it makes sense too. I can't think of anything better to explain how you splashed two German bombers with five rounds from a 03". Charles waited a bit before going on, in the hopes she would take up the slack and start talking herself. She didn't.

"My people have been on our land for over 200 years" he went on. "I know that's nothing compared to yours, but I understand becoming part of the place. Maybe not as far as your father tells it. Who knows...? In a thousand years, the Kentucky hills might start talking back to my family. Sure are enough of us that seem to already hear things that aren't there, like my Grandmother does" he said, again hoping to draw her out.

In his peripheral vision, Charles could see the girl had glanced at him with that last admission. He knew he was making progress by that, but it was time to twitch the line, not set the hook.

"I love my Gram, but she is a strange duck for sure. Ever since my grandpop died it's like she's given up caring what people think. The family knows it's just her way, but she can sure worry the neighbors at times" he was reminiscing now, but with purpose.

"She never hid it from me, even when pop-pop was alive. She'd just be talking away to the empty air. Not like someone cussing out a stubborn rock in the field" he glanced at her to see a faint blush. "More like having a conversation with family. Family that had passed on, to be pickier about it". Charles hadn't ever told anyone outside his family, and it felt weird to be talking to a stranger about it. He grew quiet again, watching the bay and fishing village.

After a few minutes had passed, Eliza spoke softly "You miss your grandparents?"

"Yes", he admitted quietly. "I've been away on duty for two years now, and writing letters isn't the same as being there. Pop-pop died over ten years ago, and I think about him every day. He was more like my father than a grandfather. He's the one who thought I should join the Navy and see something of the world".

They both lay silently on the rock shelf, watching the inlet basking in the Mediterranean sun. By now the rock peak was shading them from the worst of the sun, and the sea breeze had picked up a little. Charles wanted to get Eliza speaking so he could learn more about what her family did with the 'Ancestors' but talking about his folks back home had left him missing them more than ever. "I'm going to sleep a bit," he said. "Wake me when you get tired, or evening is coming on" as he tried to match the ease she'd shown in getting comfortable on the damn rocks. Dear God, how he hated rocks.

She looked at him for a moment and then pushed her satchel over to him. With her hands, she mimicked putting it under her head as a pillow. He smiled and did as she showed him, and then closed his eyes. If she really wanted him dead, he'd already be dead. Since she didn't, he was comfortable with her keeping watch. He was asleep in seconds.

>>>> <<<<

Eliza laid on the rocks for an hour, watching the bay and houses, before she glanced over at Charles. She was sure he was asleep because nobody snored like that on purpose. Holding back a small smile, she considered throwing her rifle sack over his head to muffle it, even though the snoring wasn't too loud.

Charles had spoken of his family the way her father spoke of theirs. Like they were his reason for living. She needed to think about that, and luckily had hours ahead of her to do exactly that. Meanwhile, she watched the fisherman's houses more than the inlet. The ancestors had told her the danger came from that direction, and not from Charles as he lay sleeping. She still didn't understand why they allowed him to live after what he learned about them, but she was slowly warming to the idea. Even as he snored in her ear.

⇝⟫ ⟪⇜

As the sun was reaching the horizon, Eliza noticed Charles's breathing change. Rather than miss the chance if he woke on his own, she gave him a quick kick while prepared to cover his mouth with her hand. "Wake up noisy mule. Time to take watch. I'm going to rest a while before it begins. Wake me in an hour".

She rolled away to her chosen nook in the rocks, taking her satchel back as she did. Laying with her back to him, she closed her eyes and used the bag to cover her smile as she quickly drifted into a very light sleep.

Charles was startled fully awake in seconds and replayed the last few moments in his mind.

Damn, but that girl was aggravating. He moved to his watch position and resumed his surveillance of the inlet and fishing village. Every so often he glanced her way, but she remained asleep. The sleep of the innocent he supposed, although his shin still reported the boot she'd given him.

As soon as the sun was below the horizon, he watched the British tender move off, and then the two submarines surfaced within moments of each other. Immediately he heard their diesel engines fire up as they began recharging their batteries. Just lying on the bottom for the daylight hours should not have reduced their charge much. It was the propulsion motors that really ate up the battery life. He guessed they'd be ready to set out within an hour or two.

Taking that as his cue, he woke Eliza by the simple expedient of tossing small rocks at her till she cursed him. "Awake sleepy head?" he said as he smiled. The look of doom she gave him made it worthwhile, even guessing she'd make him pay somehow.

"The subs have surfaced, right where they were this morning. I expect they will sortie within an hour or so, to make the tide" he advised. "Any ideas what we should be looking for?" he asked her. The fishing boats were coming home now, one by one, puttering into the small bay and heading for their home docks.

"You watch the inlet and the subs. Lend me your binoculars, please. I wish to watch something of my own" she said while holding out her hand. He handed her the small optics, wondering what she had in mind. Out of the corner of his eye, he saw her focus on the houses at the edge of the tiny village. They sat that way for over 30 minutes, each watching their section of the area.

With little happening but what looked like the final provisioning of the submarines, Charles eventually took some time and tried to see what Eliza was looking for. As he scanned the fisherman's cottages with his bare eyes, he saw one up the hill whose lights went out. As soon as that happened, Eliza laid down the optics and began preparing her rifle.

Burning with curiosity but knowing better than to disturb her, he retrieved his binoculars and studied the small building. As he watched, he saw someone climb to the roof and sit back against the chimney. If he hadn't seen him move into that position himself, he never would have seen him afterward. He blended in with the stonework so cleanly.

As he watched through his binoculars, he saw the figure put something to his face and realized it was a handheld telescope. Like those ones they had in pirate movies that extended out with a pull. The thing must have been ancient.

Next to him, he heard a click, and before he could turn his head he nearly jumped out of his skin as Eliza fired. Throwing the glasses back to his eyes he watched the figure on the roof slump over and slide down the roof. The shot was still echoing from the stone hills around the inlet as the body fell off the short building and vanished.

He looked at Eliza as she calmly ran the bolt back and caught the empty shell. She dropped it into her pouch and pulled a single cartridge out to replace it in her rifle.

"You just.... Killed that man!" He said in a strangled voice. "What the hell?"

"Fool. Are you blind as well as stupid? He was spying on the British submarines. When they set off, he would radio the German ships waiting to hunt them. They'd be sitting ducks caught coming from the bay. I thought the big bad American Navy man knew everything" as her voice practically dripped with youthful scorn.

"How can you know that? He was just some guy on a roof!" he said, still rattled. As an experienced Navy man, he'd seen his ship fire at the enemy, and they'd sunk their share. This was the first time he'd ever seen one man deliberately killed, and by a mere wisp of a girl at that. He realized he'd badly misjudged just how dangerous Eliza was.

"He is why I was sent here. That is the house I was told to watch. There is no mistake. The ancestors do not make mistakes, Navy man" She said.

"But.... That was 1000 yards away!" he whispered, still in shock.

"Yes, that is what the sight was set at. Do you still not understand Big American Man? I just aim and fire when I'm told to. The ancestors know the path of the bullet, and why it must be fired. Even you could do this if you'd shut up long enough to listen to them. We just saved two submarines full of British sailors, and you can never tell anyone about it. Do you understand now?" She said in a low and harsh voice. "My bullet killed one spy, which saved two subs, which will go on to kill many German ships and many German soldiers. Through me, the ghosts of Malta have acted to save our land and our people. Through me! Do you finally understand?".

Charles sat stunned. He stared at Eliza in shock. Not shocked at her, and not at the amazing shot she'd made, but at what she said. Yes, he did understand now and knew why he'd never be able to tell anyone. Not only would they refuse to believe him, but it would stop Eliza and her family from doing their duty to their ancestors.

Charles slowly stood up and offered her his hand. "I'll carry your bag if you like. We must leave here quickly and go home now. The British will be searching the village and will find that man soon enough. They'll guess at a sniper and may search even this far away. We can't be here when they do".

They checked their gear and made sure they left nothing behind to betray their presence. This time, Charles took the lead as they walked the pathway. Eliza followed in surprise, carrying her rifle with loving care.

After a mile, Charles stopped by some trees and waited for Eliza to move closer.

"Yes, I understand now. I won't be telling anyone about you or your family. Malta needs her secrets to survive, and we all need Malta". He said with firmness. Petty Officer Marshall had made up his mind and knew his duty. "I'll ask your father what your family needs and make sure you get it. Think about that while we walk".

As he turned, she put her hand on his arm. "I can tell you right now something I can use. Your binoculars. Those helped, and there are none on Malta we can get".

Without a word he pulled the binoculars from under his shirt and offered them. "No," she said. "You carry them for me, Big Man. You may be useful to keep around after all as the ancestors said".

He put the binoculars back inside his shirt and turned away to resume their journey. Something about her smile was weirdly unsettling him. It was predatory, but he couldn't decide if it worried or thrilled him. He decided to let the ghosts tell him the answer.

THE PYRAMID OF MALTA

KERMIT GRENOILLE

A name. A monument. A moment in time, frozen into rock, and set into the annals of human memory through the hands of master carvers. A monument to the gods that a king has joined their ranks, there to live with them evermore. Such things had my fathers, hundreds, thousands of cycles of the great Sun past, all the way through to my own father. Great towering edifices to the godhood of dead kings, crafted by the hands of slaves and free men alike, these were tombs etched with their names and ensured that time and memory would never forget them. The oldest of these towered towards the sky, proclaiming the divinity of their inhabitants. My own stolen tomb, along with those of my more recent forebears, sought to nestle closer to the underworld, to ease and shorten the journey. Such a tomb would I have rested in had events occurred otherwise. Such would have had my brother, had he not followed another. Such would have had my son. Such a tomb is denied me, for my rest is restless, and my final repose is not yet settled.

My son. My firstborn, my only son. Believe not the records of time, nor the histories of my people. The one who wore my name, who finished my reign, was not a son of the gods at all. For my son died before I, a sacrifice to a father's vainglory, with no heirs of body after, and I, the king, pursued the path of vengeance to mine own end. He who wore the double crown and took my name was of the noble caste, the highest servants of the lowest gods, but he was no god himself. Perhaps it was for the best.

Much I do not remember. Much I have lost to time. The vast and restless sleep of death has stolen many details, and buried others under the sands of the ages, washed away by the endless waves of my hatred and eventual acceptance. Perhaps I may regain them if I ever achieve the restoration of my soul. Or perhaps I am more complete without them.

My brother. My accursed, blessed brother. I blamed him for the losses. For the crop failures, for the plagues, for the tainted water of the holy river, for the deaths of so many of my people. For the death of my son. I have come to know my error, as I have come to know my place, but I did not at that time, not then. My rage blazed hotter than the fires of my forefather. It burned colder than the frigid fires of the underworld. It was implacable and could only be satisfied by the deaths of my brother and of all those whom he held dear.

My father's father began it. He believed he understood. He saw that our land's guests, granted safe haven from their homeland's turmoil, had not left, but rather increased in number and wealth, threatening to usurp our people's rightful place as the owners of this mighty land, replacing our nation with their own, toppling our gods to install their heresy. So he made them slaves, put into place controls, authorities, privileges and powers, all meant to bring down the upstarts, and remind them of their places within this country.

He never should have broken the code of hosts and guests. He brought ruin upon this land, and his line ended forever upon the death of my son, a death to the vengeance of that usurping deity, which overpowered all our gods as though they were mere mortal men attempting to control the tide. He has brought about the ruin of the lines of the gods. Far from forestalling the prophecies of his seers and the skies, he began their fulfillment, with a cruelty unimaginable to any civilized people.

My mother was his weakness. Possibly because she was born last of all my grandfather's children, when he was in his waning years and near achievement of his own godhood, he doted upon her like no other, granted her every wish, and would deny her nothing. So when she discovered an infant child of the slave race hidden along the banks of the holy river, he allowed her to keep it in violation of his own order earlier that same year. Perhaps he expected her to make a pet of the boy, a eunuch, devoted to her service. I suspect he never would have allowed her to adopt him, proclaim him publicly as her own, born of herself and her brother as our laws and gods demanded to keep the race of kings pure, before even her own first child had been conceived. And then he died, never knowing what he had wrought, what he had unleashed. What he had failed to control. And he rested with his fathers and achieved his divinity.

My father could hardly disclaim his "son," so publicly proclaimed by his wife as a sign of her love that she would bear him an heir even before they were wed! Better the small scandal of love and devotion so closely kept that she would creep in silence to his bedchambers before the requisite one year of women's moons had been completed, than that the heir was not a son of the sun at all. Better the gossip of the precocious maturity of his youngest sister, than of the whispers of a spoiled child pushing a fearsome grandfather into his dotage and tomb through a violation of the laws of the heaven. Aye, an heir born before wedlock had happened before, and would undoubtedly again, and the unseemliness was only a topic for the idle wives of the wealthy. After all, the gods were known to take back children often, especially those of the kings. The perfection of the Unbroken Line could not have imperfection in its sons, and he might not survive. His natural mother of birth was located, and although never publicly acknowledged, she was selected as my mother's maidservant, and my brother's wet-nurse. And my parents were publicly wed, in celebration of their union and heir.

One year later, I was born, then a sister, promised in marriage to the heir that the blood of the sons of the sun would not be diluted. Three years after, another son, reclaimed by the gods for imperfection, along with my mother, who found herself unable to bear the strain of the pregnancies of the heavens any further.

Both of us, adopted and natural sons, were brought up and trained as heirs to the king. My brother, being the elder and the presumed successor to our father, was trained in governance, languages, the readings of the heavens, and the relations with our people and those of our neighbors. To me was given the sword and the spear, command of all our vast armies, and the responsibilities of enacting and enforcing the will and words of our father and king. Not that we did not share lessons, for a time could come when I was away at war and he would find need of knowledge of the sword, or that the gods could take him without heir or issuance, and it would be my lot to continue the Unbroken Line. But thus, were we trained, in accordance with our expected roles, should the gods will it. And none knew the true details of his birth.

Oh, that I had a sufficiency of his governance, that I might not have fallen into the trap of my own ego! Woe that my brother lacked my full confidence of arms when he decided to rejoin his people! For the power that called him was more terrible than any spear, and I lacked the wisdom to avoid its thrust!

I won many battles for my father's favor, for my brother's inheritance. Peoples still known, and peoples now forgotten, all fell before the wheels of my army's chariots. When the time of ascendance into godhood approached, I had extended our father's rule and our borders considerably. I was widely known as a mighty, proud, and fearless warrior. None dared stand before me, and I held the favor of the gods through the force of my own arm, stronger than any had seen for many a generation.

Of my brother, he was known throughout the land as wise beyond his years, possessed with a quiet, unassuming yet intensely powerful persona, of which he seemed unaware. His modesty and mild nature combined with his intellect, assuring the people of a benevolent king to come, one under whose future rule my conquests could be absorbed efficiently and with a minimum of strife. Yet it was evident to any that knew him that beneath the meekness lay iron, and the land knew that, backed by my arm, we would be secure from invaders and poised to further expand for the glory of the sun and the holy river.

My brother threw the land and the succession into some chaos when our father died. As the heir and firstborn, he was granted access to knowledge and secrets hidden from the world. Armed with these secrets and unbeknownst to all but a few of his closest advisors, he had located his

122

wet-nurse from his childhood, who had confirmed to him his true nature and parentage. Not a son of the sun at all, but the son of a slave, of a mistreated client people, welcomed as guests and then forced to endure the weight of chains! And he had rebelled, in the secrecy of his heart, against the silks of his upbringing.

There was a murder. An overseer of little importance and less rank, full of himself and pride, though little more than a slave himself. A man of worthless life, revenging himself upon our powerless guests, and deserving of death himself. A man who I would have killed without justification, never needing such, for as the right hand of the son of the sun, I held all lives of our people in my own palm. A trifle and pittance, whose death deserved no consequence, but my brother believed otherwise.

The eve our father died, he fled. Perhaps the king's lessons of justice and responsibility overpowered his mind in the wake of the blood he shed. Perhaps his wet-nurse had filled his head with filial duty to his family of birth over that of duty to the family that raised him. I do not know. Had he taken the place all the people knew to be his by birthright and by training, perhaps even then the visions of the magicians could have been avoided. But he disappeared, and as the next fully blooded sun of the son, I took up the double crown that he discarded.

I was given access to the secrets of the sons of the sun, lessons given to my brother in anticipation of his ascension. I learned which rituals were called for to bring a successful harvest. How to curse our enemies and grant our people favor. Which kings were born not of brother and sister as the sun demanded, but of more distant relations, due to a lack of male offspring of the line. Which queens were kings in their own rights, wearing the garb and wielding the flail by their own power. I learned the history of our land's now-unwanted guests, and how our own people had been granted the favor of their god for giving them refuge from the east.

I learned the truth of my brother. That he was no true son of the sun, but an interloper, an unwitting usurper to the throne, that I was the firstborn, the only son born of our father. That he was a slave, elevated to position unworthy, and granted secrets and lessons untold to others. That he had delved into these secrets in preparation for his ascension and gone seeking his true kin.

For that, I should have been grateful. That a son born of slaves instead of the holy fire of day should reach so closely as to have the reins of power nigh unto his fingertips was an abomination before the sun! It was only right and just that he should fall! All my battles won, my conquests achieved, my lands subjugated, were never in his domain, but for my own domains, my own slaves, my own glory. And yet, I began to hate him.

I hated him for daring to reach for that which was not his by birthright. I hated him for maintaining that reach even unto our father's death. I hated him for claiming that which was not his by blood, for inheriting that which to him did not belong. I hated him for his lessons in governance, which I would now have to enact even as I learned, for his deeper knowledge of my people than of his own only so recently uncovered.

I hated him for throwing it away as well. That he should be granted such glory, such power, and abandon it for the tears of a slave, that he would kill even the least of my people in defense of even the greatest of his. As lowly as that worthless overseer had been, his life was more valuable those of a thousand slaves! And I hated him for leaving me to learn the lessons he had absorbed since the cradle, sucking them along with that supposed "wet-nurse's" fodder.

124

I hated him for abandoning the sun for a god that would grant rich harvests to a host nation, yet abandon his own followers to the whims of that nation's rulers. I hated him for abandoning his only opportunity to improve the lot of those slaves. I hated his petty, insignificant deity. I was the true child of the sun, and he would be made to pay for his transgression!

I expanded my army. I sent them into the slave camps, seeking my traitorous brother. I followed the lessons of my grandfather and strengthened the chains holding the slaves. No atrocity was too great, no slight too small, that they would be spared its despair. If they would not return the usurper to me, I would dig him out!

My search was fruitless. I dared not disclose whom it was that I sought, lest the deceptions of my grandfather, my father, and my mother be discovered, and disgrace the Unbroken Line with its near disaster. Nor did I dare allow the slaves to discover how close one of their own had come to taking up the double crowns, for even bent and broken, they were a proud people, and the knowledge would have spelled disaster. So, my soldiers searched instead for any not on the rosters of the slaves, every and all man, woman, or child, not recorded on the tablets of their overseers, with orders to kill all such they found, and send me their heads.

None were his. Either the slaves were masters at secreting away those they wished to protect, or my brother, the unseated, dethroned, now-fled usurper, had truly vanished.

Years passed into decades, and my rage, while never forgotten, did recede. I had the business of my people to attend to, and my borders to expand and defend. I ruled sternly, but forced back my harshness. I married my brother's betrothed, and we had one son and several daughters before the waters of the holy river reclaimed her life as its own. Of those children, my son and three daughters were judged by the gods as worthy of retaining life themselves. I made certain that my son grew strong in the laws of the land and the strength of his arm. His wisdom grew, and his armies were strong. Of him, it was said that he had all the gifts of the gods granted to both my vanished brother, and of myself, combined and amplified into one. He would be the one to lead our people into an era of power and prosperity unseen in our lands since the gods granted us the twin gifts of fire from the sun and water from the holy river, a paragon of the sons of the sun, the living emblem of the Unbroken Line.

And then, *he* returned, along with his brother of birth. An unassuming, unsure, quiet man of gray hair and years, leaning upon on withered stick, dressed in drab clothes as far from the finery of his youth as is the crocodile's scales far from the plumage of the egret. The brother of birth was arrogant and obnoxious, confident, and blustering. And yet...

My brother's iron will and fiery temper, both long concealed (though well understood) were on full display as he entered my court, not as beggar or supplicant, nor as merchant nor mendicant, not even as a long-lost family member, but as a ruler and king equal to my own throne! No, superior! His delve into the secrets of the Unbroken Line had led him not only to his own line, but to the minor deity which they worshiped, and he strode, hobbled with age though he was, into my court, stood unbowed before my throne, and demanded I release his people from bondage, as though he had never left, as though the Double Crown was his to direct, and inferior to him! My rage returned in full force, and it blazed hotter than ever before.

The people rejoiced. The prodigal son had returned, with full royal bearing, to claim his own. Not that I would, or should, ever surrender the throne. For once crowned, we kings are immovable by all but death. But his return was seen as a homing of a wise advisor, or a kindly and humble uncle, and was the cause of joy and celebration. Certainly, through our combined efforts, though our roles were reversed, our lands would see wealth and prestige the world wide, and dominion over all!

The people were not privy to the councils of the rulers. They knew not what he demanded. They only knew that the abdicated son had returned, and so I was unable to directly enact my revenge.

I should have welcomed him back. I should have inquired what Power he had found that he could so brazenly, so confidently, so arrogantly, assume I, king of the greatest and most powerful land, should bow to his will. I should have called him brother, and given him his people to be king over, as I was king over mine. It cost me everything.

Much has been lost to the sands of time and the waters of memory. I still remember enough of my life that I rejoice I cannot recall all the details of that terrible time. But I do know this. All our magics, all our power, all our wealth and prosperity and might, stood as for naught before the magics and power and might of that drab figure and his minor god. Our waters were poisoned. Our stocks of grain rotted. Livestock starved, even as vermin proliferated. Our health failed. The very earth and skies turned against us as the sun and the holy river forsook us, and my hatred grew. The dethroned usurper, not content to flee his stolen birthright, nor to steal thousands of slaves from the land of his childhood, now dared to assault the very foundations of the earth. Worse, he dared to succeed.

But I did not acquiesce. I did not budge. Surely the power of the son of the sun was too great to assault! And so, even as I bore my will and force upon the slaves when my brother abandoned me, I once again imposed every punishment, every strike, every retaliation, every recompense I dared compose, against his people.

With each successive plague, I bore down harder. With each bearing of my will, the plagues became more unbearable. And with each turn of the sun, we two brothers each became more implacable and immovable, he in his demands, and I in my steadfastness to not surrender one head of grain or one finger of a slave, to one who would give up everything, only to demand half of all I owned.

My son. Woe to me, woe to the Unbroken Line, for it was not my father who severed it, but I! Woe that I cannot forget that final blow! One final plague had my brother in store for me.

My son, my scion, my heir. A sudden violent and terrible sickness overtook him, aye, he and all those firstborn in the land among my people. Of the slaves, there was no death, no sickness, no disease. Of my people, death roamed the streets, prowled the alleys, crept along every roof and beneath every door. Not one heir, not one firstborn in the entire land, was left by morning. The final account of those lost would never be compiled, could never be, so great was the devastation.

In grief and despair, I exiled my brother from my court, from my lands, from my kingdom, both he and all those he called his own, along with all that they had touched and tainted. A cold and frozen ball was my heart, untouched by the light of the warm sun which gave its sons warmth, unfeeling and unthinking. Even as I surrendered my son's body to the embalmers, so did every father, every mother, every family across the land. Hated and accursed were the slaves, and the power of their godling so feared, that the slaves were given freely not only opened shackles, but all they could carry, if only they would just go. We were ruined.

My son, who should have succeeded me as king, was prepared for burial. No heir of my body remained. My birthright, my inheritance, was finally well and truly stolen, usurped, destroyed. My tears, the tears of a king, the son of the sun, were unfrozen. My heart thawed. And my anger burned anew.

Who were these people, that they should steal the wealth of a nation? Who were they, that they dared bring ruin upon us? Who was this man, my brother, that he should steal the crown rightfully mine and of my blood? My people would starve this winter. My treasuries were depleted. My son was dead. But I still retained one force, one asset, one last remaining sigil of the mightiest nation under the sun. I had my army, my thousands of chariots, my tens of thousands of blooded warriors, experienced and tempered by my decades of conquest and pacification. I had my arm and my spear. I determined that I would complete my grandfather's legacy. I would destroy my brother's people as he had destroyed my land and expunge their plague from the face of the earth.

I set out in pursuit of the slaves and their upstart king. Though they had left weeks before, they were afoot, and greatly burdened by the spoils of my lands and the remains of my people's flocks and herds. They were traveling east, towards the smaller seas, and the impassable shores there. What they believed they would find, I did not know, nor care. Three hundred thousand chariots and spears I embarked in pursuit, intent on the death of every man, woman, and child in their entire caravan. I did not intend to return until I had completed the utter destruction of their entire people, a pittance to the loss of my heir, and reclaimed the butcher's tax they had enacted upon my subjects. Along with me, in a new carriage specially made, rode the body of my son, that he would see in death the vengeance enacted for their petty god's claim upon his life.

For seven days we rode. The slaves were burdened with cattle, grain, and the gold and jewels they took as their due for departure. We were provisioned lightly, and possessed horses fleet of foot and chariots of speed. We would not need sufficient supplies to return, for had they not in their possession a surfeit of food, all the livestock which remained, wagons to bear them, and oxen to pull? Rapidly we followed their path, and the distance between my force and their caravan of spoils diminished.

I laughed, bitterly, eagerly, and long, when I realized where their new king was leading them. My brother, the fool, was taking the path of least difficulty directly towards the sea. No city, no harbor, no fort existed upon that coastline to provide safe haven. No fleet of ships would be available to bear them across the sea. Nothing but barren desert, rocky shores, and drifting sands awaited their arrival. They were trapped and could be eliminated at the pleasure and patience of my army. No succor would they have, save death by my decree.

We trapped them upon an isthmus, narrow and short, with nary sufficient space between man and beast in their convoy for an ox to swing its tail, packed nose to jowl. From the low hills overlooking the shore, I watched their panic, their anger, their despair, turn to rage against their would be king, my brother. I saw his face, terrible and desperate, and I could taste his fear upon the wind, flavored, enhanced, and amplified by that of the slaves. Now he knew the bitterness of destruction, of the knowledge that his entire people was ruined, of helplessness in the face of a power greater than his own.

Then he turned towards the sea, raised his arms, shouted words to the sky, and struck the shoreline with his staff. And the unthinkable, the unimaginable, happened. The earth shook, and the winds changed direction, bearing down from the hills upon the water. A causeway through the sea was revealed beneath the churning waves, a path providing escape for the slaves! This could not be allowed!

The shouts of the officers, the nickering of horses, the cries of war and doom, the thunder of the chariots' wheels upon the ground! The last of the slaves entered their causeway, a narrow road between towering walls of water. We bore down, intent on their destruction, and I led the charge, the chariot bearing my son's body following, that he might share in the glory, even in death. A hundred bowshots' distance lay between my horse and their following wagons. Fifty. Thirty. Ten. Five. The last slave in line, driving an old carriage bearing barrels of grain, turned and met my eye with a wild face of fear.

The wind changed, and once again the earth shook. The water fell upon me, my eyes clouded, and my lungs filled. All became dark to my eyes, and I followed my son into the path between worlds.

I beheld what truly was, that which never would be, and that which ever should be. Time slipped.

I saw the slaves escape the ravenous ocean. I saw them in riches and rags, feast and famine, sometimes obedient to their godling, often not, but always surviving. I saw my brother's burial along the banks of another river, that would one day have a moment of holiness, but was itself just water.

I saw my army, my last great glory, drown beneath the crashing waters. Their faces rushed past my own in the seas, exuberant, fearful, bloated, and dead, either rushing towards or fleeing from the heralds of the underworld.

I understood that I was not yet permitted to accompany them.

I saw my legacy forever tainted, and a halfling son of the sun, not of the purity of blood preserved through endless lines of brother marrying sister, took my throne and my name in my absence. My name, once a herald of conquest, glory, and expansion, was etched into stone alongside mundane accounts of harvests and taxes. The halfling wore my own death mask into my tomb, and I was forgotten.

My people entered a long period of decline, but also survived, and would later provide refuge and succor to another child hidden from those who would kill him.

I saw my fathers and their fathers' fathers. I saw the breaks in the line of the sons of the sun. We none were descended from its fiery grace, all children of usurpers of usurpers. The blood was not diminished; it never was. We were not gods, nor would we ever be. We were men, as was my brother. The holy river, defiled with blood, was mere water as well, a fitting match for my brother's grave.

I saw the followers of the slaves' god, altered in form and manner of practice, become an influence upon the world. Their faith, their minor religion, would become one of the mightiest forces governing ruler and ruled alike, across the entirety of that which would be.

I saw the deity of the slave race, no longer pitiful, but revealed in glory and power. Of him, I will speak no more, for I am not worthy.

I saw a redemption.

I beheld two mighty armies, battling across land and sea, each in the name of their own gods. From shore to bloody shore and across deep waters to other beaches further than I imagined possible, their war raged across the world, sometimes bearing this name, sometimes that. Faces and peoples changed one into another in service to each, but the gods served remained. At many points did all seem lost for this faction or that, only for fate and chance to intervene – and occasionally an intercession of divinity, or a chance that permitted those such as I to lend their aid.

Far across land, sea, and time, I beheld an island. A small, rocky point of land protruding from the waters, unremarkable and unnoticeable. Here would be the rallying cry of a people near defeat, harried and desperate, servants of the god of my brother, to rise and overcome those who sought to enslave and kill them once again, as I had sought to do to my brother's people. Here would banners be placed, that would lead others to assemble a mighty force to crush the armies and navies of their oppressors. From here would grow hospice and hospital, orders of warrior priests and physicians, safe havens and safe harbors, all bearing the name of this tiny, insignificant knoll.

But before they could do so, before that cry could be called, there had to be hope. Survivors. A victory. Without that boon, there would be no rally. A small group of servants of that god ensconced themselves upon the island, facing forces beyond their capabilities. Here they would die without intervention.

My spirit now bears no feet to walk upon the sands or shores, nor do have ears to hear, eyes to see, or tongue to speak. Yet mayhap I shall allowed one last influence upon this world of my brother's god. For me my hatred, my kin. I cannot forgive myself.

I was once a mighty warrior. I won many victories in my own name, learning tactics, strategy, and all the many details needed for a successful campaign. A glorious tomb prepared for me was gilt with the gold of my defeated enemies, a fitting farewell from the world for a god's ascent to divinity.

I was a defeated warrior. I knew the confusion from facing forces unknown and beyond mortal comprehension. I knew death, even my own and my son's. I knew utter destruction, and the watery tomb of the oceans never carried a marker bearing my name.

Here on these rocky shores shall my spirit await the proper moment to sow confusion, arrogance, and fear amongst the enemies of my brother's god. Here I shall enter into service alongside him, that a people might be free. Here I shall bend my own knee, and pray to that minor, that glorious and powerful deity, that I might have one tenth the effect upon his enemies as my brother's plagues inflicted upon me. Such effort shall be the beginnings of my penance, and my plea for forgiveness, from that deity, to the slaves, to my son, to my brother, to his people. For forgiveness from myself.

My name. I have remembered my name. I was Amenhotep. This island, though none shall know it, will be my edifice, my tomb, my redemption, my entry to my afterlife, and my supplication to that which could defeat even the seas and the sun. This island will be my pyramid.

I will be the Ghost of Malta.

CROSS OF BLUE

Jonathan LaForce

"Papa, do you think we'll see a shooting star tonight?"

The curly haired blond boy tugged eagerly at his father's hand as they strolled along the pier. High above his and his parents' heads loomed the imposing bulk of Fort San Angelo. Time had not diminished the former bastion where once the Order of Saint John had turned back Ottoman invaders.

"Perhaps, Anthony," the boy's father replied with a gentle smile as he admired the child's spirit.

So innocent, so good. Perhaps the very best thing I have ever done, Anthony's father told himself, *was to bring this boy into the world and try to raise him right.*

"My name is Anthony. Just like yours."

"Aye. And just like Grandpapa's."

Little Anthony frowned at this recitation. "Why did grandpapa leave us?"

"Because son, it was his time to go."

"I wish he didn't leave us. I miss him."

"I know you do."

"I miss him teaching me about the stars and all the constellations."

"Did he teach you how to say that big word?"

"Uh-huh."

"He taught me those when I was your age."

"He did?" Anthony s his father's confession.

"He did."

"Did you ever get t see shooting stars with him?"

"I did."

"I wish he were here now so we could watch them together."

"Me too son, me too."

#

The staff car rolled through the busy Wilhemshaven docks in the afternoon sunshine at a stately pace. Everywhere a man could look, they would see the signs of the ever efficient German war machine going about it's business. The man seated in the car's rear compartment on the left saw none of it, his mind busy elsewhere.

Lean, handsome and imposing, Friederich "Fritz" von Osten had spent most of his life at sea. First in the *Kaiserlich Marine* where he had risen to the rank of *Fregattenkapitain* by war's end, then the languishing years of IvS and the *Reichsmarine*. Now, at 46, he was a *Kapitän zur See* in the Kriegsmarine. Nor was he alone in such experience.

Of the five Unterseeboots in his wolfpack, three were commanded by men he had served with in the heady run up to Jutland. The lone exception, U-637, was commanded by von Osten's godson, a Prussian scion cut in the same mold as his daredevil father. A man equally capable of the task to which he had devoted his life. They had been together, officially, since '37. Other boats had come and gone, but the original quintet remained.

And now I must take them very far, very fast, Fritz told himself as his mind processed through the mission given him by Vizeadmiral Speer.

Malta.

Already an island fortress in the Mediterranean, it was now an unsinkable aircraft carrier. Held by the British since Napoleon I, the Wehrmacht needed Malta to fall, just like Crete had in '41.

"Fritz, this new convoy is called 'Pedestal,' and it's even bigger than the previous two," Vizeadmiral Speer proclaimed in his office as he tapped a map of the Mediterranean.

"What does that have to do with us in the North Atlantic?" von Osten asked as he leaned forward, dark eyes flashing beneath the equally dark hair women loved to play with when he was being seductive.

Speer leaned back in his chair, lighting a pipe as he studied his subordinate.

"Only last week our brilliant Reichsmarschall declared that the Luftwaffe has established complete superiority over the allied air forces," Speer said dryly.

"Of course they did," Fritz said with cold anger. "That's why I lost a very talented officer to an aerial night attack in the Norwegian Sea."

Speer waved a hand deprecatingly. "Minor details, Fritz. Very minor, the Reichsmarschall assures me."

"If the Luftwaffe could do their jobs properly, there would already be Fallschirmjagers on Malta," Fritz remarked, lighting a cigarette.

"Ah, you noticed that, did you?" Speer asked casually. He puffed again on his pipe. "Field Marshal Kesselring sent a message by courier, make of that what you will. He needs my very best wolfpack on station, ready to ambush Pedestal when it comes through."

"Hence why you called me back from patrol for a full restocking."

Speer leaned back in his chair. "That, and OKW gave me no choice in the matter."

"I can't imagine why," Fritz replied.

Both men knew about von Osten's familial connections, and where his loyalties lay. Beneath the handsome exterior and the modern uniform, was a man Prussian to his core. Most younger officers (and many older than him) quietly called his command "Wolfpack Max." Fritz von Osten's loyalty, and that of his officers, lay not with the party in power, but the people of Germany.

The men knew it, the Gestapo knew it, and they knew the Gestapo knew it. While the trench coat-sporting bastards couldn't have him shot out of hand, they would certainly see to it he was sent into harm's way.

Had it not been for Uncle, I would likely already have been arrested Fritz reminded himself. *That and the Blue Max.*

Absently, his left hand reverently stroked the blue cross edged in gold which rested on a ribbon at his neck. He had received it at the hands of his Emperor decades before, as a young Kapitänleutnant, just like Heino, Lothar, and Walther, the U-Boat captains under his charge. Men who wore this medal rarely concerned themselves with dying in their own bed.

"I am genuinely sorry about the loss of Otto," Speer stated. "He was up for his own command at the end of this patrol."

"It will be a hard spot to fill," Fritz admitted.

"I have a replacement for him," Speer proclaimed.

"Sir?"

Speer motioned and for the first time, Fritz noticed the young man sitting in the corner behind them. Broad shouldered and barrel chested, he had hair so blond it was almost white. Fritz quickly noted that younger man bore the sleeve lace and shoulder boards of a Korvettenkapitan. The bigger surprise was the cross worn at his throat, black on a ribbon of silver, black and red. Given how young he looked, it seemed impossible for him to already hold the Knight's Cross of the Iron Cross.

"Korvettenkapitan von Yorck recently distinguished himself in a night action, when he saved U-57 from a bomber sortie while they were raiding a Soviet convoy."

"I saw U-57 in the yard on my way here, but hadn't heard how she was damaged."

"The bombers learned that 88mm rounds are rather undigestible," von Yorck declared.

It was a dark declaration but entirely in keeping with how Fritz himself viewed such matters. His grim mien split oddly as he smiled. "And the Bolshevik convoy?"

"Last seen at the bottom of the Barents," Speer explained.

"Outstanding." Fritz nodded towards the young officer. "Shouldn't he be recuperating or on one of Goebbel's propaganda campaigns?" Fritz asked, noticing how the younger man openly bristled at the mention of the Reichminister's name.

"von Yorck requested an immediate patrol assignment. After your casualty report came in, I thought you could make good use of him." Speer lowered his voice. "He's one of us Fritz, you can trust him. After all, we trusted his father when we were new ensigns."

Fritz's eyes widened. "That von Yorck?"

"Ja."

Fritz's smile became genuine. "Danke mein admiral. I have use for exactly such a man."

"Gut. How soon will you be finished with resupply?"

"We'll be finished shortly. I planned to give them a night in port for rest, and we can leave after sunset tomorrow."

"I expected no less. Wilhelm will drive you back."

Fritz started to protest, until Speer came around the desk, clapping a hand on his subordinate's shoulder. "You have always been my most reliable captain, Fritz. I have something waiting for you at the pier. Enjoy it, old friend."

#

What does that crafty old fox have cooked up now? Fritz asked himself as the staff car pulled up to the quay. Teams of men moved with commendable efficiency, though the torpedo haulers from the naval magazine were no longer in sight.

Good to see my Obermaats haven't lost their touch.

The car came to a stop, and Oberst Wilhelm Vetter, Speer's batman held the door open for him. Stepping out, Fritz approached the foot of the gangway, bringing his right arm up in a salute to the Reich ensign, when he stopped, arm in midair.

A pennant hung from the halyards on the conning tower. White, with black iron cross insignia, it was split tailed at one end.

Why on earth do we have a Kommodore's pennant? I wasn't informed about any special visitors!

"Sir, the Kommodore is out of uniform."

Half turning, Fritz saw the white-haired Oberst had a blue uniform jacket in hand. Where the separate stripes of a Kapitan zur See would've been found on the cuffs was now an unbroken band of gold.

"The Vizeadmiral's compliments, he felt Herr Kommodore would prefer the company of his men for the occasion."

"Yes, yes I would."

"The Vizeadmiral also has a new jacket for Fregattenkapitan Von Yorck" Vetter announced.

"Huh? What?" von Yorck's serious mien broke at the suggestion until Vetter produced a new jacket for him, laden with the single-starred straps of a Fregattenkapitan.

Shrugging into the new jacket, Fritz felt his men's eyes on him. They knew what this meant to him. Just as he knew what it meant to them.

When they had finished dressing, Vetter gave them a once over, bade them good day, then drove off.

"Fregattenkapitan, let us review the men," Fritz declared.

"Jawohl, mein Kommodore."

Fritz started forward when a fresh breeze caught all the banners resting on the conning tower, unfurling them in glorious fashion. It was a perfect moment. And it pleased his soul.

"Boat!" a sharp voice barked.

The sailors milling about came to the position of attention, as Feldwebel Lehman stepped around the conning tower in his dress uniform, saber hanging at his side, followed by the several chiefs found on the boat.

"Atten-hut!"

Belatedly, Fritz realized that all fifty-four men of his crew were on deck. In fresh service uniforms.

Bosun Prater's pipes shrilled out the notes as Lehman's voice gave the order. "Kommodore, arriving! Present arms!"

Fritz brought his hand up, saluting them all, then back down.

"Chief, is the boat ready to depart?"

"Yessir!"

"Excellent. Is the watch set?"

"Set and armed in all respects."

"Crew, well done. I am proud of all of you. We leave tomorrow night. Crew is released to liberty until watch changeover tomorrow morning."

"Crew, dismissed!"

The men filed past down the gangplank, shaking his hand and congratulating him on his promotion as they headed towards the knocking shops and bars one expected to find in any portside town.

"And where will we be sir?" Fregattenkapitan von Yorck asked.

"We have a patrol to plan. Send runners to the other boats. Captains' call in 20 minutes aboard the flagship."

"Aye aye, sir."

#

Just after full sunset the next day, Wolfpack Max departed Wilhelmshaven, bound for the Mediterranean. For all that stood against them, they gave little thought toward the odds. They had fought against such multiple times, and it was no different now.

Running the straits of Gibraltar was not entirely a new task. They had brought their boats out of the shipyards in time for a shakedown cruise and run to Marseille in an effort to prevent the French Navy from breaking out.

Now though, the british were trying hard to interdict the Strait. Fortunately for Wolfpack Max, low lying clouds and fog made it easy for the U-boats to hide as their diesel engines charged the massive electrical batteries. Coming out of the strait, Fritz had his command dive and turn northeast, headed for deep water. He wanted to be well away from land before they came up to recharge once again.

Away from land and away from Allied planes, because everybody knows that dumbass druggie Goring couldn't do the job right even if you promised him free coke and the Crown Jewels of England, Fritz complained bitterly. *Why did he have to survive instead of von Richtofen?*

Stepping into the bridge, Fritz heard the XO bark. "Captain on deck."

"As you were. XO, anything to report?"

"No sir."

" You stand relieved."

"I stand relieved."

"Enjoy your rest." Fritz smiled thinly. "I think we will be busy tomorrow."

#

"Torpedoes in the water! Bearing 150. Range 5,000 yards!"

"Make your depth 400 feet, speed 3 knots. Do not cavitate!"

"Aye captain!" the helmsman barked in response to von Yorck's commands.

Around the boat, men moved with a purpose. Four days they had been engaged in vicious combat, four days that had seen both sides pushed to their very limits.

HMS Eagle fell first on the 11th. U-69 had reported two groups of merchantmen, one escorted by the light aircraft carrier south of Cape Salinas. Fritz wasted no time maneuvering to within 400 yards and launching a full spread of torpedoes at the massive target. Minutes later, *HMS Eagle* was taking on water and quickly sinking. The attacks continued as U-69 took down *HMS Manchester* and a pair of merchantmen over the next twelve hours, U-49 sank HMS Cairo and U-637 made eight shots for six vessels sunk. Ships burned, their sailors praying the destroyers would see them even as sharks gathered in the water.

The wolves did not have it all their own way though. On the second day, 49 barely avoided a depth charge and 637 went to protect her sister vessel. A destroyer escort and two more merchies fell to her before HMS Wolverine committed a dangerous ram, sinking 637 with all hands lost. Wolverine, barely able to maintain steerage, fell out of the convoy and slowly drifted home toward Gibraltar.

Day three saw 49 take out HMS Foresight, and damage the carrier *HMS Indomitable* before she fell victim to depth charges. Through it all, Anton von Yorck could not remember feeling more angry, more alive, or more excited than any time prior in his life, even as his own boat bounced about from the shockwaves which claimed 49.

The crew had been uncertain of their new officer, stranger that he was, until halfway through the first day of combat. Trying to evade the depth charges which came as retaliation for the sinking of HMS Eagle, he'd heard a shout from the damage control officer.

"Forward torpedo room is in trouble!"

Running forward before Fritz could countermand him, von Yorck arrived in seconds to find a torpedoman partially stuck under the weight of a fallen weapon. Grabbing the chains used for exactly that purpose he'd not even slowed in his movements as he swiftly hoisted the heavy load just enough for the Matrose to remove their fallen comrade. Swiftly organizing the ratings streaming into the compartment, von Yorck managed to re-se-cure the heavy weapons and drop the wounded man in the galley where the ship's doctor went to work on him. It was an act of pure strength none of the sailors had thought possible before the XO put his mighty shoulders to work.

"Everything alright, XO?" Fritz asked calmly when Anton stepped back into the conn.

"Alles in ordnung Herr Kommodore."

"Gut."

That night, the story spread around the mess of von Yorck's feat. If the Kommodore heard he said nothing. But his men knew the what they had seen. And a legend came into being.

Right then, Anton von Yorck wasn't concerned with legends or feats of daring. He was busy enough managing damage control as depth charges rocked the boat side to side.

This stupid grin on my face only comes out like this when I'm truly in the shit, Anton told himself as he raced toward a valve to turn off the pressure, a thick cloud of steam filling the tight room.

The idea that anything could be wrong right then didn't seem possible till he heard a Maat shouting as he pointed towards the plot board.

"The Kommodore is dead! The Kommodore is dead!"

The cry was taken up and von Yorck knew he had to regain control quickly. Kapitan Fritz was the beating heart of this vessel, and they could not afford to lose him, or their nerve, now.

"Silence on the bridge!"

It was a bull roar, more fit for charging infantry following an artillery barrage into the assault than the conn of a submarine. But it worked with equal ferocity.

Von Yorck had a hand pressed against Fritz's head, working hard to staunch the bleeding.

"He's not dead yet, get the doctor to the bridge and man your stations!" Von Yorck ordered.

That harsh voice brooked no argument, and they immediately did as ordered.

"Helmsman, ensure our bearing is 158, depth 300 feet, make your speed two knots. Maintain steerage," Anton ordered.

"Bearing 158, rising to 300 feet, speed 2 knots. Maintain steerage"

"Steady as she goes, man. We're not dead yet," Anton stated.

"Steady as she goes, aye captain!"

The doctor appeared, satchel in hand. Dropping to his knees, his quick fingers began probing the wounded commodore.

"Sonar, I want to know the instant that destroyer comes back," Anton ordered.

"Aye sir."

"Chief of boat, get me a status on our torpedoes. I need aft tubes first."

"Understood, sir."

That calm, deliberate voice continued giving orders, much as their Kommodore did. The men could work with that, and by degrees, order reasserted itself. This was a German vessel after all, commanded by a Prussian.

It took hours for the allied ships to move out of range, allowing for the boat to surface and recharge her electric batteries. But once they were well out of danger, he went over the intercom and spoke to the crew.

"Herr Kommodore is still alive, according to the doctor. He is breathing and for the moment all is well. Stand down from general quarters."

#

"Herr Kapitan, we are well and truly stuck in."

"Yes, Oberst, yes we are," Anton said as he ate a sandwich from the galley.

The rest of our Wolfpack has perished. We have only a quarter of our fuel load, seven torpedoes, and a full complement of deck gun ammo. But we're not dead yet. He half smiled at a memory from his academy years, a memory spoken in bitter French. *The bell has not rung, cadets! Until it rings, you will strike!*

He studied the plot board as the reports continued to come in, ate and considered what was happening above them on the surface.

Some elements of the convoy had already arrived in Malta. The big tanker, SS Ohio, was still moving, despite air raids, holes in her rudder and hull. The defensive net around that ship had increased too.

I know what I need to do, he told himself. But making it worth the effort will be difficult.

"Penny for your thoughts, sir?" Chief Josephs asked.

"Really wishing the Kommodore was available, I could use his advice on how to make the most of this."

"Aye sir, but you haven't done bad. Not at all, Josephs assured him.

"Thank you Chief, I appreciate you saying that."

"Kommodore on deck!" a Matrose shouted.

Every man in the conn turned about, jumping to their feet as the man they all relied upon loomed in the hatchway.

"FregattenKapitan von Yorck, what have you done to my boat?" he said seriously.

"Shot and sank and kept the allies running," von Yorck replied.

"That is well."

For a moment, Fritz swayed, but he steadied himself and resumed his walk into the conn area. As he did so, he studied his men, knowing their body language and attitudes well. Despite his absence, they were still in good spirits.

The young man has done well for himself, Fritz decided.

"Kommodore, are you sure you should be up?"

"I blame the bandages, once we get them off, I won't look quite so awful," Fritz jested. "What problem vexes you right now, Fregattenkapitan?"

"The tanker. It needs to go down."

"I see." Fritz really could, but he was not going to undermine his XO in front of his men. Especially not when it appeared that he had continued to run the boat with a furious vengeance.

No, I cannot do that to him. Anton checked the clock, and the calendar below it. *Not after nearly two days recovering from that hit to the head. He doesn't look like he's slept in all that time.*

"XO, I have the conn."

"I stand relieved."

Fritz clapped a hand on his shoulder. "You've earned this rest. I will summon you when I need you again."

"Jawohl, mein Kommodore."

A great weight shifted off those broad shoulders and he slowly moved from the conn at a walk. When he'd finally left, Fritz looked to Lehman.

"Don't ask, sir. You don't want that answer."

"Humor me, chief."

"He hasn't left the conn except to use the head every few hours. I didn't know you could drink that much coffee and still function."

"Surely—"

"No sir, he wouldn't listen to us. We got sleep. But he refused to hear of it for himself."

Fritz shook his head, checked the clock once again. "How much battery life do we have?"

"Seven hours. Maybe."

"Wake the XO in four hours. Have the crew rest and relax."

Fritz looked back to the plot. *If we move against the tanker, it will be our deaths. The challenge is making sure our deaths count. And I think I know how to do that.*

Four hours and eleven minutes later, Anton von Yorck stepped into the conn, looking far more human and refreshed so many hours before.

"Mr. Yorck!" Fritz said cheerfully, catching his attention at once.

"Jawohl, mein Kapitän."

"I must ask a favor of you."

"Anything."

"I need you to live."

"Sir?"

"You have served this ship and it's crew with all the skill and courage one expects of a sailor of the Fatherland. Your father would be proud of you. Just as we are proud of you."

Fritz von Osten took a seabag, placed it's straps in von Yorck's hands. "Ensure that our families receive these letters. And know how we died for them. On your honor as a Prussian."

Understanding filled his eyes. Proud scion that he was, Yorck refused to let the gathering tears burst forth even as he saluted.

"Attention on deck!"

The room snapped to, and Fritz spoke again, voice clear amid the panic and uncertainty.

"On my authority, I promote you to Kapitan zur See, with all honors, customs and courtesies associated," Fritz declared. "You will find a letter attesting to such in the bag, along with the appropriate rank on your jacket. I also give you this."

His hand reached into his pocket, withdrawing a small oilcloth bag which never left his possession.

"This was given to me by my Kaiser on the 14th of May, 1919. I deliver it into your hands. Wear it in good health the remainder of your days."

He made a show of removing the medal from it's protective bag, and draping it about von Yorck's neck, then removed it and replaced it inside the oilcloth bag, and into sea bag Anton now held.

"Obermaat, assist the Kapitän to the conning tower and get him in a life jacket."

"Jawohl!"

"Chief, prepare to perform emergency surface. Weapons, load all tubes. Deck gun crew, prepare for combat! We must give the captain a fighting chance to get away!"

Anton moved swiftly as the ship rose, mindful of the precious cargo he was now entrusted with. Two life jackets were wrapped around him, and two more jackets lashed onto the mail bags lumpy form, and he swallowed as he looked toward the two sailors helping him.

"Good luck sir," both proclaimed.

The handwheel spun, flew open and then Anton surged up the ladder as sea spray and rain streamed into the compartment. Balancing precariously, Anton made his way across the wet deck, listening to the deck gun crews as they ran for their positions. There was neither the time to look back nor the desire to. He had to get away, quickly. If he did not do so, none of their sacrifice would be worth the effort.

Leaving his shoes behind, Anton looked toward the horizon, where he spied a Union Jack fluttering above what looked to be a destroyer.

That one. I will head straight for her.

Determined not to fail, Anton dove forward into the thrashing water, seabag in his arms.

Even in August, the dark blue Mediterranean water was cold. Salt stung at his eyes. Far off, he could still see the destroyer, bearing down on his position. Releasing the seabag to follow behind him on a lead rope attached about his waist, he began side stroking, bare feet kicking steadily.

Anton von Yorck had been an excellent swimmer back in his academy days as it kept him in shape for boxing. Now he fought, not for medals or glory, but his own survival. The dim gray shapes of royal navy warships could be seen in the distance, moving closer as their guns bellowed, throwing up geysers in the water.

Must get clear before the depth charges arrive, he told himself. His stroke lengthened as he swam. *I have sworn upon my honor to do this for my captain and crew. May God judge me accordingly.*

Behind him, his boat rocked about as torpedoes lanced through the water, deck gun booming and smaller crew serves chattering relentlessly. U-593 would go down, but not before she left her mark on her enemies.

#

"Sir, man in the water!"

"How the blazes did one of ours end up in the water?" Commander Calvin demanded when he heard the report, even as his forward gun batteries bellowed.

"No sir, one of the jerries," the lookout replied.

"What?"

Calvin stepped out onto the destroyer *HMS Bengal's* starboard wing bridge, binoculars in hand.

"There, sir," the lookout gestured. "three points off the bow and making a beeline for us. He's covered in life jackets. I think he's pulling something."

"Could be a mine," the XO opined.

"If he's towing a mine to kill us, that's the strongest Jerry I've ever seen," Calvin retorted.

"Shall we have the machine gunners deal with him, sir?" Master Chief Hobbes asked idly as he lit his pipe.

"Nonsense. The least we can do is bring him aboard, see what he wants. Then we'll decide if he's fish food," Calvin replied.

"Fair enough sir. Oh Master-at-arms!" Hobbes called out.

Just before the man came aboard there was an incident, one which Calvin found utterly hilarious given the circumstances. The man had come within hailing distance of *Bengal* when a shark appeared, fin breaking the water as he surged toward his prey. The lookout on *Bengal's* crew shouted a warning and the German had looked backwards to see the threat looming.

Rather than scream for help or surrender to his fate, the man pulled a knife from his belt. Even as the shark clamped onto his leg, the German sailor refused to go down, slamming the knife into the shark's face repeatedly with fury.

It was an odd sight for *Bengal's* crew and they forgot about throwing the life preserver toward him, engrossed as they were in watching the bloody spectacle. Some cheered the shark, others the unknown man. It ended only when the shark decided that today was not the day to try for food which fought back with such violent ill-intent. Bettors cheered or groaned as they were wont to do.

"Master Chief, I do think that lad's not interested in dying today," Calvin observed.

"I hadn't noticed, sir," Hobbes remarked.

Sheathing his knife, the man resumed his sidestroke toward *Bengal*, stopping only for the life preserver cast by a Bosun's Mate from the deck gang.

"Master Chief, I'm not entirely sure about this," Calvin admitted at length.

"Aye sir. I'll have the Helsman pull the ship back to range and use the main guns to do away with the blighty bugger."

"That's not quite what I meant Master Chief. But while you're at it, tell me this," Calvin asked, "What are you going to do if you miss him?"

Master Chief Hobbs sniffed indignantly. "You have no faith in me, sir."

"Me? Never. Not I." Calvin gestured toward the streaming blood trail leading out into deep water. "But I'm not a betting man today."

The thoroughly bedraggled man who came aboard HMS Bengal was larger than Calvin could've imagined. He brought himself to attention as best he could, leaning on a petty officer for support as he studied the Commander and crewmen around him, eyes settling on Calvin once he'd counted the gold braid on his shoulder straps.

"Kapitan zur See von Yorck, l'autorisation de monter à bord?"

"A bloody Boche who speaks frog. Will wonders never cease?" Master Chief Hobbes said dryly.

"Accorde," Calvin saluted back, appreciating the courtesy demonstrated.

"You speak frog, sir?" the surprised seaman holding up von Yorck asked.

"It's a handy when you want to make friends in Marseille, my boy," the Commander smiled and winked.

"Je suis ton prisonnier," Kapitan von Yorck declared, hand extending with the blade he'd used on the shark. It was a combination trench knife and knuckle duster, a wicked looking piece of work such as Calvin had seen in his own family's collection.

Explains how he didn't lose hold of it while he did his best impression of a monkey with a switchblade. Accepting the weapon, Hobbes nodded toward the medicos now appearing on deck.

"Master-at-arms, escort Captain von Yorck to sickbay and see that he's extended every courtesy."

"Aye sir."

The knife was extended back toward the German Captain, who recognized what he'd received. Nodding respectfully, he sheathed the weapon, then reached for the large bag he'd brought along. Steady hands shouldered that load and he stood upright.

"Merci, capitaine."

"Somebody radio ahead to Malta, tell them we've got one to drop off," Calvin declared. "Navigator, get us on course for home and a pint. Best speed."

"Aye, sir!"

\#

"Matron, we've received word from the pier," an orderly announced in the silence of the hospital's emergency room.

A woman appeared in an office doorway, curiosity written on her diamond-shaped face.

"The pier?" she asked, tucking a stray curl of strawberry blonde hair back behind her ear.

"Yes, ma'am. They have wounded incoming."

"Did they say how many?"

"One. Not ambulatory."

"Two orderlies to the entrance then and let's prepare properly for him."

"They said he's not a small man."

"Well then make it four orderlies."

"Aye ma'am."

It had been a quiet night thus far for Roberta Griffiths. Nearly twenty-six, she was the presently the senior-most Nurse on staff at the Army hospital in Mdina, Malta, and by default, the commanding officer at the hospital. It was rare, but not impossible for them to get casualties at this time of night, what with all the German and Italian air raids. Of late, those had tapered off as the various axis air forces had refocused their efforts toward the convoy coming into the harbor right now.

What Roberta enjoyed was the independence of night shift. No officious oafs looking for photo-ops to bother her, save the occasional senior officer and even those tread warily in her hospital. As the temporary commanding officer of the hospital, she had her pick of shifts, and she chose night-paperwork got done at night. Her nurses could get their natural rest at night too.

Soon enough, the heavy doors swung open to admit four orderlies carrying a stretcher. On it, a man was strapped down, standard procedure when moving wounded via jeep from the airfield or the pier back to the hospital here in Valletta.

What made Roberta Griffiths pull up short was the four men who entered the emergency room area, close on the heels of the stretcher-burdened orderlies. A burly, iron-haired chief, and three seamen wearing Shore Patrol brassards, all armed with pistols and billy clubs.

"Good evening ma'am," the Chief greeted her.

"Is there a reason you're in here, Chief?"

The Chief, wearing the crown and laurels of a Master-at-Arms gestured with his club at the man still on the stretcher.

"Wounded man is a POW, ma'am."

"Oh." Roberta refrained from making a face.

"Commander Shropshire was worried he might try to make a break for it."

"Let me have a look at him."

Dropping the man none too gently onto a gurney, he was maneuvered into an exam area. Roberta began a cursory examination, while the orderlies watched warily and the Shore Patrolman fingered their pistol butts.

I guess we're all tense she told herself.

Even with the convoy's arrival yesterday, things were tight still here on island. The Luftwaffe had seemed utterly determined to bomb them into oblivion, and all of the residents bore a grudge for it.

Hopefully I can get everybody to relax, Roberta told herself.

She had come here from England back in 37, straight out of Uni. Nobody expected much from the fifth (and youngest) daughter of a middling Earl, except for her to be married off like a prize cow at a county fair.

Sod that for a game of soldiers she had proclaimed, preferring instead to join Queen Alexandra's Imperial Military Nursing Service where she quickly found something she was good at. Now twenty-seven, she enjoyed the rank and prestige she'd earned for herself, far from her family's shadow or responsibilities. Matron Roberta Griffiths received a different kind of respect than Lady Roberta Griffiths ever had.

His blue eyes watched her malevolently as she began He seemed to be in excellent health, aside from the bandages wrapped around his leg and several odd bruises.

"Orderly, how many do we have on the ward tonight?"

"Right now, none, ma'am," Hopkins reminded her.

"Thank you."

Pulling aside the bandages on his leg, Roberta found deep marks and angry bruising. Almost as if something had tried to bite the man, take a chunk out of his leg. That the leg had been broken was obvious. The splint told her the sailors had at least tried to treat him somewhat. But deep puncture wounds were harder to deal with on a rocking boat.

What monstrous creature could've done this? she wondered.

Looking down at the man on the stretcher, Roberta tried to conjure up the words a German nanny had taught her while growing up at Seven Oaks.

What is the word for shark? It's not fish, but that's the closest I've got—

Reaching out, she tapped the man's sternum twice, to get his attention. His blue eyes engaged hers with that serious look and she found herself trying not to stare back. They were a strange mixture of gray and blue, almost like gunmetal.

"Der fisch?" she asked, gesturing at the leg.

"Nein, fraulein. Eine hai." His voice was full of anger.

I don't think it's aimed at me though. Something is off about this whole mess.

"Hai?" she asked, using her hands to mimick a shark's jaw closing repeatedly.

"Jawohl, fraulein," he smiled, causing her to blink.

"Wie?" *With?*

"Mit einem messer."

Messer, messer? Knife?

Reaching for a tray of tools, Roberta selected a scalpel and held it up.

"Messer?"

"Jawohl, fraulein."

He's being so formal with me. I need him to relax. Hell I need all of these men to relax. Gah, men, Roberta exclaimed within herself.

"Ein am major," she said, motioning towards herself. "Du?"

"Kapitän zur See von Yorck"

Captain von York. She re-examined his face. *He doesn't look any different from a boy out of Cambridge or Oxford on holiday.*

"A captain?" she said.

"Der Marine," he corrected.

His words made no sense. Roberta's face scrunched up as she stared at him, confused.

"Begging yer pardon ma'am, I think I know what the problem is," the Chief declared, hand still lingering over his pistol butt. "It's a common issue for us navy types when dealing with landfolks."

"How so?" Roberta asked.

"In the Navy, captains are senior officers. In the army, captain is much lower rank."

"How much different?"

"Navy Captain is like an Army Colonel, ma'am."

"Oh."

"I'm ta be thinkin' he's right likely the highest ranked prisoner on island."

"Was he brought in carrying anything?" Roberta asked

"Yes ma'am, it's on the jeep."

"Go get it."

None of the orderlies or sailors moved.

"That's part of the problem, ma'am."

"Oh?"

"We tried taking it from him when we went to fetch him, and he laid out two Shore Patrolman. It took all of of us to hold him down and we still barely made it here."

"Well then it clearly must be important to him."

"Yes ma'am." The man paused. None of them wanted to meet her eyes.

"Thing is ma'am, the General's Intelligence officer says all prisoner's private effects go straight to his office. He can't keep it, ma'am."

Roberta looked from the Master-at-Arms to the prisoner who was flexing his hands impatiently. He clearly wanted out of the straps binding him.

"Chief, when the Intelligence Officer is the one down here ensuring the safety and well-being of my staff from angry, violent Germans, he can have a say. Until then, the prisoner's effects will remain with him."

"Yes, ma'am."

"Go get them."

"What about your safety ma'am."

I say again, Gah men, Roberta groaned. Rising up to her full height of six and a quarter, Roberta drew on the imperious voice of command she had learned whilst managing the family estates.

"Master-At-Arms, is the prisoner properly strapped down?" Roberta demanded.

"No. Er, yes, ma'am."

"And he certainly can't run away with this broken leg, can he?"

"No, ma'am."

"Then bring his things here and be on your way, understand?"

"Yes, ma'am." He turned, looked toward one of the Seaman assisting him.

"Cartwright, bring his things here, make it snappish," the chief ordered.

Touching his helmet with his hand as if saluting, the Chief came to attention. "By your leave, ma'am."

"Carry on, Chief." Roberta looked to her orderlies. "Hopkins, you and the lads give them a hand, then be back about your tasks."

"Yes ma'am."

They left and Roberta sighed.

Gah, men. I am not dainty.

"It is good to have such loyal subordinates," a man said aloud.

160

Roberta's head whipped around to look at her charge, still flat on his back. She stared at him, then glanced around the empty ward. *I could've sworn that came from his direction. But it sounded so properly British!*

Yorck said nothing more so Roberta continued examining him. Twice, she found shark teeth lodged in his leg. Plucking them out with pliers elicited no response, and she took the time to study them before dropping them in a tray.

The triangular daggers had serrations on either side and she shuddered as she considered the damage inflicted.

What would make a man want to go out in the ocean with such creatures present? She asked herself. She dared not ask Captain von Yorck.

She was finishing making notes on her clipboard when the orderlies returned with Captain York's possession- a large lumpy sea bag. He eagerly accepted it, checking the lock's hasp before his scowl disappeared. Roberta pointed at the floor and he gently laid the semi wet load on the floor..

"Bring me a suture kit and alcohol. I'll take care of his stitches," Roberta ordered.

"Yes ma'am," Hopkins declared, nodding with his head at one of the slightly smaller men in the quartet.

"He's got a splint, we'll see how it's holding up in the morning. May not need to rebreak the leg to set it in a cast," she continued, thinking aloud.

"Tis a pity if that's the case, ma'am." Hopkins paused. "Sure you need to handle the stitches, ma'am?"

"It's a slow night, Hopkins, I'm not up to reading the same book for the fifth time. It still ends the same way."

Hopkins seemed to remain unconvinced. She sighed.

"I promise, if he tries to start anything, I'll scream for you to come kill him," Roberta promised.

"Yes, ma'am. Hope you do ma'am," Hopkins replied.

The other orderlies took their cue from the large man and withdrew for the last time, the quartets' footsteps disappearing as they traversed the hallway back to the aid station.

"This is going to hurt," Roberta explained as she threaded the needle. "We'd have anesthetic but we used up the last of our supply a week ago Tuesday after a bombing raid."

Why am I talking to him? He doesn't speak any English. Is it nerves?

"Remember to hold still and I'll be done soon enough," she said as she began.

Had she looked towards his face before she bent over to begin the stitches, she would've seen that brilliant smile. It remained, despite the pain as she went about her craft.

When she finished, she stood back up, wiping her hands on a cloth.

"There. Try not to move around and you'll be fine," she ordered.

"Parole?" he said quietly.

Roberta looked at him in surprise. *That sounded like French.* "Excuse me?"

"Si je vous donne ma parole d'officier, retirerez-vous les sangles?" *If I give you my word as an officer, will you remove the straps?*

"Tu parles francais?" she asked, shocked at his smooth baritone and polite speech.

"Oui. j'ai fréquenté l'académie de saint cyr." *Yes I was a student at St. Cyr Academy.*

"Ma mere est de Bois d'arcy." *My mother is from Bois d'Arcy.*

"Si je vous donne ma parole d'officier et de gentleman, est-ce que ca marchera?" he repeated.

Can I trust a german? Roberta asked herself. She'd spent a war hating men like him, believing them all to be evil, but here and now, she'd met one. And he wasn't doing anything to justify being hated.

What about him is worth trusting?

"Sur mon honneur et mon nom as a Prussian, vous avez ma parole," he stated.

His honor and his name, Roberta translated. *Wait, "von" is an honorific, like "Lady" is for me. Is he from one of the old Junker families like nanny Gertrude talked about?*

"Etes-vous un junker?" she asked politely.

"Jawohl fraulein, Ich bin Preuße junker."

"Sur ton honneur alors," she declared, moving the surgical implements well out of his reach. *Best not to tempt him.*

Reaching down, she released the straps from his waist and legs, then his chest. For a moment, she half expected him to fly out of the bed, Luger magically appearing in hand as he shouted "I knew you'd fall for my cunning plan!" like a villain from a Basil Rathbone cinematic.

Instead, he came up slowly, carefully, rolling his bull neck and those massive shoulders about.

"Mieux?" *Better?* Roberta asked.

"Beaucoup. Merci beaucoup Fraulein Major."

"Je vous en prie." *You're very welcome.*

"Quel est ton nom?

"Griffiths."

"Danke Fraulein Griffiths." He leaned back on the bed, closed his eyes, and began to sleep, leaving her to wonder about the man as she continued with her rounds for the night.

#

Captain von Yorck's condition has improved, and he seems to be in much better spirits since his arrival. His wounds have mostly healed over the last two weeks, and his prognosis is very positive. He should be able to leave in another month.

Roberta paused, re-reading what she'd finished writing in the log. Since his arrival, they had spoken a great deal, entirely in French. Prior to his arrival, she'd had no use for the language here in Malta. Their conversations made the night shift far more bearable. Roberta was not looking forward to coming off this shift at the end of the current rotation, or for von Yorck to leave her ward.

He was a strange man. She had not heard him speak English once since that first occasion, if it had even been him speaking, and even now, she was never quite sure if he understood what she or others were saying when they spoke around him. But his eyes never stopped watching.

Roberta's thoughts went back to that time she had seen him, stripped to the waist. What night was it? Had to be the third or fourth. She was making her rounds when she heard a familiar tune being whistled. It was tugging at her memory but she couldn't immediately identify it right then. Still, it gave a sashay to her step as she walked about.

Stepping into the last ward, Roberta found Captain von Yorck standing before a sink, toweling off his face. He was bare to the waist, having traded the hospital gown for a pair of pants with the legs cut off below the knees.

I'm not sure we have any shirts on island that would fit him. Might have to borrow a sail from a fisherman.

Anton (as she now knew him) was immensely broad in the chest and shoulders, built like a prizefighter. The way patches of his skin still gleamed, she could guess he'd just finished giving himself a sponge bath to avoid issues with the stitches or the plaster cast on his leg. She kicked herself mentally for having forgotten to check that was happening. Brilliant light bulbs highlighted the muscles of his torso as he moved about easily, despite the impediment of his fractured leg. The second shock she felt came when she saw his face. The heavy beard he'd entered with was gone. Without it, he looked young. Almost younger than her and strikingly handsome.

"Anton?" she said, voice squeaking in surprise.

He turned at her voice, surprise written on his features.

"Bonne soiree Fraulein Griffiths." *Good evening Miss Griffiths.*

"Ta barbe?" she said, stroking her cheeks before gesturing at him. *Your beard?*

"Je ne suis plus en mer. Il fallait que ça sorte." *I am not at sea anymore. It needed to come off.*

"Ah."

As if that answered everything, he went back to his bed, not noticing how she watched him. Nor did he seem to notice how distracted she remained until he covered himself with a sheet once more.

Roberta hadn't been sure of herself until she made it back to the privacy of her office. She knew men watched her, she had known it for years. Their eyes enjoyed drinking in the pronounced curves of her womanly physique and classically beautiful face. Certainly, there had been plenty of suitors at

Seven Oaks, even after she joined the Nursing Service. But none of them had ever taken her fancy before.

So why him? Why does a German captain have this effect on me?

She had asked herself that question repeatedly since then, to no avail. Now, two weeks since he had first arrived, she still didn't know what to do about Captain Anton von Yorck.

Would've been nice to meet a boy like him on holiday. Without a war going on around us. Or between us.

She heard shouting and the sound of men yelling.

What is that commotion? She wondered.

Stepping out into the hallway, Roberta saw a soldier on the floor, unmoving. Anton was trying to get the at the pair of soldiers who remained upright, despite the best efforts of several orderlies and nurses. as they tried to leave the ward and make for the exit.

"Who the blue blazes are you and what are you doing in my hospital?" She yelled.

The fighting ceased, heads swiveling about as she stalked towards them, temper rising to the boil.

One of the soldiers, smarter than his fellows, spied her rank and popped to attention. "Evening ma'am! We was sent over by Brigadier Dudley's staff to collect some items."

"Items?"

"Yes, ma'am."

"What items?"

"The bag that jerry brought in. It's needed for analysis."

Roberta had a very good idea what bag they were talking about. And it did not please her to consider what they were doing. The man's personal effects were his. Non-negotiable. This held true even for prisoners of war.

But somebody on the Brigadier's staff seems to think it's highly important. Bully for them.

"That jerry happens to be the equivalent of a Colonel. Do you suppose he might take issue with a mere sergeant trying to take his possessions?"

"Umm. Yes. Ma'am."

"Never mind that you thought you could walk into my hospital, do whatever you please, then walk out?" She snarled.

"Um. Uh."

"What's his name?" She demanded.

"Uh— who—?"

"The Intel officer. What is his name?"

"Leftenant G. Daniel-James."

"Daniel James?"

"Yes ma'am, he has two last names. Quite proud of it he is."

Snatching up a phone, Roberta held it out. "Call him."

"Uhmm—"

"Are you in the habit of disobeying direct orders from a commissioned officer?"

"No, ma'am."

He dialed a number from memory and passed the receiver to her, then stepped back.

The conversation which followed was memorable for it's short, pungent exchange.

"Is this Leftenat Daniel-James? It is? Tell me, do you use two last names because your mother couldn't decide which drunken Irish stablehand she'd mounted was the the real father?"

Pause.

"Now that I have your attention, come get your filthy piles of pig vomit out of the hospital. Otherwise I'll leave them with redcaps."

Pause.

"Shut up you piss-poor excuse for a British officer."

Pause.

"Do you know why we're talking?"

Pause.

"That's right, you sent them into the hospital. Without permission."

Pause.

"No, I don't care who you work for. The army has laws. And you will follow them."

Pause.

"No, I don't care who your father drinks with in between rounds of buggering each other at the club, or how much cock your mother sucked so she could get her worthless whelp into a second-rate boys' school."

Pause.

"Impolite, after what you pulled? If you, or any other member of the Headquarters' staff wish to receive treatment ever again on this island you're going to shut your mouth right now."

Pause.

"Oh you don't? You should try asking my rank. Who am I? I am the Acting Chief Matron. This is my hospital."

Pause.

"That's what I thought. Don't ever send your bully boys around again. Or I'll call the redcaps to refer charges. And I promise, they like me more than they will ever like a you."

The receiver slammed down in it's cradle, and she looked toward the soldiers. "Get out, stay out, otherwise I might forget to be civil.

"Yes ma'am."

The three scrambled out in a clatter and Roberta looked toward the orderlies.

"Clean up the mess and carry on with your duties. Captain von Yorck!" She pointed toward her office, speaking in very precise German. "Immediatement!"

She did not wait to hear a response from any involved as she stomped back toward her office. *Gah, men.*

#

"Anton, why are you so important?"

Roberta had waited for him to be seated before she began her interrogation. Normally, she was far more considerate with her questions, but here and now, Roberta was too mad to bother with politeness. Even for him.

"Me, important?" Anton asked, his voice mild.

"Yes," Roberta insisted.

He leaned back in the seat, working his jaw around before he spoke.

"I was an officer on a U-boat," he admitted.

"What was your duty onboard?"

"I was the executive officer to Komondors von Osten."

Roberta breathed in. "That. That would be quite important. And the bag?"

"Letters from my crewmen. I am to ensure their families get them."

169

"Is that even possible?" She asked.

He shrugged.

Roberta thought about what she was dealing with, and where her loyalties lay. *I am an Englishwoman. I love my empire and serve it with all my heart. But I am also a doctor. And I am trying to keep the peace in an island which has seen enough war already.*

"You gave me your word once, as an officer and a Prussian," she said carefully.

"Yes, and I have not broken it," he assured.

"I know." She breathed. "I need you to give me the same trust."

"Why?"

She pointed at a cabinet on the near wall. "Leave your bag there. It will be safe."

He stared at her.

"On my honor as an officer and a Lady of the British Empire."

"You are a lady?"

Reaching into her desk drawer, she produced a brooch, kept as a reminder of calmer times than these. Pushing it across the scratched wood top, she let him handle it, inspecting the familial crest on it's face.

"I am a Griffith of Seven Oaks. My father is an earl."

"I see," Anton said.

Standing, he walked over to the cabinet, placing his bag inside. She produced a key from her pocket and locked it sharply.

"The only key to this is in my hand."

"You think this will work."

"If the Leftenant they mentioned is the same one I remember from the Christmas party, he's a fat, unimaginative idiot who pretends to be clever."

"Shame he doesn't run your navy. We'd already be in London."

"Touché."

Roberta breathed as his anger visibly dissipated. This close, neither of them spoke, though Roberta felt fairly certain her skin crawled as if electricity were running across it.

He looked levelly at her with his gunmetal eyes in that moment.

"Please, do not make me regret this. Their families deserve to know." Before she could think of something to say, he was out the door, closing it with finality.

She sat down hard, staring at the door. Heart still fluttering.

What do I do about you, Anton?

\#

"Anton, I'd like you to take a walk with me, before I go off shift for the day." Outside, the sun had not yet broken the horizon, but it was getting lighter. Roberta had walked in on Anton getting his morning exercises in. By all rights, he should've left the ward days ago. The paperwork hadn't made it to her desk though, and Roberta presently felt disinclined to acquiesce to any such request.

"Why?" Anton asked.

"We have a prisoner camp here, and I think you can help it."

"Who's there? Germans like me?" He asked, pointing at himself.

"Yes. Maybe a few Italians too."

He grunted, then moved toward the door and held it open for her.

"Lead on."

Nobody was moving when they arrived, which he seemed to prefer. The corporal of the guard allowed them inside the perimeter, inviting Anton to look around. The tentage was minimal, and the grounds did not look

171

like much. His nose wrinkled at the trash littering the ground. Eventually, he returned to where Roberta stood.

"I can fix this," he declared.

The venom in his voice was apparent.

"How soon?"

"A few weeks. I think."

"Why?"

He looked back towards the camp as the gate slammed shut behind them.

"It is— hard to explain. You must trust me."

"Of course."

In the next three weeks, Roberta did not see much of Anton during her shifts. But she heard about it from the staff.

"That jerry captains always doing pushups in the ward," an orderly remarked in the hospital kitchen to a cook while Roberta was doing a walk-through.

"I see him throwing lots of punches, like he's boxing his shadow," the cook replied.

"I heard him ask for a jump rope the other day," a maid declared, stirring milk into her tea.

"A jump rope?"

"Yes. He's been practicing with it."

"Wonder what he's doing?" The cook said.

"Dunno. Maybe he thinks he can skip his way off-island," the maid suggested.

Through it all, Roberta held her peace. She had her own matter to handle. Answers took time, but she found them, and was surprised at what she learned. Then came the day she had been waiting for. Anton knocked on the door of her office, dressed in rough work clothes.

"Madamoiselle Griffiths, I need gloves," he told her in French.

"How many?" Roberta asked.

"One pair, leather."

"I can make that happen," Roberta promised. *I'm certain I can find something that fits.* She glanced at his massive hands once again. *Maybe. I might have to sew them together myself.*

It took hours to find gloves which she thought might fit, and when she returned to drop them off, Roberta found him patiently sitting in a chair, staring out towards the hill where the prison camp resided.

"He ain't moved once ma'am. Just sat there and waited," the duty corporal, Baker, informed her. "Ain't even bummed a cigarette off me like most of them do."

Roberta stared at him, and felt a chill running down her spine as she watched those gunmetal eyes swivel towards her. Predator eyes. He was planning violence. Possibly even mayhem. And it scared her. Then those eyes took her in and they softened considerably.

"Ma chere dame, did you have any luck?"

"Yes, I found these," she said, holding up the leather driving gloves she'd found in a half-destroyed haberdashery.

He tried them on, flexing his hands in the black leather.

"Gut."

"What are you going to do?" she asked.

He looked up the hill towards the camp. "Those men. They have forgotten how to soldier. I will fix that."

He stood, bowed slightly at the waist, kissed her hand, then stepped off, marching up the hill with a determined purpose and stride. Roberta wasn't sure if she should cheer or cry.

"Ma'am, you think he'd mind some company?" Corporal Baker asked politely.

"Corporal, I'm not sure you or I want to be there for it."

The Corporal looked significantly at the marching figure. "Ma'am, you might not, but I'm feeling the need for summat more than reading the same old book again."

He stood, slinging his rifle and followed along behind the Captain at a slow walk, leaving Roberta alone with her thoughts.

The first sign that she'd made the right choice came when an orderly appeared at the emergency care doors carrying a prisoner, escorted by a very cheerful Corporal Baker.

"Ma'am, this man needs some help. He fell down and hurt himself bad."

"Fell down. Yes ma'am. Fell down the hill and busted his nose in. Like to think it's broken."

Three more men came down that first day from the camp. All shared similar fates- they had fallen and injured themselves. Roberta watched the procession, trying not to laugh as she did the examinations and paperwork.

The very worst damage came a week into Anton's assumption of command at the camp. To the surprise of none, especially not Master-at-Arms Gill, the injured party was Oberscharfuhrer Dietrich. An SS commando, he had made repeated trips to the solitary confinement cells for a variety of crimes, including escape attempts. Fanatical, and driven, he had sworn the british would not be able to contain him.

On this occasion, the Oberscharfuhrer's visit was vastly different. His face had been badly lacerated, ribs partially stove in, and both hands were broken. He had to be hauled down in a wheelbarrow from the camp, and he struggled to do more than moan piteously through the jaw smashed in two places.

"Corporal, please don't tell me this man fell down."

"No ma'am, wouldn't dream of it," Baker said carefully.

"So what did happen?" Roberta asked,

"Would ya believe me if I told you that he was trying to move lumber for fixing the camp and the stack fell on top of him?" Baker replied.

"It fell on him?"

"Yes ma'am. Who knew wood could do a number on a fella like that?"

Roberta clucked her mouth disapprovingly, filled out the paperwork and carried on with her shift.

With another nurse, the Corporal might've had success, but not Roberta Griffiths. She'd grown up attending the prize fights with her uncle Damon when they went down to London on business for her father. Roberta knew exactly what leather driving gloves could do when given to a man skilled with his hands. Anton had sliced the SS man apart as surely as a surgeon at an operating table with a fresh scalpel.

She had enabled a man to commit violence against his fellow man, and she felt no guilt over it. If anything she felt pride. Her man was making a difference on this godforsaken rock.

My man? She stopped in her tracks, as she realized the enormity of what she had just told herself.

And I want none other.

He came in later that evening, just as she was coming on deck for the night's duties, dusty and dirty from working. There was a slight bruise on his jaw but he looked none the worse for the wear.

"I do not think you'll have any more trouble from them."

"You don't? How?"

"I am Prussian. We have our ways."

She poured him a glass of locally made wine and he drank, grimaced, then continued drinking till the glass was empty.

"Thank you. I miss proper beer, but that was good."

"You're welcome."

"Have a good evening madamoiselle Griffiths."

"You can call me Roberta, Anton, it's alright," she told him.

"Only when it's just us, like this. I would not want others to speak badly of you."

"Since when have you cared about that?" She asked, surprised at his forthrightness.

"Since you showed me you were worth trusting.

\#

Five months after he'd first arrived on island, Anton York looked at a calendar and felt a strong pang of homesickness.

It's almost Christmas. I miss watching Mama set up the tree with candles and tinsel. He missed the food too, but that was easy to replace. A home? A place full of love and laughter and people who cared about you? Not so much.

Who knows when this war will be over? He asked himself. Certainly not I. Will I even have a home to return to?

There had been the socializing too, various families visiting their friends and neighbors with gifts in hand. He'd enjoyed the attention of the pretty girls that came around, trying to catch his eye. Anton von Yorck knew he was a catch.

Strange, I can't think of a single one of their names, or faces any longer. There was only room for one woman now, even if he didn't know how to put to words what he felt.

What do I do about her?

"Sir, men are formed for evening inspection," iron-haired Stabsfeldwebel, Schulz declared, breaking off his train of thoughts.

"Thank you Stabsfeldwebel. How are the men doing?"

"Well sir, though there are questions about Christmas."

"Understandable. We'll see what we can do."

"Yes, sir."

Walking into the hospital ward where he slept every night, Anton saw clothing laid across the wardrobe. It was a blue and gold-trimmed service uniform, neatly cleaned and pressed. Two medals, suspended on ribbons untied, rested nearby. Besides them was a note, written in flowing cursive.

The Red Cross got all the letters off island. Most have now been delivered. Your honor as a Prussian is intact.

At the bottom there was no signature. There was no need. He knew that cursive, just as he new the paper would smell faintly of her perfume.

Ye gods and little fishes, what a woman Anton told himself. *All the beauties of Brandenburg, Berlin, and Bremen I chased, but how did I find an Englishwoman who outshines them so brilliantly?*

It mattered not how he had found her, simply that it was time to show he appreciated what she had done for him, and for his men.

#

Father Brendan Kelly stood outside St. Paul's Cathedral, greeting parishioners as they approached for the Christmas morning Holy Mass. He'd awoken this morning with the feeling that something momentous was going to happen to day. He just knew it.

Standing outside in the nippy morning air, he wasn't sure what that momentous thing was. But the Father knew he ought to be ready for it, whatever it was.

"Morning Padre," Colonel Sylvester said, shaking hands with the priest, followed by his Regimental Sergeant Major, McLaglen.

"Colonel, RSM, how are we doing?" Kelly asked.

"Doing well. Thank you. Though I suspect that my Sergeant Major wishes he were still in bed right now."

"Yes sir, I do sir. Nothing good comes of being up this early."

Behind the colonel, a group of QAMC nurses was approaching, followed by several nuns from the convent and a pair of families.

"Colonel darling, we've got company," McLaglen said cautiously, hand straying to his service pistol. "That's a sight more Germans than I wants to think about right now.."

They came up the street, two abreast in good order, led by an officer in the uniform of a senior captain. Curious eyes peered through curtains, even more curious people looking outside, wondering if they'd somehow missed a German invasion, muttering at the indecency of attacking on Christmas morning. The worries only ceased when they saw Corporal Fitzsimmon's squad of infantrymen and gaolers, following along behind with bayoneted rifles at the ready.

"Links. Links. Links Rechts links. Zeit markieren! Halt!"

The cadence caller stopped the formation just outside the church, barking an order in harsh German. When he finished, the captain in the lead marched to where Father Kelly stood.

"Good morning Father, I am Captain zur See von Yorck."

"Good morning to you too, Captain. Can I help you?"

"Yes. We are here for communion and the Christmas service."

His smooth English shocked all who heard it and Father Kelly felt himself positively beaming as the large German officer spoke with him.

"Please, do not be alarmed. My men will cause no trouble," he assured.

"Very well," Father Handley said. "Are you sure they'll be able to follow? We do Mass in Latin, and the sermon in English after all."

"These are good German boys, Father. They'll follow just fine." Von Yorck flexed one massive black-gloved hand. "Or I'll teach them to follow."

The Captain looked over his shoulder toward the double column.

"Stabsfeldwebel, send them in after me." He turned back to the door, paused, looked to Sylvester and the RSM. "By your leave, sir."

"Oh yes, yes of course."

Stepping inside the chapel, Anton genuflected, then set himself just so in the aisle. As each column quickly filed inside, they found their Captain waiting for them, directing them to the rearmost pews.

When all had passed, with much of the parish staring after them, Father Kelly chuckled.

"Well, that's one Christmas miracle for the books," Kelly said cheerfully.

"Father, we need to talk about your definition of miracles sometime," McLaglen muttered.

The entire service passed with ease, even if it was spoken mostly in English, rather than their native German. When it had finished, the Stabsfeldwebel and Captain repeated the procedure, swiftly moving the men out of the building and back up the street to the POW camp.

"It's the darndest thing I've ever seen, Padre," McLaglen admitted as he watched them go, impressed by their conduct and neat drill.

"God's children are as varied as the rainbow, my son. Still I wonder how they knew what time to be here for morning mass?"

Behind them, the new Chief Matron mulled over the question. *Matron Griffiths has been working on that German captain, von Yorck. I thought the Intelligence shop said they were done with him? Oh well, can't be any harm in her keeping all the prisoners in line. I wish all my nurses were so productive.*

#

Anton heard soft music playing from Roberta's office that evening as he went past. No light escaped under the door, and he wondered if all was well with her.

She's just as far from home as we are, and she hasn't been back since she first came here. I hope she's alright.

Grasping the knob, he turned it and stepped inside.

Within, Roberta sat at her desk in a half dark room, light coming from the waning moon above. A bottle of wine, unopened, rested on her desk.

"Roberta, is everything well?"

She sighed, looked at him. "I am missing home, Anton. I miss Christmas at Seven Oaks."

"What do you miss?"

"The smell of a good fire. Watching chestnuts roast and waiting on the goose to finish in the oven."

He sat down across from her, studying her as she spoke. Not that he needed light for the matter. Anton von Yorck was deeply familiar with

180

every curve of her face, the way her lips moved as she spoke, how her eyes batted when she was nervous.

Everything I want to say about you is on the tip of my tongue, Anton chided himself, listening intently to what she said.

"Is there anything I can do to help?" He asked when she paused.

"I'm not sure. I don't know about our family, but mine always set up the tree in our Great Hall. It's big enough to hold many guests."

"Many guests?"

"Nearly a hundred. Mother would play waltzes all night, rather than carols, and encourage people to dance." She looked towards the now silent phonograph. I thought playing music would help but its made the melancholy of my heart far worse.

An idea struck him, as if lightning thrown down from on high. Standing, Anton walked over to the phonograph on a cabinet and looked through her collection of records.

"See something you like?" Roberta asked.

"Oui." He paused, holding up a record.

"You have Strauss?" he asked.

"You listen to Strauss?" she replied.

He made a face. "Do I know Strauss?"

Putting the record on the machine, he set the needle then walked over to where she sat and bent at the waist as he extended his hand.

"Madamoiselle Griffiths, puis-je avoir cetter danse s'il vous plait?"

Roberta felt her heart flutter. Whatever fear she might hold on the matter , but fear had been bashed aside as she came to her feet.

This can't be real she told herself. Even as she said it, Roberta felt her hands guided to where they ought to be, and one of Anton's broad palms

181

slipping down to her waist. Then he began to lead her through the steps and she forget about anything else as the violin strains of "Gold und Silber" filled the air.

#

The music had stopped playing long ago. The couple had slowly come closer together, hands moving of their own accord till both of his palms rested on her hips, her arms wrapped around his neck as they slowly revolved around a patch of moonlight streaming through the open window.

"Anton?"

"Oui, ma chere?"

"I don't want to let go," Roberta admitted

"Neither do I."

"What are we doing?"

"Falling. In love."

"You think so?"

"I know I am," Anton declared.

Roberta looked up from where her head comfortably rested on his shoulder, all the while thanking her lucks stars she'd found a man who stood on her level.

"How?"

"How could I not love you?" he asked. "I know about your fight with that pompous Intelligence officer. And I know you are the one who took care of my uniform."

He kissed her, gently, in the quiet dark, and Roberta felt her world begin to coalesce.

"You knew?" she said, surprised.

"I can speak three languages dear lady."

He'd spoken in English, with only the very slightest trace of an accent. Roberta stopped moving, letting her eyes lock with his.

"It was you!" she snarled.

"Hmmmm..."

"That first night you were here, in the emergency room!"

"Oh, that? Yes. And you've since proved I was right. You are a woman worth being loyal to."

"You— you scoundrel!" Roberta hammered against his massive chest with one balled fist, before he caught her hand in his.

"Please don't my dear, you're liable to hurt yourself doing that."

"Damn your eyes, how are you so shameless?"

"I am Prussian."

"Nanny Gertrude used to tell me stories about the Prussia she grew up in, before the Great War. I had thought she was exaggerating."

"And now?" Anton's eyes twinkled merrily as he asked.

"She was right."

"Of course she was. I wonder what she'd say right now."

"That you are a lion-headed scoundrel," Roberta replied, running her fingers through his curly blond hair.

"I suppose, but only if I can be your scoundrel."

"What about the war?"

He shrugged. "What of it? Eventually, it will be over. And we will still have our lives to live."

#

One day after Admiral Donitz's surrender to the Western Allies, Roberta Griffiths became Mrs. Roberta York, with the Chief Matron as Maid of Honor and Orderly Hopkins giving away the bride to her husband, An-

183

thony York. Any commentary which might have been made on the matter was very quietly silenced by local society, all of whom adored Matron Griffiths for her role during the Siege of Malta. If they had reservations about her husband, those comments were likewise kept quiet.

Anthony York would live to see his third grandson come into the world, a healthy baby boy with a head full of cornsilk blond hair, born on a quiet morning in Malta, forty-nine years to the day after he first came ashore. Those final years were spent with a wide-eyed boy who listened and learned from his grandsire about the sea, the stars, and how a man conducts himself. In the midst of it all, Anthony York found peace.

#

Above the family, standing on the ramparts where they could watch the light show with an uninhibited gaze stood a score or more of specters, unseen by mortal eyes. Here a knight of the Order of St. John, still attired in his maille and surcoat, the latter emblazoned with the white Maltese Cross on a field sable. There, a Janissary, alternately playing with the ends of his mustache or else consuming great quantities of popcorn. The horsehair plumed helms of Hoplites rested alongside a Fallschirmjager's drab green Stahlhelm. Tonight, as the stars rose, they welcomed the newest member of their association.

He had been old when he finally passed, his Teutonic features worn with age like a great stone beneath a waterfall. There came a popping sound and an old man made young once again stepped into the space. He shook himself, looked at his hands, no longer crippled with age or rheumatism, then to the uniform he now wore. Shaking, unsteady hands, reached up to his throat, brushing against the blue cross edged with gold which rested there, beside a second cross, on a ribbon of red, white and black.

"Welcome!" the Knight boomed. "We've waited a long time for you!"

"Herr Kapitän!" the fallschrimjager barked, rendering a salute as his boot heels audibly slammed together.

Anton returned the salute. "At ease Feldwebel," he commanded. The Prussian looked to his host. "Am I dead? Is this the afterlife?"

"Yes, you are, and yes, this is."

"I never thought Hell would look like Malta. I always expected more lakes of fire and pits of damnation."

The Knight laughed.

"A Prussian with a sense of humor. I thought that only happened after you'd had enough beer to float a ship."

Anton smiled. "Why am I here?" he asked.

"Why are any of us here?" A corsair rejoindered. "We died fighting here. Some the island keeps, some it passes on to God."

He clapped a hand on the Captain's shoulder and led him to the edge of the rampart.

"Normans, Spanish hidalgos, French hussars, we've even got a Roman or two. Should hear them argue with the Italians."

"I can imagine.

"It makes the time far more pleasant to pass," the corsair grinned behind his majestic mustachios. "And that's before we get to the beaches."

"True. Now I don 't have to worry about having a stroke every time some lovely young thing trots on past to remind me I was once young."

"Exactly."

"Come brothers, it is time," the Knight called.

"Time for what?" Anton asked.

The Knight gestured out to sea.

"Look, and behold."

Anton stared hard. Saw nothing save the wind and waves.

"You're a spirit now, lad. Try looking deeper."

Anton focused his will on that. And in a moment, his vision changed.

He was underwater now, watching an undersea vent wreathed in smoke and lightning open, a corona of cascading energy pouring out of the hole. Water frothed under the lash of writhing tentacles, propelling a series of multi-eyed monstrosities driven by an insatiable hunger across the Stygian gloom from which no man returns. Just as their kind had since time first began to count, creatures of chaos and fury drawn to the world of the living.

Driven? Aye. And drawn by the presence of life uncorrupted. Driven to wantonly consume without regard. To rage without ceasing. To drive the sons of Adam and Daughters of Eve into wild paroxysms. Such was the Covenant by which Chaos made war.

Anton shook, feeling cold and clammy.

"What are those?" he asked.

"Chaos," the centurion declared.

"Before man came to the earth, a third of the host of heaven fell. Where did they go?" the knight asked.

"I— I don't know," Anton admitted.

"What if I told you that Malta exist next to an undersea volcano, one which was so violent when it erupted, it ripped a hole in reality and now serves as a gateway to Hell?"

"A month ago, I'd have said you were insane. Why have we not heard of these before?" Anton demanded.

"But we have! Where do you think all the old sea stories came from?"

His eyes widened as he considered the information.

"What changed?"

"Men. Men changed. We made ships. And when wood was not enough, we made hulls from iron and steel."

"Who— How—"

"Watch and learn."

Chaos moved, destroying that which lived. He saw now the multi-teethed beaks, capable of crushing wood and stone with ease. The way their tentacles flexed as they moved, the wide footpads which would allow them to move across the land.

And yet, in their course, Chaos stood opposed. For another came. Another who chose their own track. And these would not be denied, neither by man, nor by beast, nor even by eldritch horrors beyond human reckoning..

Gray hulls gleamed with inhuman phosphorescence as they sliced through the water, so many metal wolves on the prowl as they circled their prey.

"Sonar makes three contacts coming up through the layer, bearing 359, 310 and 029. Designate Sierra One, Two and Three respectively!" a sonar-man called out in a familiar sing-song voice.

Behind him, Oberbootsmannmaat Lehman marked the plot board, listening to the swirl of information around them and recording it all.

"Match tubes one and two on the Sierra One," a calm voice ordered and Anton felt his jaw drop as he recognized that man.

"Matching!"

"Fire tubes one and two."

"Tubes one and two, away!"

"Close doors and make ready tubes three and four in all aspects."

"Torpedoes in the water, U-49 has made their shots."

With only 2,000 meters between the target and U-49, it'll take maybe 30 seconds for impact, Anton computed.

The deadly weapons struck true, exploding on contact with hard chitin, breaking off chunks or smashing the plates inward against the soft rubbery flesh beneath. Thick green blood oozed out from the lacerations and punctures, filling the water with the dark, viscous fluid.

They were not dead, not yet. They began to move more swiftly now, fighting to break for the surface and reach dry land, where their tormentors could not follow.

Bodies floated toward the surface, as invisible to the mortal eye as a puff of the wind. Outside the reach of grasping tentacles, those gray wolves rose swiftly. U-637 broke the surface first, her surefooted crewmen scrambling out of the conning tower toward the powerful deck gun. A round slammed home in the breech, handwheels spinning as the barrel swiftly rose to max elevation. Patiently waiting, the gunner checked his sights, adjusted a handwheel slightly.

"Hanzi you bloody Pomeranian, what are you waiting for?" an ammo hauler called out.

"For the little focker to get where I want him, Peter," Hanzi replied.

Peter gave his old friend a smile. "Ever the master of showmanship, that's our Hanzi."

"That's my boat! That was my wolfpack! What are they doing here?"

"Your comrades are still on patrol, senor," the hidalgo explained casually.

"It's been over fifty years! They should be dead!" Anton protested.

"Of course they are. These men are spirits now, fighting in a realm unseen by human eyes. In defense of all humanity."

A roar filled the air, one only inhuman ears could articulate and a deadly red lance punched a gaping hole through the abomination's torso. A second roar and the creature's head burst asunder this time.

"That's a man who knows how to double-tap right proper," a Frenchman in the stripes jacked of a Sergeant of Hussars declared. "I'll give him credit, even if he is a Boche."

"Quite," a bearded Englishman beside him declared.

Hearing a familiar laugh, Anton stepped forward, automatically recognizing the small boy playing down below.

"Oh my boy, my beautiful boy," he murmured. "What I would give to spend more time with you."

A hand fell on his shoulder. Anton looked to see the hidalgo.

"He knows, senor. Just as he knows you love him. He has always known that. We have too. We have watched your care for him, and you have done well."

"I wish I could rejoin him," Anton admitted.

"I know. Our duty is here though."

"Till when?"

"Till the Horn of Judgement sounds," the Knight declared.

"And what is our duty?" Anton asked soberly.

"To protect the world of the living, from Hell."

Anton squared his broad shoulders, blinking away unspoken tears. "I can do this."

"We know," The centurion replied. "There's a lady here been telling us all about you."

Anton heard heels click-clacking against the stone walk, heels which broke into a run as she caught sight of him, standing head and shoulders as he was above the other men present.

"Anton, you made it!" she shouted breathlessly.

He managed to catch her as her arms wrapped around him, enjoying the feel of his wife's touch for the first time in nearly four years. Before the cancer had taken her from him.

She was young again, young and alive in his arms.

"I would've gone anywhere it took to find you, ma cheri," he declared, kissing her as he did so.

She giggled, in a way which made his heart flutter just as it had the first time he heard her speak.

"Of course you would, mein Kapitan."

"And now that this reunion has occurred, can we get back to watching the good stuff?" the centurion declared. "Because as much as I hate this fecking island, it does give me a glorious source of entertainment."

All four submarines had risen to the surface now. The deck guns were hard at work, hammering round after round into the hellish creatures. Nor were the heavy cannons alone. Aft of the conning tower, 3.7cm guns slammed out a lethal staccato, punishing the foul monstrosities with furious lashings of fire and steel.

Drained of so much of their life's essence, ethereal bodies began to rise through the air. They rose above the above the rain squalls, the cumulonimbus clouds, even the ice-laden cirrus clouds. For a moment, the bodies hung in the sky, silhouetted by stars and moonlight before they began to fall. As they did so, flames appeared, licking at bloody ichor and mangled wounds.

The creatures screamed, agonizingly shrieking for relief. But in space, none could hear them scream. None save the deity who they blindly followed. Succoring them was beyond his remit. And so they fell, cast back down to earth once more.

"Look Papa!" a little boy's finger pointed toward a spot above the horizon where a brilliant blue corona streaked across the sky. "There's four shooting stars! One for you, one for mama, one for me, and one for grandpapa!"

"Very good Anthony! Good eyes lad!"

Scooping the tired boy into his arms, Anthony York let the cherubic face rest on his shoulder as he patted the fine blond hair with one calloused hand. It was perhaps an incongruous sight, a Major of Her Majesty's Royal Marines holding a child like this, but Anthony York cared not for the opinions of men on the matter. His father had taught him well on that count. All else was dross.

"Papa?"

"Yes, son?"

"Can the next shooting star be for grandma? I miss her too."

"Of course, my boy."

High above them, on the ramparts, Anton von Yorck wrapped an arm around his young-old bride's waist.

Dream well small boy. Dream well, a Prussian scion commanded. *We shall not fail you.*

PRECURSOR

Evan DeShais

With my throbbing left hand, I grab at the wrist of the unconscious tribal fighter. The man's loose Jebba and weapons are of higher quality than the other dead rabble around me. I glance around the roundabout of Rue Ali Belhaouane. The place is still and quiet. The port of Sousse trade center building lies in ruins. This man's team unloaded a half dozen of their mortar rounds into it before attacking it and the three of us defending it.

I glance at the corpse of Sous-Lieutenant Pierre Boisclair. His right arm is missing from the neck to under his armpit. He was dead before the body hit the floor of the ramshackle port authority building. The other man was a Corporal. I did not know him. I didn't know all 3,500 of us that set out for Sousse. The bandages on his chest cover his ID tag.

My captive is the man who had used a Forward Elliptical Educational Display (FEED) unit before the attack on our hardpoint. I pull down his right sleeve and find the FEED system's wrist band intact with its single haptic power nerve.

These are supposedly new un-hackable tech that lives on the mesh net. The nerve generates power from the human body's heat and electrical current. The cuff looks like an expensive model with a large five by seven and a half-centimeter holo display. I tap the stud on the stud worked into the wrist cuff, but nothing happens.

My frustration blooms. I hear sirens and clanks far away. I slam my eyes shut when my body dumps rage, the engineered cocktail of endorphins into my system. I've lived with this rage all my life, from the very first memory. This is what it means to be a precursor, variant K-37.4, from Putin the ninth's holy Rus army.

I fight back the torrent of adrenaline and phencyclidine that clouds my mind and think. I look at the moaning man and drop him to the ground. I touch the stud on his wrist cuff with his left hand. Still, nothing; the word 'thumbing' works its way to my mind. I push his left thumb to the stud, and the FEED display pops to life. I enter the message address and hit send.

"Ops officer," A young male voice says.

"Legionnaire first-class Franc reporting," I say. But unfortunately, my voice comes out as a whisper when I try to swallow the dust from the firefight. "Sous-Lieutenant Boisclair is gone. I have found no others."

"Thank you for the report Legionnaire Franc," The OPS officer says. "We saw the mortar rounds impact the facility. Retrieve their IDs if you can." The FEED screen goes blank for a moment. "The Captain isn't going to bring the ship near the port nor risk his cutter. Can you make it to the end of the jetty?"

"I believe so; it is a few hundred meters distant," I say. "I've enough ammo, but I am leaking heavily."

"We are launching the cutter now," the Ops officer says. "I will see that the ship's medic is on board."

"Franc out," I say.

I look down at the unconscious man as I let go of the FEED system. It is still on and displays the message address of the Franco-Prussian Legion (FPL) ops center aboard the ship. This mission was a cluster-fuck from the start. Our tooth-to-tail legs were days behind when we left to rescue the Tunis royalty. As far as I know, I am the last alive. Thirty-five hundred brothers in arms lie dead or missing.

I close my eyes as the images of the men and women of Tunis Royal house staked to the fort atop Jebel Ech Chambi flood my mind. Corpses burned by hot bitumen and then set afire. A wave of memory floods my senses, the stench of burnt tar and roasting fat. The sounds of gunfire in the middle of the night. The memory of the mortar shell blowing a wheel of a god damned donkey cart. The memory of waking with that broken wagon wheel atop me the following day.

I let that rage I am holding at bay leak out of control. Not many people live from a stomp backed by 180 kilograms. The body doesn't even have enough air left to gasp. The man wakes from his unconscious slumber. His eyes blink a few times after opening, and the pupils contract and fix upon me. I grind my heel in his chest, and the eyes relax, losing focus. The man's life ends, and the FEED display slowly fades into nothing.

I pull the *plaque d'identite* from my two dead brothers. The Corporal's name had been Valentin Schumacher. I check the wrapped bandages about my body. The rage dulls the pain to a mere inconvenience. My left hand doesn't feel right, and I realize that two of the fingers are badly bent. My sides have a dozen harsh pains, but the bandages hold.

Today isn't my first war. I check the rifle I have on me. The rumblings of a track-driven machine reverberate down the roadway. Thankfully it is the opposite direction I need to go. I pull the last two smoke grenades from the

Corporal and toss both. The smoke mixes with the viscid haze of Sousse's week-old fires.

With that, I leave the shell of the old port authority building. I attempt to jog at first, but I do not have it in me after the last five weeks. We force-marched from our Franco-Prussian Legionnaire (FPL) base in Alger to Kasserine. I spent the next two weeks in a protracted battle from Kasserine to Sousse, where our FPL ship was supposed to be waiting.

When I arrived in Sousse a week ago, the city was in a raging battle with the remainder of the Legionnaires that had made it this far. I contacted the ship's Ops officer, and he directed me to the fighting where I could be of most use. But instead, I found my brothers dead, mutilated, butchered, or burned in bitumen pyres. The last of the holdouts had made it to the port.

I turn and look back at the length of the jetty. I see several tracked vehicles rumbling through the rows of shipping containers. They are looking for me, as I have haunted the tribesmen since the battle at Kasserine. Then, a flash from a signal lamp near me causes me to turn around. A small inflatable cutter is making its way to me on the seaside of the jetty.

I stumble down the boulders, and my weight here is a significant disadvantage. My third step is my last step on the African coast. I slip on the slime-coated rocks and plunge into the water of Homer's wine-dark sea. The inflatable lining expands when it contacts saltwater. It hardens in seconds, and I bob up to the surface. With a painful effort, I swim towards the cutter.

My progress is minimal, and I pause to unload useless gear. Two pistols leave my waistband, and the rifle falls into the sand somewhere below. Knives, grenades, and food all drift away from my body. I push forward stroke after stroke.

They help yank me up over the side and from the ocean when I near the cutter. I fall into the inflatable dripping vast amounts of its salty sea into the vessel. The water around me is red with my blood. The motors hum to life, and I let my mind fade out.

The rough tang of smelling salts drives me awake. I sit up and vomit over the side of the inflatable. I sit up and find us tied to the gangway of the FPL landing craft Camaron. Someone helps me up and out of the way. Ships men are loading fresh power cells onto the little cutter. I move near the gangway, but the ship's Legionnaire lifts his weapon.

"Legionnaire Franc," says a raspy older voice. "I am Capitan Monroe of the Camaron. I am afraid, brother, I must treat you poorly. "

I try and find the voice as the little vessel bobs up and down in time with the gangway. There, near the entrance to the ship. I spot the Captain. He's got this scar across the left side of his throat where something almost ended him.

"I know what you did for our brethren Franc," The Captain says. His eyes are laden with regret and sorrow. "We can do you no favors here aboard this ship. The world knows about you now. They call you the' Der Phantom-Teufel' now. The world is looking for you, and if they find you on this ship, we will all hang."

I can feel the rage starting to build; my left-hand cracks and pops as my fist clenches. The old Captain swallows. "I will not turn my back on you, Franc," he says. "I've 1271 men aboard this vessel I have to think about,

196

though. King Leopold and his adjunct minister of war are blaming you and all of FPL for the murder of the Royal house of Tunis." He stoops a bit behind him, disappearing from view for a second. "They are saying FPL had no authorization to march to Kasserine."

His eyes find mine as he returns to face me. I glance at a fourth power cell when wheeled down the gangway. The Captain lifts a bag and hands it to the Legionnaire on the gangway.

"I know that is a lie," the Captain says. "I was there when his majesty's adjunct war minister delivered the orders."

The canvas bag sails through the air, and I catch it. It's not heavy.

"I can give you this, though, a cutter stolen from Syracuse," The Captain says. "There are enough power cells to see you anywhere within 1,500-kilometers. We included some credits on a fob, a standalone FEED unit, and a workman's jumpsuit." His face goes grim. "You will be hunted, Franc; the world knows you and your face as the 'Butcher of Sousse.'"

I look at the bag of meager offerings and let it fall near my boots. I lift my plate carrier over my head and strip the empty medical bag from it. As I pull, the slight clack of hundreds of myomere tags emanates from it. I pull off my plaque d'identite and ad it to the bag. I seal the bag up and toss it to the Legionnaire on the gangway.

"I couldn't get them all," I say. I flex my sore left hand again. "There are over 200 in there. Maybe they will let me die with my brothers." I let a sad smile play across my face as I look back towards the port of Sousse. We are too far out to sea to spot any land; nevertheless, I know what direction it lies. "My time, Captain, all 48 years in the FPL is over. I've buried over five hundred brothers in that time. If you count the tags in that bag, over seven hundred. I am done with this life. I have soldiered enough."

197

I pick up my plate carrier and let it fall into the ocean. I shoulder the canvas bag the Captain gave me as the last man steps back onto the gangway. A moment later, the cutter drifts free, and the FPL landing craft slowly pulls away under its powerful motors. I strip off wet bandages and my uniform and do my best to clean my wounds. The saltwater stings and the ship laborer's jumpsuit smells of old sweat and grease.

I drain a couple of liters of water from a bladder in the bag as I start to put the little cutter under power. What direction do I head? I have no idea, not to Sousse and not following the Camaron. So, for now, I will be satisfied with anywhere but here.

It takes me a while to initiate the standalone FEED system. I know one man outside of the FPL, and we have exchanged letters for decades. I don't know if Dr. Peter Alverez can help.

"Franc?" Peter says his bushy eyebrows and a thick beard are now going white, a stark contrast to his midnight skin. "I was worried about you, my boy," Peter says, his head moving out of view of the FEED pick-up. "I heard a newscaster talk about this dreadful FPL blunder in Tunisia and assassinating the Tunis Royalty. When will that upstart Franco-Prussian King learn."

"Doc," I say. My voice is thick, still with blood, dust, and grime. I clear my throat and spit globs of bloody phlegm into homer's wine-dark sea. "I need help. I was in Tunisia." I pause, and Peter's face slowly comes back into the FEED displays field of view.

"Der Phantom-Teufel," Peter says in horror.

"I am not what they say," I remark. If anyone could believe in me, it would be Peter. "It is time for me to retire from soldiering."

Peter's gaze is unfixed as he looks off to the side still.

His right-hand waves up and down at the FEED pick-up to silence me. I wait as he thinks things through. To say Doctor Peter Alverez is brilliant is to insult him. He is to human logical thinking and science as I am to physical destruction and pain. I've known Peter for 51 years, give or take. He visited me in prison, and he was a scrawny 18-year-old twig of a boy then.

"I'm working for the Family now," Peter says. "We are en route to Malta; Stewart Sr. has me looking into a couple of medical research corporations that Stewart Junior is considering purchasing." Peter pauses, his mind once again working through something. "You can make it to Malta?"

"I believe so?" I say, looking at the FEED systems small map. "I am close to Pantelleria now, and It looks like a 16 to 20-hour trip in this cutter."

"There is a," Peter says, and for the first time, I hear another voice, "a little inlet some short distance from us. Il-Prajjet. Can you make it there?"

"I will try," I say. "Who were you speaking with?"

Peter looks directly at me, "Stewart and his mother are here with me on this trip." His head moves out of view of the FEED pick-up again and does not return for a number of minutes. "We will meet you there in 22 hours. It will be well after dark then."

"Thank you, Peter," I say.

My fear and worry are barely kept at bay as the FEED message dies. I look at it and decide I have no other choice. With a sigh, I drop the standalone FEED unit over the edge and watch as it sinks to the bottom. While at the conning station with the cutters onboard map booted up, I turn the little craft north away from Pantelleria.

I lied about how long it would take me to get to Malta, but not by much. I want to distance myself and the Camaron before heading southeast to

199

Malta. After two hours of speeding north, I turn the little ship southeast. I am close enough to Marsala that people might think I am headed there. I head to meet my friend with the throttle open as wide as this little cutter can handle.

I've heard of the Family. The Jankowitz Family has the world's largest hedge fund, the world's most advanced adaptive science program, and most of all, they are the Family that opened the Gates. So if Dr. Peter Alverez is working with his friend Stewart Jankowitz Jr, he might have the clout to help me. I hate trading on my friendship with Peter like this, but I am a man out of time, out of place, and with literally only one friend left in the world.

I arrive after dark. I've drained three of the power cells running the cutter up on plane to get here. I am battered, soaked, and need a long night's rest. I pull slowly into the little inlet of Il-prajjet after making it over the breakers. The harbormaster waves me over. The portly man swallows hard when I tie up and step onto the little dock. I am twice his height and almost double his width.

He lets his instrument wave over the little cutter, "you are a long way from Syracuse," he says in Maltese.

"I am," I answer back in my best French. "I got lost on holiday, and a passing container ship helped get me back on track."

He looks down at my boots and swallows.

I look down at them; the tan brown of the boot is a rusty red with what can only be blood. I am ready for a fight; the rage dumps into my system.

"It looks like it was a big fish," the little harbor master says; a gleam settles in his eyes. "It broke all your tackle, and you lost all your fishing gear. A tragedy. I can give you a three-day pass for 200 credits?"

"That is appreciated," I say more harshly than I feel. When the rage dumps into my system, it is more than a physiological readiness change. My whole body reacts, my voice gets deeper, and more of that gravel permeates everything I say. Finally, I turn and look at the vessel, "how much to deal with that?" I ask, letting the suggestion be unspoken.

"I've got a cousin," He says, rubbing his chin, "His son is getting married and starting on his own."

"Sounds like an excellent wedding present," I say. "My congratulations to them both." At a wary glance at me, the old pirate nods. "The original owners will not come looking for this."

He puts a thick plastic sheet into his little instrument with a nod. He looks the machine over, head bobbing, as he types.

"Welcome to Malta, Mr. Ronaldo Montaigne. You have three days to appear before the immigration offices in Valletta with your passport and papers," He says.

I pass over a Credit fob and pray the Captain loaded it with more than 200 credits. The name is a poor one. No one will think of me as Ronaldo Montaigne, the lead striker for the Madrid football league. The little thief's eyes brighten as the transaction completes. He hands the fob and my temporary made-up ID to me.

I lift my little canvas backpack and start walking down the dock to the small village in the distance. I need a place to sleep and something to eat. For the last two weeks, dried protein bars have left me wanting to eat a whole cow raw. I spy in the back of the promenade, a place that deals in large slabs of meat.

I ease my way past the many smaller people and come to a complete stop. In a chair at a table sits Peter Alverez. His tall thin frame waits for me with a wide bright white smile.

"Hello," he says as he gestures to a seat. "I thought you might arrive early. After some research, I figured this might be where you would show up. A man, your size needs substantial calories."

To say that I am gobsmacked is an understatement.

I am about to reply when a young woman steps up and says, "This is your other party?" Her eyes look at me in disgust. Then, she turns to Peter, "we have a jacket and tie requirement."

"We will take everything to go," Peter says.

The woman blinks; once again, she looks from him to me.

"The faster you get that done, the faster we leave for our hotel suites," Peter says. "Ramgeet will pay you."

Peter's hand waves to the man behind himself. Ramgeet steps from the background shadows. I spy his armor first, a modern plate carrier, and the rifle second. The rifle is the North American Compact's newest and greatest. This man, though, this Ramgeet, isn't a CM soldier. No, he's too central Asian for that. It clicks then, the knife at his hip. I turn to Peter, who looks back at me.

My thick finger pointing at Ramgeet, "One of the 40?" I ask.

"My Segundo," Peter says, looking to Ramgeet, "I'm not keen on the idea, but it comes with having a seat at the Family table."

A few silent minutes later, a pair of trays with boxed food in bags arrive. Ramgeet pays, and Peter stands. I follow as we make our way up a couple of streets to a waiting sleek Mag Lev Roller. A second member of the storied

40 stands guard. We enter the vehicle, and it speeds down the road for a few minutes.

Two hours later, I've eaten, and Peter has reviewed my wounds. He re-bandaged a number of them.

"You will need an MRI to find the slugs," Peter says.

"My healing will deal with the slugs," I reply. "Right now, I need sleep."

"We have a meeting tomorrow," Peter says. "Can you be ready by 09:00?"

"I can," I say, looking down at my stained jumpsuit.

"Ramgeet will have some things delivered here," Peter says. "You'll have them waiting for you in the morning."

〜〉〉〉〉〉〉　〈〈〈〈〈〜

Peter knocks on my room door at 08:55 in the morning. The new suit is different from any clothing I have worn. I understand the concept of a dress shirt and tie, but I have never worn one. The over jacket seems a bit much in this heat. Also, there isn't a suit that can hide the scars, bruises, and stapled-together lacerations on my face, hands, and neck.

We pass along several hallways out onto a veranda with a view. The space has this trellis that sports many new vines striving to work their way up and over us. A woman, almost two meters tall, turns from watching the surf when we enter. Her glance at me is insignificant. I don't mean that I am insignificant, just that she has little care about me being here.

I spy another of the 40 only feet from her. His wicked Kukri hangs on his left hip. He has his rifle slung behind his right shoulder. He glances up at me and returns to making two cups of coffee.

The man finishes and offers one to the lady. I catch a whiff, a bite to the odor of the coffee. She accepts, and they clink cups; the two are drinking a moment later. Ramgeet brings over a second coffee service for us and sets it at the table. I decide to follow Peter's lead.

I drape my suit jacket on the back of the chair and sit. I wait my turn and make up a tiny cup of coffee. I've finished my second before the woman finishes her first cup of coffee.

"Do you like it?" her canto-like voice asks.

"I do," I say. "It beats the coffee in the FPL."

"And the prison Coffee?" She asks.

"We had coffee in prison?" I ask back with a bit of amusement laced grumbling.

The sound of her laughter is well worth the joke. She takes a deep breath of sea air and turns. In three steps, she is at the table and sitting across from me.

"I am Teresa Jankowitz," She says. "Dr. Alverez is my son Stewart's best friend." She lets the challenge to my relationship with Peter stand. I don't disabuse her of that.

"Peter is my only friend," I say.

"I think I see," she says as her eyebrow lifts a little as her other eye narrows, "Exactly, what are you?"

I look at the woman, the leading lady of house Jankowitz. A woman of no small means of her own. She has many of her accomplishments in the corporate world before marring Stewart Sr. The two make for a dynamic combination of brains, money, and looks.

I spot a knife-edge of pain that creases at the corner of her eyes. I look from them to the coffee cup and back to her separate pot. The acrid scent wafts to me ever so slightly. Focusing on smells isn't a skill I have used often, and now that skill lies unpracticed. However, I detect enough to confirm a few things.

"You are ill?" I ask carefully, wary of the power her money and influence can bring.

Her eyebrow climbs to the top of her forehead as she smiles tightly and looks at Peter, who shakes his head. When she turns her attention back to me, I know that is as much an answer as I get without explaining myself.

"I am a precursor," I say. "The last of us, if my suspicions are correct."

"Which variant?" She asks without hesitation.

"Variant K-37.472," I say.

This time both her eyebrows rise to the top, her mouth parts a little, and she seems to take me in injury by injury.

"A Rager?" she whispers. "The K variants were hunted mercilessly when Putin the ninth fell.

"I watch as every member in the 40 comes to full attention, hands at the ready. She must have heard the shuffle of boots and gear: her long-fingered hand lifts, and the 40 return to a less immediate death posture.

"The King and his warmongering minister have blamed the FPL," Teresa says. "You know that, right? But, do you also know that you are outed as the 'Butcher of Sousse'?" At my nod, she hums for a moment in contemplation. "You are bleeding," she says.

I look down at three widening spots on my right side, and two more spots on my left breast bloom through the shirt fabric at my movement.

"Tell it to me, Rager," Teresa Jankowitz says.

"My name is Franc," I say slowly. "As in the old Swiss Franc, you know, before their adoption into the Franco-Prussian Kingdom. The term Rager is off-putting," I explain.

"My apologies Franc," Teresa says. I begin with my stint in Putin the ninths Rus army. My 31 days of training after leaving the birthing lab. My nine years in the Sino-Rus war. During my time in prison where I met Peter. I relay my early days learning to be a real soldier in the FPL. I end with the mission to retrieve the Tunis Royalty. Teresa listens intently, her eyes delving into my deepest depths as I let those memories up from my soul.

Spurts of the rage dump into my system as I relive the horror that is my life. I relay every fight, battle, and war. I hide none of the gruesome details. When I finish, the spell that is Teresa Jankowitz's eyes, lets me go. I look at my arms and see that my shirt is damp with my blood. I grimace, a hazard of being me. When the rage dumps, the healing can be quite aggressive.

A good wound heals from the inside out and pushes foreign material out of that same wound tract. So in bloody balls of puss, my body has expelled the foreign material in each wound. In some cases, it is rock, dirt, or grime. In others, little shattered bits of bullets, their jackets, or hard metal cores.

"I am sorry for ruining the shirt," I say. "It was my first nice shirt."

Teresa's eyebrow goes up a bit, and she looks at Peter and Ramgeet. Then, when she settles back on me, she asks, "What are you hope we can do for you, Mr. Franc?"

I bite my lip because my predicament is quite dangerous. My face is wanted now all over the world. I watched the news on the room's FEED system display.

"I asked Peter for help," I say. "I have nowhere else to turn. I need time to heal," I lift my right arm slightly. "Even as fast as this seems, the actual healing will take months if not a full year."

"I'll think on it, Mr. Franc," Teresa says. "I've seen the hints in your eyes. The rage has been dumping into you during our conversation, hasn't it?"

I nod with a slight weary bow. If Teresa knows I still utilize the rage and that the cocktail of endorphins keeps coming, I suspect that I have little hope for help.

"Get some rest while you are here, Mr. Franc," She says. "We will be along in a couple of days with an answer. You should be safe enough here. The staff will not bother you here. So take some time to visit San Blas beach."

She stands, and Peter stands also. Teresa pauses at the doorway, "There are those in the world who know the King is lying about FPL. The question is, Mr. Franc is that lie enough? Are the promises he is handing out sufficient?" Then, with a tight smile, she steps through the doorway.

I return to my room and step out of my bloody clothes in the shower. Fragments of twisted metal, sharp copper, and bi-metal zinc flowers fall out of my clothing. I strip the bandages and grunt as the wounds start oozing blood that is nearly coagulated. When the blood stops flowing, I am woozy and tired. Finally, I lean against the shower's wall and fall asleep.

>>>>⟩ ⟨≪≪≪

I awake to the sound of the room's front door opening.

"Franc," Peter says with some caution.

"Yeah," I grumble, "Shower."

Peter pokes his head into the bathroom and stares. His eyes dart over me and the myriad of wounds.

"Shower again," Peter says. "I'll get those dressed up and food ordered when you finish."

I nod and try to stand but slip on the film of my blood coating the shower's floor.

"Could you," I look at Peter nodding my head to the shower's handle. "Just turn it on. I'm a little out of sorts."

"You are in a vast caloric deficit, even for you," Peter says as he steps to the handle. "I doubt that even you can push much further, Franc."

An hour later, I am showered, my wounds glued, stapled, and cauterized shut. I have a pair of large fuzzy pants and a thin armless shirt on when the food arrives via Ramgeet.

"Why?" I ask.

"Why what?" Peter says.

"Why help me?" I rephrase. "Yes, we have known each other for many years, but."

Peter's dark face frowns, and his eyes go sad. "You believe I think so little of our friendship?" Peter asks. "You have known me before anyone save my parents, Franc. We met before I met my wife, kids, and Stewart."

"I've had brothers and sisters in arms," I say, looking at the bags of food on the table. "But only you could I consider a friend." I lean forward, pull one of the bags, and remove the cartons. "What I meant more is why help me now when the world turns against me."

"I know you, Franc," Peter says. "I knew it the first time we talked. You are more than Variant K. I know that; I think Teresa knows that. Her concern, I will wager, is whether you know that." Peter pulls the other bag over to him and starts pulling out more boxes. "You decided when you told me your soldiering days are over. The question is, what will you become going forward?"

"I have not thought about that," I reply as I open the first food box.

Peter stands and heads to the door.

"Give it some thought Franc," Peter says. "I'll be back to let you know what Teresa has decided."

I look down at my food, clothes, and hotel room. Each of them provided for me, with no question about repayment. I start in on the food. I've been adrift from one battle to the next my whole life. I've learned to read, think, and question. Maybe I made a mistake staying in the Franco-Prussian Legion so long. I wonder if I should have retired years ago. What would I have done?

"You would have fought," I mumble to myself. "You were a Rager then, and you will be a Rager forever if we aren't careful."

The idea is out there now, even though it remains un-spoken. I understand it clearly and know if I give it words, I will gift it life.

"I want more than killing," I say. "I need to be more than blood and death."

Fifty-seven years of soldiering is enough; I am done. A knock wakes me from my food-induced sleep the following afternoon.

I open the door expecting Peter. Instead, Teresa stands there, her member of the 40 off to the side where he can see me. "The Franco-Prussian King has denounced you by name," Teresa says. "Have you seen the news?"

"I have not," I say, rubbing at the back of my head. I retreat from the doorway. "Would you like to come in?"

Teresa tilts her head and smiles. She enters my room with only the slightest hesitation. Her member of the 40 steps up to the door and pulls it closed. I turn to her in surprise. "I decided yesterday to help you," Teresa says. "Peter is a friend, and I would have done it on his request alone." She smiles as she pulls a chair at the table and sits. "I had never met a Precursor before and wanted to meet you. You're mistaken, though. I know that five of you live. You five are all that remains of your 9,000 brethren."

"Do you know the variants?" I ask.

"Two Alpha's, a Beta, two Charlie's, and now you," she says. "A 'K' no other nonprimary Precursor survives. Putin labeled you beasts and tossed you at the unbreakable walls, fortifications, and every form of chemical attack they could not break." Her long fingers tap silently against the table.

I'm at least a dozen feet from Teresa, but I feel her eyes pull at my soul. They dig into me, pull me along to plumb their depths. I shake my head and wince with my eyes tightly shut.

"I did not mean to stare," I say.

"King Leopold has defaulted on loans to the Family," Teresa says. "He's outed a friend of the Family as perpetrating a crime." Her voice now carries its weight; gone is the sing-song canto. "We leave Malta in two hours," She says. "The Tram will pick you up here. Will you be ready?"

I nod as I am speechless. Finally, I have a life, an opportunity for something other than mindless rage.

I cleaned the room. I bagged the trash and hid my bloody clothes inside. I have my small canvas sack with only a few spare bits left. I look around the most opulent space I have stayed at.

The whine of a Tram's nacelle builds as I step from the little suite into the hallway. I walk down the small path leading to the Tram landing areas. A second Tram is only a few hundred meters behind the first.

A bit of rage dumps into my system when I spy the logo on the first Tram. The Emir of Malta or his people is here. I glance at the second Tram and find the Family's Corporate holding company logo.

I watch as a trio of people exit the first Tram. One is a shorter woman; the two others are men with bushy beards. They wait in the lee of their Tram as the second one lands. It buffets the space in fine dust and pebbles. Mrs. Jankowitz exits her Tram after members of the 40, and Peter follows not far behind her. Then, as a group, the two parties head in my direction.

I let my canvas bag fall from my grip as a familiar smell wafts through the landing area. The stench of my kind isn't something you forget as a Precursor. The first days of our lives reek of blood and the offal from our slain brethren. I tilt my head and give a big sniff. I stink a little, likely from that last dump of rage.

Teresa nears, as does the tall men with beards.

"Franc," Teresa says. "This is the Vizier of the Emir. He is going to help us today."

The Vizier's eyes flicker from Teresa's own to me. He has to lift his chin to look into my face.

"Mrs. Jankowitz," the Vizier says. "Formalities first," he turns to the small woman. "Finder, what can you tell me."

The diminutive woman steps near. A scent of deep floral musk mixed with loam slips from her. Her eyes are mostly black, with only faint rings of brown.

"Belen," the Finder says. "I've told you, Malik, and your brother the Emir that my name is Belen." Her eyes flick from me back to the Vizier. "What do you want me to know?"

"I need to know if doing what Mrs. Jankowitz asks will bring shame on the Emir," Malik says.

Belen looks from him to me and nods. Her eyes focus, but the halo of brown that is her iris stays the same. I feel the tug at my rage, almost as if she plucked at it to see how I would react. I tilt my head at her.

"Little bird," I say. "That isn't polite."

A toothy smile widens across her face. Her teeth are not pointed, but I catch the glint of serrations on the very back edge. I do not know what this little bird Belen is, but I recognize her as a predator. Her staring at me isn't comfortable at all. I feel as if she is weighing every decision I have ever made.

"Come here often?" I ask, trying to lessen her scrutiny or break the ice.

"First time," Belen mumbles, "It's a job. I find things."

Her head turns to Malik, and she gives him a single nod before stepping away and heading towards the Tram. Malik's hand waves forward the second man in his group. That whiff of stale Precursor hits me again. Belen's scrutiny of me must have had me sweating something fierce.

Teresa steps up, as does Peter. Their shadows, the men of the 40 mere feet behind them. Teresa looks from Belen to Malik, to me.

212

"We have a deal then?" Teresa asks. "The Family will build you a Gate to a Dimensional Iteration of your choice for making Franc a lifelong son of Malta."

"We have a deal," the Vizier says. "It's a piece of fiction, and you know that. No one will mistake," his hand waves from my feet to the crown of my head, "him as a son of Malta."

The second man steps forward, and his virulent green eyes are solely for me. He pushes forward some papers to the Vizier. Malik impresses his signet ring on some wax. The ring flashes as its power cell warm the signet enough to mold the wax. That damn odor hits me again just as the hairs on my neck stand up. I breathe deeply, and my nostrils flare as my hands flex into fists. Again, Malik's servitor's green eyes blaze brightly.

The full force of the odor hits me. We, Precursors, know each other. It is more pheromones than real sweat stink if my studies are correct.

Rage dumps into my system as the papers push forward to Teresa. Her hand reaches out to grab them. I will never know what tipped off the 40, was it a reaction to me tensing up or the uncanny look Malik's servitor gave us as he shoved the papers toward Teresa.

I am injured but not dead. Stiff and sore I might be, I know what the servitor is. He is my death sentence if I don't intervene. If I do step in, it is my death sentence. If I don't stop him, it is the death sentence for those here to help me. My left hand wraps around his wrist, and I clamp down with all my might.

"He is a Precursor," I growl as the rage pumps throughout my body.

I watch Teresa yanked backward from around her waist. I hear Peter mumble something as Ramgeet shoves the much taller Peter back. My distraction almost costs me an eye. A glob of spit hits my cheek, and I hear as much as I feel the sizzle as it begins to burn down my face. My hand starts to swell as the Precursor's nature infects me.

"Well, well, well," says a cultured voice. There is barely a hint of old Rus in his accent. "A 'K.' Good old King Leopold did not warn me that I would be doing a 'K' today." His eyes flash deep green, and I feel the venom slide into the skin of my left hand. "If I had known that, I would have done this job for free. A Jankowitz, the Emir's brother, and a troublesome brother variant. It is truly a trifecta of a day."

I yank with my left arm as more rage builds. As the Precursor flies towards me, I roll onto my toes with my forehead leading. The headbutt causes him to wobble. All of my kind can take a beating. I know it won't hold him, but it brings him out of reach of the Emir's brother. My right fist goes for a kidney shot and lands a glancing blow. The Precursor, a variant 'B,' twists deftly at the last moment.

"Barabbas," I growl, using our slang term for Putin the ninth's assassins. Their very skin can become a lethal venom injected by thin hairs that penetrate the skin of their targets. A touch can be fatal. "Not today Barabbas," I say. I knee him once in the stomach and land a second blow with my fist to his temple when he doubles over.

B's left fist hammers at my left knee. I stumble under the pressure of the blows. My right leg isn't set to take my weight, and I have to let go of his wrist to keep from falling to the ground. A right jab lashes out at my cheek as I work to gain my footing. Our kind are strength personified, built to take abuse and wounds plenty. With his hands free, he wades in, landing blow after blow.

I catch them on my arms and shoulders for the most part. Each of them leaves a stinging burn of venom. I more rage dumps, I lash out with a pair of low kicks to the leg. The first one lands and B hops after the blow. The second misses as he dances back. He closes in and finds another kick to the same leg before his hands land on my throat.

I grab his left and right collar bones in my own hands. We squeeze; we each emit howls of pain. Like two rival saltwater crocs, we are now grappled in a death roll. The first to flinch will die.

"Die Rager," he growls, "you will be my third 'K' kill."

I feel the venom attack my throat, my airways. I pull up a glob of the envenomed blood and spit it back at B. His head dodges the bloody mess. I head butt him a second time.

I see my friend Peter then. Tall and willowy, a man of medicine and science scrambling to get away from Ramgeet in a vain effort to help me. I don't know what is said between the two. I struggle to knee Barabbas in the chest. I spy Ramgeet looking over his shoulder at me and back to Peter.

I have been a soldier for 57 years of life in war, in a military, or battle between bruisers. I thought I knew what being a soldier was. For the third time in my life, I was wrong, so very wrong.

Ramgeet gives Peter a final shove and turns to Barabbas and me. I hear the Kukri sing as Barabbas head buts me, then knees me in the groin. I know any blade of man will not harm Barabbas much. But, when my eyes open and focus, I see the weapon lodged in the side of Barabbas's ribs. Ramgeet is in the air, his little Karda knife in his left hand.

When Ramgeet lands on Barabbas's back, his right arm snakes around his throat. His added mass drives the two of us Precursors to our knees. Ramgeet lets his cheek rest against the left side of Barabbas's head. Ramgeet's eyes find mine. I know now what being a soldier is.

It is service, not of yourself, your country, or other people. It is selfless service; it is that fading moment in Ramgeet's eyes. I have no words to encapsulate the depth of service Ramgeet gifted to me.

Ramgeet's eyes go milky white as his tiny Karda knife saws at Barabbas's throat. I watch as a member of the 40 teaches me what 57 years of war and two armies could not.

I have not done it since the last time I fought a Precursor variant B. It was the end of my ninth year in Putin's army. We K's had broken the walls of the forbidden city, and Putin feared our might. So with his blessing, B's came for us.

I find that place in my rage and flip the switch from off to on. A pink haze creeps in from the edges of my vision. My hands clamp harder on Barabbas collar bones. When I stand, Ramgeet's corps falls free.

"Barabbas," I growl. "You will be the second 'B' that I kill."

The rage is no longer a hit, a taste of the raw fury that is me. Instead, it melds humanity's greatest endorphin cocktails in a shell housing a juggernaut.

I clamp down so hard that I feel my fingers dig into his skin. A moment later, his collar bones crack under my might. His eyes blaze green, but it is too late. I know the healing that this level of rage brings.

I don't plan to rip Barabbas apart so much as flex him back and forth until he tears in two. My shoulders and muscles are screaming under the pain, under pressure. Then, when his body starts to split, I let out my rage in one decisive expulsion of force. The yell I let loose pulls the last of my rage into my system.

When my tears come, I have two halves of a Variant 'B' in my hands. Then, finally, my hands release, and I collapse to the ground.

"Lie still," a voice whispers. "Let ol' Belen do her work."

"What are you doing?" Peters's voice asks. I slip back unconscious.

A jolt rattles me awake. I blink my eyes open. Peter is off to the side, head lolling as he sleeps.

"He is awake," the little bird says.

"Thank you, finder," Teresa says.

"You are recovering, Franc," Teresa says. "We are taking the tram back to the North American Compact."

I waggle my head in a nod. I try to glance around to see if everyone is there. My eyes land on the body bag in the middle aisle of the Tram.

"Ramgeet," Teresa says, "did not survive. The rest of us did, thanks to the two of you."

Her hands shift out of my line of sight for a moment. She holds up paperwork, but I can't focus on it.

"You are a son of Malta, a subject of the Emir with a permanent work visa to the Family." Her eyes soften, and they flit to Ramgeet's ever silent form. "You two were awarded a boon for saving Malik, the Emir's brother. So the Emir knighted the both of you. You are the first living Knight of Malta in nearly 300 years."

I try to speak, but my body is still too weak. Even that effort is too much as it drives me back into slumber.

VIRTUES OF COMMAND

RAY KRAWCZYK

Master Sergeant Don Burkett unhooked the buddy cable from the charge port on Private Keppler's scout suit. He watched his suit's Tokamak rings spin down to nominal output now that he'd finished charging Kepp's fusion bottle.

Slapping Keppler on the shoulder with a gauntleted hand, he said, "All done, Kepp. That should hold you for a week, if you lay off the grav assisted bounding. How's the mag bottle on your fusebox holding up?"

Keppler paused, probably due to switching to his maintenance display, before replying. "Ah, it shows fifty-eight percent integrity, sergeant. Any chance you're going to send me back to Malta for shutdown and refit?"

Burkett shook his head. "No chance, Kepp. We can't spare you. How are the ACV fish pens doing on Cominetto?"

"We're down four fish for only two confirmed kills on Combine subs."

"What does that leave our fish count at?"

"One hundred and fifty-one swimming the sensor line, as of this morning. Twenty-eight fish down for repairs and maintenance."

"Command wants no less than one hundred and twenty swimming the IMT sensor line. Do what you can to up the active numbers."

"You got it, boss." Keppler said, turning to leave.

"Keppler, one more thing," Burkett said.

"Yeah, boss?"

Burkett ignored the lack of military discipline. Keppler had always been lax, and his NCOs had allowed it back when they weren't assigned to a forgotten outpost on Comino in the Maltese Archipelago. "I know when you're in the maintenance bunker on Cominetto you get out of your suit. I don't care about that. But do me a favor and stop bragging about it. Some of the guys topside have been sealed up in their suits for a month. If you pop off in front of Oleastro and he decides to use his ape suit to rip your arms off, there's no way I can stop him."

"Uh, yeah. Sure thing, boss."

Burkett tossed a salute at Keppler. "That's all, dismissed."

Keppler returned the salute, turned and left Burkett's command post.

Command post. The term was laughable. It used to be his maintenance shack. He was the single, surviving engineer the company assigned to the air defense position on Comino. They'd been placed there nominally to defend the Italy-Malta-Tunisia undersea sensor line. Asian Combine submersibles had to slow down when transiting the shallow part of the Mediterranean in the gap between Sicily and Tunisia. The Union had decided that it was a perfect bottleneck to prevent the subs from transiting through the Suez, dashing through the Med and escaping into the North Atlantic.

Trouble is, the Combine had figured out that the sensor line had to be anchored there. Missiles targeted at the facilities in Italy and Tunisia had to transit a corridor controlled by air defenses based further east of the anchor points. But Malta only had open ocean east of it. Scramjet powered hypersonic missiles dropped on them randomly. A two-ton missile didn't even need a warhead when it was travelling five times the speed of sound. Kinetic kills were good enough. Comino, once an idyllic, if arid, island with former citrus and olive groves and some scattered buildings, now looked like the war zone that it was.

They'd landed with ninety effectives, twice that number in humanoid drones. He'd set up in a subbasement of an old church. The subbasement was still there, the church, and most of the other structures on the island were scattered about the landscape as widely separated debris. Along with half of the company, all of the officers, every NCO senior to him, and most of their pulse lasers. They'd landed with twelve, they had a cache of kinetically challenged parts, and three functional lasers that some wag had named Faith, Hope and Charity after some ancient aircraft from the second global war.

Burkett was not amused by this course of events.

Of even less amusement was the loss of all of their fusion generators. Faith, Hope and Charity were being powered by the company's only remaining ape suit. The heavy weapons suit wrapped around Sergeant Oleastro was the last survivor of one assigned to every platoon. When the company was on the move, one of the pulse lasers would be fitted to the suit in place of one of the railguns they normally carried. The ape suits had enough surplus power that they could fire them on the move. Instead, they had Oleastro bunkered up in another subbasement, reinforced with cerametal plates scavenged from the destroyed laser mounts. His suit's twin

220

one-meter Tokamak rings were powering the lasers with enough juice to fire two of them at the same time.

The only good note was the supply situation. With so many casualties, they had plenty of protein bars. The suits could create fresh water from the abundant salt water surrounding the island and they had enough DT bars to keep the suits with Tok rings powered up for the near future. But since they only had three suits with Tok rings, that was scant aid. His, Oleastro, and one of the company medics in a logistics suit, Nguyen. The other suits were either scout suits, like Keppler's, or the more common line suits. Those suits were powered by a fusion bottle called a fusebox. Which Oleastro, Nguyen, or he had to charge. Since one laser had to be online at all times, most of the charging was handled by him or Nguyen. Unfortunately, Nguyen couldn't help with all of the administrative tasks that would normally have been detailed to the officers of the company.

For two weeks he had been submitting his daily sitreps to silence from battalion command. Last thing he had heard, they were part of the Union drive across Egypt to cut the Suez and make his position superfluous. The battalion operations officer had told him that he was lucky he was in a safe, rear area. The battalion was taking it on the chin on the front lines. Since that brief response to a request for resupply and reinforcement, he hadn't heard anything from higher.

The news from home was just as bad. The Combine had driven a broad wedge in the heart of North America. After they'd sent their Tyrant tanks across the bottom of the Bering Strait and along the southern coast of Alaska, they penetrated into Canada, turned south and scoured the country of population. Last week they'd razed Denver to the ground and they were making a concerted push against Wichita.

To say the issue was in doubt was an understatement. He could understand why higher wasn't sending reinforcements. There was nothing to send.

Burkett sighed and turned to the exit for his command post when his comm sounded. He checked the ID of the comm and was surprised to see it was a Major Zubia, listed as Brigade Operations Officer.

He authorized the connection and said, "Twenty Second Air Defense Company, Master Sergeant Burkett speaking."

"Burkett, I want to talk to your CO," Major Zubia said.

"Ah, sir, I am in command."

"What? Crap on a cracker. How bad are things there if a master sergeant is in command?"

"I'll send you the precis of the sitreps I've been filing, sir. It's pretty bad. We're down to half effectives, no fusion generators, and only three lasers left. We are averaging two missile attacks a day."

"Well, shit."

"Yessir. But the worst of it is that we don't get any advance warning. The Combine is trying to knock out the IMT line. The head stations in Italy and Tunisia get advance warning from stations further east. We get warnings from Israel, sometimes. Other than that, we get less than a minute's warning from the station on Malta's east coast."

"Well, damn. I figured something was up when my staff told me that we were getting sitreps from a company in a battalion that didn't exist any longer."

Burkett's breath caught in his throat. "Doesn't exist, sir?"

Zubia paused before he began in a softer tone. "I'm sorry, Burkett. They were either laagered on a volcano mine or somebody's fusebox let go."

Burkett thought over the people in the other companies that he'd never see again. His heart hurt, but it was too much to process right then. He coughed to clear his throat, "Yessir. Thank you, sir. What's the situation?"

"The Combine is throwing the kitchen sink at us to prevent us from reaching the Suez. Once we do, we restrict their only viable path to the Atlantic. We've got sensor lines stretched between Antarctica and Tierra Del Fuego and South Africa. Canada, Greenland, Iceland, the UK and Norway have the North Atlantic sensor line bottled up. The Pacific is a mess, Japan is completely blockaded. Australia is on her knees, but until we kick the Combine out of North America, we can't get any relief to them. The Russians are holding the Combine at the Baikal line, but they're in danger of getting flanked because the 'stans are evaporating like spit on a griddle. Thank God the terrain is so rough there. The Combine can't use their big tanks and walkers on that route, and that robs them of most of their firepower."

"They still have plenty of infantry."

"That they do. But plenty is not the same as unlimited."

"Yessir."

"For now, lieutenant, I'll see what I can do about getting you some generators. At all costs you must keep those lasers up and defending the IMT line. If the Combine can break out into the Atlantic, they'll cut our supply lines to Europe and North Africa."

"Uh, master sergeant, sir."

"Not anymore. For your sins, Burkett, I'm brevetting you to First Lieutenant."

Burkett watched the rank icon next to his name change from three chevrons and rockers to a single, silver bar. His stomach dropped as his rank increased.

"Yessir," he said with resignation.

"Can't have a master sergeant commanding a company. It makes us look like we don't know what we're doing."

"Yessir."

"Send your sitreps to Brigade ops from now on. And keep on keeping on. We're going as fast as we can. Zubia out."

Lieutenant Burkett grumbled to himself about the fickle finger of fate poking him squarely in the ass. Lieutenant! At least he wasn't a butter bar. Time enough to grumble later. It was time to walk the line, talk to the troops and inspect the situation. He turned to leave his command post just as Brigade posted the orders to Battalion. The command network distributed it to all personnel to make them aware of command changes.

The text scrolled across his heads-up; *55th Brigade Combat Team to all personnel, 22nd Air Defense Company. Command transferred to Brevet First Lieutenant Donald Gordon Burkett, effective immediately.*

Burkett sagged in his armor and heaved a sigh. Another line of text appeared in his heads-up, this time from Staff Sergeant Pompey, his nominal executive officer. *Sorry, buddy. And, congratulations, Lieutenant. I guess I have to salute you now, huh?*

Burkett toyed with the idea of giving a two-word reply, that was not 'happy birthday', but relented. All communications were archived and it wouldn't do to get gigged for conduct unbecoming with only minutes on the job. He replied, *Roger, and understood.*

Gathering himself mentally, he headed out to inspect the positions on the island.

Comino is in between its larger cousins of Gozo and Malta. Barely a kilometer across in either direction, with a highest point that had been approximately eighty meters above sea level, it has rolling hills that end abruptly in cliffs at most points on its perimeter. When they'd arrived there were a few abandoned fortifications dotted about the island, a couple of churches, an ancient pig farm, a recently abandoned hotel, and an old quarantine hospital that dated from the British colonial period of the 19th century.

Now, various points of the cliffs were badly eroded. Most of the buildings were completely disassociated debris, and there was very little surviving vegetation. The highest point was somewhat shorter than it had been, thanks to a Combine missile hit on what had been one of their observation and detection clusters.

Burkett observed a squad of drones digging a trench to bury a cable that stretched from Oleastro's dugout to where Hope was emplaced. He recalled that the old cable had taken a direct hit in yesterday's attack. He closed up on the work detail in three bounds.

Staff Sergeant Wiliam Tecumseh Pompey met him with a salute as he landed. "Sniper check," Pompey said.

Burkett returned the salute, "Up yours. What's the situation, Bill?"

Pompey dropped the salute. "You want the good news or the bad news first?"

"Good news. I've already had all of the bad news I can deal with for one day."

"We'll have the new line run to Hope by the end of the afternoon."

"What's the bad news?" Burkett asked.

"Hope is deadlined until we get the new cable laid in and connected."

"About what I expected. Brigade says they're going to try and get us some generators. Assuming they show up, get them positioned in a cave on the north shore. Below water, by preference."

"Are they rated for underwater use?"

"They're rated for all weather, and they are sealed units, so, I don't see the issue. And, by placing them underwater and out of the diving trajectory of the damn Quails. Hopefully they'll survive," Burkett said, using the brevity code for a single land attack cruise missile.

"I'd like to know how the damned Combine figured out that we're here. I mean, if they were dropping missiles all over the island chain, fine. But all of the hits have been on Comino alone."

Burkett used the palms up gesture that armored troops used instead of a shrug. "Combine's got ships in space too. One of them could have a big enough telescope to image us from outside the LaGrange points."

"Assuming there's no human asset feeding them information on our placement and disposition."

"Now you're just being paranoid. Although, if you see anyone on this island running around with a cloak and dagger, you have my permission to shoot them."

The ululating wail of the attack alert sounded in their ears followed by the on-duty controller's voice. "All Malta units, incoming Covey of Combine missiles, four tracks, splash in 55 seconds."

Staff Sgt. Pompey took a cone shaped object off his armor's harness, tossed it a few feet away, and said, "Foxhole out!" on the local channel. He bent away from the plasma charge, dropping to a crouch.

Burkett assumed a similar stance, ass to the blast, but didn't reach for a charge. He activated his plasma cutter on his right gauntlet and thrust his hand at the earth. His Tokamak ring spun up to provide the extra power as he called for a six-foot lance. A hair-thin stream of plasma shot out. Dirt and loose rock blasted away from the lance in a gout of dust and pebbles that rattled harmlessly off their armor.

As he carved into the body of the island, he also issued a command on the company net. "Drones, air attack, cover positions." As he finished excavating a foxhole to hide in, he watched the work party of drones scatter and find holes to hide in.

He glanced behind him to see Pompey already hopping into his foxhole, so Burkett followed suit. The lance he'd used was 10,000 degrees Kelvin, but the amount of plasma was so tiny that it was mostly expanding gas that had excavated the hole. The interior was probably a couple hundred degrees, but his suit could handle that for the duration of the bombardment.

Burkett tuned to the company net and listened to the local O&D clusters track the missiles. "Quail one, bearing seventy-five, entering engagement zone."

"Faith firing."

"Hit, expanding gasses. Good shoot."

"Quail two, seventy-seven, in the basket."

"Charity firing"

"It's tumbling, good shoot. Quail three, seventy-five."

"Laser's cycling."

"Quail three is diving."

"Faith firing."

"Falling parts. Quail four seventy-eight, in the basket."

"Charity's still charging."

"Quail four diving. Target Comino."

"Charity fir..."

A huge impact made the very bedrock of Comino tremble. One side of Burkett's foxhole bulged in on him. Using one arm and one leg he braced the soil to hold it in place. He took a moment and scanned his life support display. His suit was dumping the excess heat picked up from the foxhole walls into the heat sink. As soon as it was safe, he could get out and let the suit dump the heat to atmosphere.

The air raid all clear sounded in his helmet, a steady wail instead of the rising and falling warning of an imminent attack. Flexing his one leg still holding him up he leapt out of his hole. The unsupported wall caved in as he cleared the mouth, and the hole turned into a depression in the earth from the displaced soil.

"Crap," Pompey said from nearby.

"What now?" Burkett asked.

"The drones. It looks like a half dozen of them grabbed some shelter in one of the old dugouts we'd made for one of the generators. Something big hit them. Maybe the Tok reactor from the missile? Anyway, they're slagged."

"Great. So much for the genius programs the drones are supposed to run. But better drones than troops. Get Hope wired back into the power. I'm going to go check on Oleastro and figure out why it took so long for Faith and Charity to cycle for their second shots

Burkett ducked under the arch of a door to enter Oleastro's dugout. The ceiling and the north, south, and eastern walls were lined with plates showing nicks and scars from earlier damage. They'd been welded together. Inside, Oleastro's ape suit was sitting on what Burkett guessed had been a massive lintel for one of the doorways of the former building that had been above them.

"Oley, what's new? How're you doing?" Burkett asked.

"Morning sir. I see the Combine is still sending us love letters morning and evening."

"Yep, and we mostly intercepted all four letters. They did manage to take out a half-dozen drones with their last Quail, though. The lasers weren't cycling fast enough."

"Yep. That's cause the power switch in here died," Oleastro said, indicating a gray box with a dozen power ports on it. One of the power ports was blackened. "I've got private Orne scrounging around in the trash heap for another one. I don't know how many we had in inventory, but hopefully one of them survived."

"Ah, crap. That's bad news. Those things die on a good day. How'd you get power to Faith and Charity without a switch?"

"Suits with Tok rings have two buddy ports. One on the belly, one on the back. Orne pulled Faith's power cable out of the switch and plugged it into my back and I plugged the other one into my belly. But I screwed up, uh, sir. I accidentally plugged in Hope. I swapped it out as soon as I heard that Charity wasn't ready, but it was a little too late."

"Well, that explains it. I'm not going to gig you for making a mistake under fire, let's just get a couple of the switches out of the scrap yard and stockpile them here. Just in case we lose another one."

"Yessir. I don't suppose the particulate count is low enough to unbutton my helmet? It's getting kind of claustrophobic in here."

Burkett shook his head. "Sorry, Oley. The pieces of the Quail that hit and took out the drones probably had a Tok ring on it. I'll have Nguyen check it out, but if it was, there's no telling what kinds of secondary radioactives it fused when it ruptured. Until we get the all clear, nobody on Comino can unbutton."

Oleastro's response was interrupted by the attack alarm.

"What the fuck?" Oleastro said.

The same controller's voice sounded over the all-troops channel. "Incoming Covey, two. Low angle, twenty seconds. Quail one, seventy-nine, in the basket."

A second later, a different voice. "Faith firing."

"Hit, impacted the water. Second Quail, low angle, ten seconds, seventy-nine, in the basket."

"Charity firing."

"Detonation."

Burkett looked around, the attack warning had come so suddenly and unexpectedly that he hadn't even thought about taking cover. Even though Oleastro's dugout was excellent cover, the thought still hadn't crossed his mind.

"Shit, sir. Looks like the Combine's changed up their game on us," Oleastro said.

"Quite a bit. Follow up attack barely an hour after their morning attack. Low altitude and slower speed, but a shorter engagement range since we can't detect them over the horizon. Check on Orne, we need that switch back here, pronto! I'm going to walk the line and check on the lasers and see if we can get Hope tied back in sooner rather than later."

⇛⇛⇚⇚

Burkett arrived at Hope's firing point on the bounce to see Pompey plugging a power cable into the power connector on the laser's mount.

"I thought the cable wouldn't be dug in until this afternoon?" Burkett asked.

"It won't. But the cable is laid out right next to the trench. The drones can move it into the trench while it's energized, so, we can save a few hours and get Hope back online."

"Except we can't. The switch Oley was using to connect to the guns failed. Orne is looking for a spare in the scrapyard."

"Well, shit. I think our TOE only allocated us three switches and one spare," Pompey said.

"Wait. The SOP for battery setup had each three-gun battery, with three generators supplying them, right?"

"Yeah, we can call Specialist Dietz, he's our power systems MOS."

"Right. But the point I was getting at, is that they weren't connected one-for-one. Each trio of generators was supposed to be plugged into a four-port bridge. Then each battery of guns was also plugged into a bridge. Then the bridges were connected with a single cable," Burkett said.

"So?"

"What happened to all of the power bridges?"

"Shit, sir. For all I know they're all still sitting in Valletta harbor. Things were sort of chaotic when we landed. I'm not sure we ever got a full accounting of all of the gear."

"Bill, find out who has the highest containment status on their fusebox. I'm going to detail a couple of guys to go scour Valletta and find those missing bridges. Meanwhile I'm going to go find Orne and see what he found in the scrapyard."

Burkett spun up his power plant and engaged his grav system so he could make long bounds across the island. Along the way he contacted Oleastro. "Oley, do Faith and Charity have a full charge?" he asked.

"As far as I know, lieutenant. I'll confirm with the gun crews."

"Once you do, plug in Hope and let its capacitors soak up a full charge. Staff Sergeant Pompey's connected the gun to the power cable."

"Roger that, sir."

"Lieutenant?" Pompey asked over the same channel.

"Yeah, Bill what's the word?"

"The troops with the best fusebox wear are, and you're probably not going to believe this, Specialists Dietz and Meyers. They're at 85% and 89% wear."

"We're going to have to rely on the E4 Mafia? Ah well, at least they're deniable," Burkett said.

Burkett opened a channel to Dietz and Meyers. "Listen up you two shammers. Some critical equipment went missing when we landed in Valletta. Get your asses over there and find the shipping container with our missing power bridges. Dietz, you're a power systems specialist. You know what they look like. Find them and get them back here pronto and you can have the next two days off."

"Yessir. Any limits on what we shouldn't do?"

"The Hell if I'm going to document anything like that to you two. Just keep requisitioning through unofficial channels to a minimum. But I need all of the power bridges you can find. Or, if you can find an unused power switch, bring that."

"Yessir. One question, sir."

"What is it?"

"What's the difference between a switch and a bridge?" Meyers asked.

Burkett sighed. "A switch takes multiple connections and allows one port to transfer power to any other port on the switch. A bridge makes a simultaneous connection between any port and all the other ports."

"Okay, got it. Thank you, sir."

"Lives are in the balance, gentlemen. Now get it done." Burkett wondered if he was assigning this job to the correct troops.

A final bound landed him in the scrap yard. Orne was nearby, lifting a badly damaged gun mount to inspect the power connection.

"Orne! Tell me some good news," Burkett said.

"Sorry, sir. Looks like we're fresh out of good news and switches. One of the guys on the 2-1 gun said that one of the switches was laid nearby. 2-1 took a direct hit, in fact, this is the mount for 2-2, taken out in the same hit. There's nothing of 2-1 that I can find. The switch is probably in pieces, Orne said.

"Good effort. Get back to Oleastro and stand by to assist. The Combine looks to be spooling up their offensive to take us out before our forces make it to the Suez."

"Yessir."

By eighteen hundred hours they'd suffered through ten more air attacks. The cost was climbing. They'd lost a dozen more drones, two troops killed, and a half dozen more injured and evacuated to Gozo. Along with another trooper whose waste recycler had failed and contaminated his water with feces. Off duty troops had taken to resting in their holes and expanding and improving them with available materials. Burkett had given authorization for the three remaining active gun mounts to go to a single troop manning them in case of local failures.

In ten attacks, six missiles had made impact. Oleastro and Orne had done a great job keeping three guns up, but the last wave of missiles had eight missiles in it and even if they'd had a generator, they couldn't cycle the guns fast enough.

It was going to be a long night.

Burkett wished he could get a catnap in. But he'd advised Oleastro to sack out, leaving Orne on duty. His eyes felt gritty. He'd kill for a cup of coffee right about now. He settled for a shot of caffeine and winced as he felt the injector pinch his deltoid.

"Don, you've got to see this," Pompey said over the command channel.

A window appeared in Burkett's heads-up display from Pompey's point of view. The compass hash marks at the top of Pompey's heads-up indicated he was looking slightly southeast, from a cliff on Comino, facing toward Malta. A grav truck speeding across the water, a military CONEX box hanging off the back of the bed. Pompey zoomed in and two familiar line suits were crammed into the truck's cab designed for unarmored humans. The one in the passenger seat was waving furiously.

"Bill, is that who I think it is?" Burkett asked.

"If you think it's Dietz and Meyers, then, yes," Pompey replied. "Don't ask them where they got the grav truck."

Dietz and Meyers parked the truck and opened up the CONEX box, to display a variety of smaller containers. One of the containers visible displayed the logo, BRIDGE, FOUR PORT, POWER, PLASMA, ONE EACH, 40 KG WEIGHT.

"Unload it and get them distributed; two at each gun, three at Oleastro's dugout. Bill, lay two cables on different routes between each of the guns. Let's failure proof our power."

A trio of acknowledgements followed while Burkett opened a channel to Nguyen. "Nguyen, get over near Charity and build yourself a dugout. We're going to tie you into a power grid we're making to keep the guns up."

By the time Nguyen signaled his acknowledgement, Burkett was already moving, a bridge container in hand, on his way to Faith.

Halfway there, another air attack siren interrupted him. He looked around, but no shelter presented itself, so he carved one out of the soil of the island with his plasma cutter, making sure it was large enough for the bridge he was carrying, dropped in, and sat out the attack of six missiles coming in on a low trajectory. One missile was aimed short and hit the water east of the island without being engaged. With Hope aiding, Faith and Charity were able to down the remaining five.

Once he was at Faith, he carved a larger dugout in the earth. This time shaped like a W. There were three troops manning the gun. They all came out to see what he was up to.

"What's up sir?" One of them asked. Burkett's heads-up identified him as Corporal Essa.

"We're short on power for the guns. We're going to tie all of the suits with Tok rings into an improvised grid and we're going to protect the IMT head station until our troops cut the Suez. Any questions?" Three negative replies to his question made him feel the weight of command. "How're you men doing? Holding up? What's your fusebox state?"

Essa replied first, "Forty-four percent, sir."

Private Boyle answered next, "Thirty-one percent."

Finally, Private Varma replied, "Eighteen percent, sir."

"Eighteen? Okay, if you're that low, we need to take action." Burkett opened a channel to the company. "Attention men. Anybody whose fusebox is below forty percent, evacuate to Gozo. Wait on the head land closest to Comino for further orders. Anybody whose fusebox is below twenty percent integrity, shut down once you get there. The prevailing winds out of the west should clear any contamination from the bombardment. If not, go further inland until you get a green light on your environmental monitor and shut down there."

Having finished his general order to the company, he opened a channel to Dietz and Meyers. "Dietz, Meyers, get up to Faith. They're undermanned and I know your fuseboxes are both above forty percent."

"What about those two days off?" Meyers asked.

"Needs of the service. You'll get 'em just as soon as we're not in danger of letting the IMT station get destroyed."

"Yessir."

Burkett opened a friendly tracker and saw at least half of the company survivors headed west across the island. He was a little surprised, Aside from Keppler on Cominetto there were only 17 effectives left manning the island. The rest were a chain of blue dots moving west, dropping into the ocean, and proceeding to walk across the bottom of the channel to Gozo.

Brigade had better hurry up or there wasn't going to be anyone left to defend Comino.

Burkett busied himself by unpacking the bridge and tossing aside the crate. He severed the power cable running from Oleastro to Faith, and plugged either end into the bridge, then pulled his buddy cable out, and plugged himself in. He then took the bridge and sat on the edge of the trench he'd dug. He couldn't detect any draw on the cable, because Faith had already been charged up by Oleastro.

Soon enough, Pompey came on the bounce, followed by Dietz, Meyers and a gaggle of drones. A pair of drones were carrying a spool of cable between them, laying out a line. When they arrived, Pompey pulled out some slack cable, cut it off the spool. Then cut off a four-meter-long piece of cable.

"I get what you were going for, Lieutenant. Local power, that's you, plugged into the same bridge as Faith and a pigtail connecting bridge to bridge, where Oleastro and Nguyen are connected," Pompey said.

"Right. And Line and Scout suits can pull power out of the one port left on bridge one. Which wouldn't be a bad idea for all of you to do now. Use the last port on bridge two to connect Faith to Hope."

The air raid alarm sounded just then.

"Or we could all climb into the trench," Burkett said.

"Shit," Dietz said. "It's only been like thirty minutes."

"Thirty-three, by my clock," Burkett said.

The trench was crowded with Burkett, Pompey, Dietz, Meyers and a half dozen drones. Essa stayed on the gun mount for local control, in case the automatic system failed. Pompey busied himself making the power network. First, he connected Nguyen to bridge two, then plugged both bridges together. With Nguyen and Burkett tied in, he disconnected Oleastro from bridge one and plugged him into two.

With all three Tokamak ring powered suits tied together, and all of them able to supply to Faith and Charity there was no pause and the three guns were able to down ten missiles in this wave without a leaker. Although the last missile was downed a bare kilometer from the island.

Pompey opened a command channel to Burkett. "They're gonna roll our defense back, just like they did earlier."

"Yeah, I was hoping they were only sending harassing attacks because they couldn't send more. But it looks like they might have been stockpiling missiles to use in larger waves."

Burkett continued on a local channel as if he hadn't been speaking to Pompey. "Get that line laid in to Hope, and tie Hope into Charity, and then hunker down. Keep the drones out, burying the cables."

"Yessir," Pompey said, rendering a salute.

Burkett returned the salute and said, "Take care, Bill. Once the cable is laid, find a deep hole and take cover. It's make or break tonight."

Pompey turned and leapt out of the trench. A moment later the bitter end of the cable on the spool dropped down into the trench as the drones started laying it out, it twitched and jerked. Burkett grabbed the disconnected end and pulled a good length of it toward him, before producing a six-inch plasma thread and cutting it off.

"Dietz, Meyers, come over here, fill up your fuseboxes and one of you go relieve Essa on the gun. The other one might as well grab some shuteye. They'll probably send another wave soon," Burkett said, lying down and closing his eyes.

The air raid alert startled Burkett from his sleep. He'd dropped into it almost as soon as he closed his eyes. He couldn't remember dreaming and his eyes still felt gritty. He ordered his Tok rings to power up to 100%, even though there was no demand yet. There would be soon enough.

The air raid controller called out an attack of twelve missiles at low altitude. They were coming almost due east this time. The power network they'd built worked flawlessly again, although this time the last missile was destroyed only 800 meters from impact on Comino.

Pompey commed him right after the all-clear was given. "Ten missiles, last one was killed a kilometer out. Twelve missiles, 800 meters out. The math ain't working in our favor, boss."

"Nope. I'm open to suggestions, Bill."

"I've got nothing for you."

Switching to a local channel Burkett ordered, "Dietz, Meyers, Essa, rotate gunners on the mount. Grab some shuteye."

At 2200 hours they sent fourteen missiles at low altitude. At 2230 they sent sixteen, but at high altitude for some reason. Those were downed further out. At 2300 they sent eighteen missiles and the guns barely managed to stop them.

At 2330 they sent twenty, at high altitude. They travelled faster, but the guns could engage them further from Comino. Again, the guns just stopped them.

Burkett knew that the next attack, at high altitude or low, would get through. He ordered everyone off the island except for Nguyen, Oleastro, Orne, and the gun crews. Pompey refused to leave.

He opened a company-wide channel. "People, we are anticipating an attack at midnight, 0000 hours. If the Combine keeps to their pattern, it will be low altitude, with enough missiles to roll back our defenses. I do not believe we will hold. However, the missile attack will target our position on Comino. I have sent off everyone but a gunner for each laser mount, the three suits with Tokamak rings, and the XO, who refused to leave." Burket paused to smile at the rumble of laughter from the troops. "I just want you to know that I am proud of the job all of you have done over the past month. We've held on with little support and no supplies. Nobody could have done a finer job than you did. It has been the honor of a lifetime to be in command of a fine group of soldiers such as you. Burkett out."

He pulled up an overhead on the friendly tracker. He was surprised to see three dots instead of two at Faith's location. "Who is still at Faith?" he asked.

"Meyers here. I'm manning the gun."

"Dietz here."

"Dietz, damnit! Was I unclear on who was supposed to leave and who was supposed to stay?"

"Clear as crystal, sir. But I figured that with this cobbled together power grid, you'd need a power systems specialist if anything went wrong."

Burkett thought about tearing a strip off Dietz's backside, but the fact is, that he made a valid point. "Fine. Just stay in the bottom of that hole unless we lose power."

"That was precisely my plan, sir."

At one minute after midnight the air raid alert sounded in Burkett's helmet. The air defense controller's voice said, "Incoming Covey, twenty, low approach, bearing ninety-five. Weapons free."

"Charity firing."

"Fireball, next Quail, low approach, ninety-five."

"Hope firing."

"Debris field. Good shoot. Next Quail, low approach, ninety."

"Faith firing."

As the urgent hum died off, Burkett kicked his Tokamak ring five percent past its rated maximum, until the draw on the power bridge died off.

"Charity firing."

He'd missed the controller's call on the Quail's bearing and angle of approach. He had noticed that this time the Combine had stacked their missiles on almost the same approach vector. That meant that the debris field from the last destroyed missile obscured the approach of the missile behind it until it was in clear air. You could only hope that your opponent would fight dumb.

Round after round, each gun mount fired, but using destruction of their missiles as cover, allowed the Combine to get their missiles closer to Comino, faster than ever. Finally, Faith splashed a missile a bare hundred meters from the island.

The controller's word came all in a rush. "Low approach, ninety-five!"

Answered immediately by the gunner on Charity, "Charity firi..."

The bedrock of the island was rocked by a huge explosion.

Burkett's friendly tracker showed one of the two blue dots at Charity go red and then disappear. But Nguyen's blue dot was still there.

"Low approach, ninety-two!"

"Hope firing. Miss!"

Again, a huge explosion. A piece of the bedrock was torn loose from the wall of the trench and slammed into Burkett. He heard one of his femurs break with an oddly painless snap. At the same time, he saw Oleastro's dot go red and disappear. His power draw gauge pinned itself at 100%.

The pain arrived as he tried to issue an order to Nguyen. "He gritted his teeth and slammed his reactor control to war emergency, 115% of rated power. "Nguyen, Tok to 115."

"Is that safe?" came the quavering reply.

"Do it or we're dead!"

Again, he missed the controller's callout, and Hope's gunner's reply.

"Hope is gone. I say again, Hope is gone. Next Quail, low approach, ninety-one."

"Faith firing."

"Hit, detonation!"

All Hell broke loose over Burkett's head. Meyer's dot turned orange. Dietz's dot stayed blue. He noted that his was yellow, indicating injured, but still in the fight. Dirt and debris were swept into the trench. The power strain gauge dropped to zero. He fiddled with his reaction control, but didn't get any response. Somewhere the connection to the guns had been severed. He tried to stand, noticing that the external temperature was spiking around eighty-five degrees centigrade. His right leg failed and the pain arrived in full force.

He fell on his forearms and screamed through the pain. And then someone was there, helping him to his left foot. "Pain meds," he said through gritted teeth.

"I got ya, Lieutenant," Dietz said. And the grinding pain of his broken femur's ends clashing together mellowed into the distance.

"Oh yeah, that's the stuff," he said, suddenly nauseous as the pain ebbed.

He was able to max the oxygen in his life support and his head cleared after a few breaths. "Dietz, find the break. I'm disconnect and Nguyen's off the grid. We need the power to keep Faith in the fight."

"Fight? What fight? If the Combine's been observing us, they know we're out. Besides, Meyer's needs medical..."

Burkett had enough bullshit for one day. He hauled off and slugged Dietz in the hip from where he was seated on the ground. "God damnit, specialist. Get me connect to Faith and find out where the line to Nguyen is broken! We're not out of this fight until I say we're out!"

"Jesus wept, sir! At least let me get Nguyen here so he can take care of Meyers! Instead of chasing ass all over the island looking for a broken cable!"

Burkett was brought up short. Dietz was right. That made one Hell of a lot more sense. Why hadn't he tried to raise Nguyen?

"Nguyen, get your ass over to Faith. We have a casualty and we need your reactor here."

"On my way. Nothing I can do here anyway," Nguyen's tone of voice carried volumes of agony.

Burkett ached in sympathy, but the mission had to come first. "Dietz, a medic is on the way. Get a bridge connected to Faith and get me plugged in, and get a cable ready for Nguyen."

"Yessir."

Burkett dragged himself over to the gunner's seat of Faith. The lower gun shield had been wrecked. The cerametal severed, and the jagged edge had

243

hatcheted through the manual foot controls and Meyers' shins. The liner of Meyers' suit had sensed the damage and clamped down on his lower legs to tourniquet the injury.

From his place on the ground, Burkett fumbled with the latches holding Meyers' armor in the seat. Suddenly Nguyen and Dietz were there, helping Meyers out of the gunner's seat.

"Help me into the seat," he ordered. In short order, they had him seated and the latches fitted to his armor. Dietz reached around and plugged a power cable into the buddy port on his belly.

The air raid alert sounded just then.

"Incoming Covey two, high altitude, ninety-two. Weapons free. Track indicates impact on Gozo."

Gozo. Where the IMT head station was. Right next to where he'd sent the company evacuees. Some of which weren't in their suits.

"Nguyen, plug in and get Meyers into the trench. Push your reactor to 120% of rated power. We're going to need it without Oley in the grid.

"I shoulda stayed in bed," Nguyen complained.

Amazingly, the gunner's console was still intact. Burkett touched the automatic control to let the mount accept the feed from the O&D clusters still in operation on the company net, calculate a firing solution, and engage the target without his input. With the pain meds in his system making his vision swim, it was probably for the best.

A vivid light display illuminated the sky and Burkett raised both of his hands in triumph. Some part of his brain registered that they had gotten one kill. The display showed charging and the missile was diving. He rammed his Tok control to the maximum. Do or die.

The laser fired a single coherent beam joined by two punctuated streams of pulse laser fire from the south.

A mellow, electronic voice sounded in his ear and he could hear Dietz and Nguyen shouting something.

"Sending station, say again," he managed to slur.

"Two-Two AD company. This is Turtle 1-1 and 1-2 approaching from the south to relieve you. The west bank of the Suez has been secured. Zubia sends."

The latches held Burkett in the gunner's seat as consciousness faded.

⊱⊰

He woke in field hospital oblivious to how he'd gotten there.

Of the eight people on Comino during the final hours, only four came off alive. The dead included Oleastro and the gunners on Hope and Charity, Sergeants Burns and Amanchukwa. He'd known they had died. But he hadn't even noticed when his old friend Bill Pompey had died. And that guilt was going to stay with him for a long time.

Major Zubia commed him to congratulate him on holding until the stormers with their built-in air defense had been able to relieve them. The grav tanks had been dispatched once ground forces had secured the west bank of the Suez. Apparently, the Union offensive had disrupted the Combine badly. They were bombarding the IMT stations long after there was any benefit to it.

In fact, the whole Combine perimeter looked to be shrinking. The war was far from over, but it was a step in the right direction. Unfortunately,

245

Zubia had already given him his orders. He was to continue in command of the 22nd Air Defense as it fell back to rear area for reconsolidation.

He'd need to rebuild his NCO corps. Fortunately, he knew where there were a couple of specialists he could recruit and promote to positions of authority. Because misery loves company.

SHIELD OF MALTA

CHRIS FRENCH

RAF Luqa, Malta, 19 April 1945

"They're coming," Grant Susman said, looking north, toward Sicily. "Coming tomorrow."

Sidney Roche looked over, and down, at the short Israeli. "How d'you figure?"

Susman continued staring at the horizon. "Tomorrow will be the first decent day of weather we've had in a while. The Italians won't set keel out of harbor without air cover, no matter what their German masters tell them to do – and that means they need clear weather for the bombers and reconnaissance planes."

"Also leaves clear skies for you and yours," Roche said, casting a glance at Susman's <u>Corsair</u> parked on the Luqa tarmac nearby. The American fighter with the Star of David on its wings and fuselage dwarfed any fighters Britain used – as well as any used by Germany, or its servitors.

Susman nodded. "Sauce for the goose, and all that. The only question is: Whose goose is getting cooked?"

Roche chuckled. "Why are your lot always so cynical?"

Susman took his gaze off the horizon, and looked at Roche. "Look at our history – Murphy follows Jews like a cloud."

Roche nodded. "Point conceded. Still, you've been doing well for yourselves the past few years. You have your homeland, you have the tools and training to keep it, and now you're helping others to get out from Adolf's heel – including people who don't like your kind all that much." He kicked at the pavement. "It's that last one I have a hard time figuring out."

"Well, there's two ways to deal with folks who hate you," Susman said. "Hate them back – and we all know where that ends up. The alternative – respond with kindness, and maybe one day they'll get it through their heads 'there's better ways'."

"Don't hate people who want you dead?"

Susman shrugged. "Oh, we can hate the National Socialists – it's just how we manifest that hate which matters, in this life, and when we face The Big Boss. This –" and he gestured to the north, towards Germany and subjugated Europe "– is just business. Dear Old Uncle Adi wanted us gone; Churchill, for all he disliked our people, gave him an outlet... someplace to resettle us, so he could go after the 'living space' in the East. I'm pretty sure neither of them quite anticipated the results of that."

"Won't argue that," Roche said. "A Jewish Empire from Turkey to Egypt, from the eastern Med to the Persian Gulf."

"Not an Empire," Susman snapped. "Definitely not an Empire. That's not what we want. Hell, we wouldn't have taken most of that territory if the damned hardliner Muslims had left us alone. But they kept on running raids across the borders, and didn't think we might conceivably come and get them, and bring an ass-walloping with us."

Roche nodded again. "And between that, and the numbers of you fighting with the Americans in the Pacific War... well, I've heard the stories about Guadalcanal, Tarawa, the Java Sea, Indochina, and what's going on in China these days. Lot of real-world experience there."

Susman smiled. "You may not know this, but: I was at Java, and Indochina. I was supposed to go to China, but when the Three Declarations were released, I was sent here."

"You, and – what is it – three carrier battle groups?"

"That's the word – Leyte, Tarawa, and Java Sea, plus their groups. And since the Germans and theirs have been tarbabied in Russia for so long, they haven't been keeping up on naval affairs... such as how naval vessels are now floating anti-aircraft batteries which will massacre the kind of pre-war garbage the Italians are using. I'd feel pity for them, but they brought this on themselves."

"And now there's nothing left for it but the actual fight."

Susman nodded. "A fight we'd better win."

100 miles N of Malta, 20 April 1945

Sunlight sparkled off the waves of the Mediterranean Sea; the only clouds in the sky came from the detonation of Italian naval anti-aircraft gun shells.

Susman ignored the display outside, focusing on the hulking shape of the Roma-class battleship ahead of him. Boring in at full throttle, no higher than fifty feet above the water, he waited for the correct moment to release the 500-lb. bombs slung under his Corsair's wings. Traveling some 350 miles per hour, that moment came quickly. Susman squashed the bomb-release button, felt the bomb's weight come off the plane.

CLIMB!

Susman pulled the control stick back hard, pressing the bomb-release button once more. While the first bomb skipped across the water like a stone, the second arced toward the battleship's superstructure. Susman's plane shot the gap just above the ship's exhaust stacks, then whipped upwards like a homesick angel. In moments, Susman was a couple thousand feet above the battle. He rolled his plane, to see how the attack was progressing.

From appearances, it was going perfectly to plan. Black smoke boiled from multiple Italian ships; streamers of smoke, and stains on the water's surface, showed where Italian aircraft had met their ends at the hands of Israeli naval air power. Susman's own target was belching smoke and fire from stem to stern, and was leaving a trail of oil behind it.

Susman rolled his aircraft upright, then pushed the nose down, looking for a ship which hadn't yet been serviced. He sighted a destroyer on the far side of the Italian formation which didn't appear damaged. *Let us rectify that,* he thought, and aimed for the outlier.

Sweeping down, he aimed for the torpedo tubes visible amidships, then opened up with his six 0.50-calibre machine guns. The results were spectacular – a four-second burst, and the ship's midsection was engulfed in a fireball. Susman yanked the stick back, and arced towards his target's stern before clawing back the altitude he'd lost. He'd seen no Italian fighters thus far, but he was not about to take for granted that there weren't any around.

Another check downward showed wakes circling around and heading north, or terminating abruptly; a check of his fuel gauge told him there was enough to get back to Malta. Having no more bombs, and no targets suitable for machine guns, Susman turned his plane south.

Happy fucking Birthday, Adolf, he thought, and smiled.

RAF Luqa, Malta, 21 April 1945

"They won't be coming," Susman said. "Not soon... and likely not ever."

Roche looked over at him. "Reports are that good?"

"Recon flights over Taranto came back. One battleship, and that one of the old ones – neither <u>Roma</u> made it back. Most of their cruisers – gone. Same for destroyers. Some land-based fighters are coming up, but they're getting slaughtered. Expectations are: Landings on Sicily this week, then Sardinia and Corsica by middle of next month."

"Damn – that puts the whole west coast of Italy under threat. And who-knows how long it'll take for the Germans to get reliable troops unwedged from Russia and out here."

Susman smiled. "Not only that – word is: Britain's repudiated its agreements with Berlin, and American ships, aircraft, and troops are arriving on the islands as we speak. Apparently Dewey's preference to fight one war at a time only goes so far."

"Can't blame him," Roche said. "Question is: How close an ally will he be to your lot? Lend-Leasing or selling stuff is one thing; I don't think he expected your lot to use it, and the fight against Japan, to build a military from scratch."

"Oh, make no mistake: We had the experience already – we'd been fighting the Muslims in Palestine for decades. Churchill just gave us the opportunity to focus our people in one place at one time, and settle the issue once and for all. Japan attacking the USA made available the equipment, plus the live-fire-training opportunities, we needed to deal with Adolf and his ilk."

"And you're making the most of it."

Susman nodded. "It's what we do. Never get in the way of a Jewish man who has a destination, a timeframe, and the right equipment."

Roche looked northeastward, towards Italy. "So, in maybe a couple months, the Star Of David will fly over Jerusalem, Istanbul, Mecca, and The Vatican. That's going to cause some coronaries out there."

Susman snorted. "You think so?" he said derisively.

"I know so. The question is: What will people say when it comes to pass – when almost all the major religious centers of Europe are being protected by Jews?"Susman shrugged." If they're smart, they'll say 'Thank you'. But I won't hold my breath."

"Then why bother helping them at all?"

Susman gestured expansively at the buildings of Luqa in the distance. "Over the thousands of years my people have been around, we've seen too many of our own buildings destroyed, our people killed merely for existing, to wish it upon anyone else – even those who hate us. That's why we're going for Berlin – remove the cancer of Adolf and his ilk surgically; then let people look around, and see who the actual threat is."

"You people never cease to surprise me," Roche said.

Susman looked up at him. "And that's why we're still around, despite some people's best efforts."

THE SIEGE

By Brennen Hankins

"Nothing is so well known as the Siege of Malta."

-Voltaire

May 1565

The Ottomans came in from the south.

We had known they were coming for weeks. Jean Parisot de Vallette, Grand Master of the Order of the Knights of Malta, had ordered the harvesting of crops, regardless if they were ripe or not, and the plowing and destruction of the fields afterward. "To deny the invaders resources," they had said. Our wells had been poisoned, too, and the only fresh water to be found on my villa were the tears pouring down Marguerite's face as our olive trees burned.

I'd had to leave her and my young sons behind. The Knights had needed men to help defend the island, and I found myself among a contingent of Knights, galley slaves, and soldiers drafted from the local population, many of whom I recognized from the village, atop the walls of Fort Saint Elmo. I

253

tried not to focus on the ominous glow of the fires reflecting bright in the southern sky above Marsaxlokk.

I had just finished loading our crew's cannon with chain shot when I heard the roar of the approaching Turkish army. My friend Vincente kneeled down with his ramrod and nodded towards the sound.

"It begins, Giancarlo," he said.

❯❯❯❯❯❯ ❮❮❮❮❮

June 1940

"What's beginning?" Mary asked as I ushered her and the kids into the cellar beneath our villa.

"An air raid," I said as the drone of planes echoed in the distance. "Maybe German, probably Italian. I've no idea. Hurry."

Explosions rocked the far northwest, towards Valleta. Clouds of smoke billowed over the horizon. Mary gasped and clutched the bib of her apron. One of the boys, Joseph, started crying. My other son, Theodore, shushed his younger brother and helped lower him down through the cellar doors.

We'd been hearing the rumors for weeks. War had broken out on The Continent, and being a colony of the British Crown, only fifty miles from Sicily and directly in between Italy and its holdings in Africa, it was only a matter of time before Herr Hitler's *qahba f'xalata* in the Italian Prime Minister's office would move to invade.

"There's wine, cheese and fitira down there, along with some dried fish, potatoes, jarred olives and bottles of oil. It should last you awhile," I told

254

Mary, passing her a couple of kerosene lanterns after she cleared the ladder. "Get to the far wall and stay as close to it as possible. "If the house gets hit, it's less likely you'll get buried in the rubble. Keep the kids close, and the cellar door shut."

"What are you going to do?" Mary asked.

"Don't worry about me," I said. I had to raise my voice a bit to be heard over the sound of the the approaching airplane engines. I gave Mary a kiss on the forehead, then closed one of the cellar doors. "I'll be back in no time!"

What was I going to do? What else could I do? Thirteen generations of my family had lived in this villa, maintaining and cultivating a living from the ancient olive groves growing on it. I bolted for the toolshed and grabbed my father's old service rifle.

Father didn't like talking about the War, and I'm pretty sure the Enfield Pattern 1914, Mark 1* (W) (F) was one of the only souvenirs he brought home with him. It served him well, firing across No Man's Land from the trenches in the Second Battle of Ypres, and was probably the impetus for the 1915 Star, British War Medal, and Victory Medal I found in his old steamer trunk after he passed away—the other souvenirs from the War.

I found a couple boxes of .303 shells in a workbench drawer. I stuffed one in my coat pocket, then made an all-out sprint to the to the ancient Bidni grove my family had tended for generations.

What was I going to do? I love my wife, but the Zammits who bore and reared her did me no favors by failing to install a sense of familial pride into her or the rest of their children, much less pride for her "olive picking" husband. Sure, olives ran deep in my family's blood, but so did defending our home, beginning with my ancestor, Giancarlo Camilleri, who fought alongside the Knights of Malta during the Great Siege of 1565. We had survived the Ottomans, the French, annexation under the British, and I'd be Zamned if I was going to be scared away from the land of my forefathers by some *demel Taljan iffurmat li terda' l-vit ta' Hitler.*

I climbed into a tree on the northernmost row of the grove, laying down on a branch that pointed towards the stone wall marking the edge of the property. The branch had a fork just far enough away that allowed me to comfortably rest the barrel of the Enfield in and still be able to shoulder it. I peered through the iron sights, lining the front sight post up on a propeller aircraft that had just appeared over the horizon.

What was I going to do?

I took in a breath and let it out, getting the feel for the respiratory pause my father taught me to learn as a boy, and chambered a round, keeping the front sight on the advancing Italian plane.

What was I going to do?

I took in another breath, let it out, and laid my finger upon the trigger.

"F'għoxx mara omm tiegħek u l-isperma li hi xorb, inti kaboċċa mingħajr bajd,"

December 2010

"WHAT DID YOU JUST SAY, YOUNG LADY?!"

I'm pretty sure I made steam come out of my father's ears upon hearing what I had to say to the high school principal. Turns out Dad may have been paying a little bit better attention to Great Grandpa's lessons than Grandpa Teddy had led me to believe.

Oops.

Principal Curtis looked confused. Probably because he didn't speak Maltese. Or maybe because he was just an idiot. Probably both. "Um, is there a problem, Mr. Camilleri?"

My father turned to look at the principal, then pinched the bridge of his nose in frustration, pushing his glasses slightly askew as he sat back down. "Don't worry about it. You were saying, Mr. Curtis?" Mr. Curtis leaned back in his chair, speaking in that annoying, slow drawl typical of Southerners and country bumpkins alike. I wasn't really sure which group Mr. Curtis belonged to.

Then again, it's not like it mattered—in my experience, those two groups tended to overlap.

"Uh, as I was saying, Mr. Camilleri, we take fighting on school campus very seriously."

"The *toqbi* deserved it," I muttered.

"That's enough out of you, Kristine," Dad said sharply, before turning to look at the principal again. "How much trouble is she in?"

"We're looking at a minimum of two days suspension," Mr. Curtis drawled. "As far as the school district is concerned, we're not going to refer this to the law, but if this becomes a habit, I'll have no choice but to report your daughter's actions to the Phillips County Sheriff's Department." He leaned forward. "I'd like to avoid that, if at all possible."

He very carefully did not say, *Because if I did, I'd have to expel your daughter from the only high school within twenty miles of your house.*

My dad sighed. "I'll handle it, Mr. Curtis. Anything you need from me?"

257

"Just a signature on the disciplinary paperwork stating that we've notified you of Kristine's suspension and the duration thereof."

Dad took the proffered clipboard, signed it, and passed it back to Mr. Curtis. "Apologies again. C'mon, Kristine," he said as he stood up and walked out of the office.

⇛⇛ ⇚⇚

"First off, I don't *ever* want to hear you use that kind of language towards an adult again," Dad said, voice raised. "That is not language becoming of a lady, period. Who taught you how to say that, anyway?"

"Great Grandpa did," I said, watching out the window of Dad's truck as the city limits of Malta faded away and the landscape turned into desolate grassland again. "I heard him mutter it at the nursing home when the orderly told him he couldn't have coffee anymore. I asked him what it meant, and he told me. And by the way, the only way *you* could've understood what I said is if you knew what it meant, too, so don't go acting all high and mighty."

"You're about to find out how high and mighty I can get, missy," Dad said sourly. "Second, you're grounded. No phone, no computer, no TV, and you're staying home with Grandpa when we go Christmas shopping in Billings tomorrow."

"But Dad!"

"No buts, Kristine. You are 17 years old. It's about time you started acting like it, and either you will, or you're going to learn to."

"But I didn't even start the fight!" I protested. "Shaelyn Neufeld—"

"I don't care *what* Shaelyn Neufeld did or said," Dad said, cutting me off. "Breaking a yard stick over her head is *not* how civilized adults handle things." I looked at my dad pleadingly, "God Zammit, Dad—"

My father eyed me. "Civilized people also do not take The Lord's name, *or* the name of their great-grandmother's family, in vain." He turned back to watch the road. "Perhaps you can think about that while you stay home doing chores all weekend."

⟫⟫⟶ ⟵⟪⟪

I watched out my bedroom window as Mom's Suburban pulled out of the driveway, annoyed at being stranded in this desolate hellhole with nothing to do for the next few days.

Unlike a lot of the other locals, we were considered to be fairly recent transplants to the area, if you consider 30 years to be "recent". Grandpa Teddy had said our family had come from "the old Malta", a little dinky island in the Mediterranean. He said our family had lived there for centuries. Ottomans, Frenchmen, and Axis douchebags were not enough to displace our family, but encroaching development and rising costs of land ownership were a different story. Faced with the prospect of either shutting down the farm or taking advantage of a ridiculously hot real estate market, Grandpa Teddy decided to sell the olive groves and "move to where it's not so damn crowded".

He couldn't have picked a "not so damn crowded" place if he tried. The way Dad tells it, Grandpa was looking up places to live and stumbled upon the story of a dinky little town in Montana's Hi-Line country with the same name as the family home. When the Great Northern Railroad was built, several towns sprouted up along the route, on land the railroad owned. Railroad officials had apparently given up on coming up with original names for towns and ended up just spinning a globe and naming them after whatever country or city their finger landed on. Despite not being an environment suitable to growing olives, Grandpa fell in love, and in 1980, he bought some ranchland bordering the Milk River north of town, and the rest is history.

Given Grandpa's taste in movies, I think that Sergio Leone's spaghetti westerns might have had something to do with that decision.

Great Grandpa was not happy about the move. He only ended up agreeing to emigrate with Grandpa Teddy after his health started failing. He passed away a few years ago, right before I started sophomore year.

I guess it's not too bad. The house sits pretty close to a bend in the river, below a small hill that hides the desolate prairie beyond, and there's trees and bushes around the immediate area—which is more than I can say for the rest of the property. It'd just be nice if there was just something to *do*.

Other than mess with cows and farm equipment, that is.

Mom's Suburban disappeared over the hill, and with it, any hope of anything fun or exciting happening for me this weekend. I sighed, and went to change into my work clothes. It'd been cold, down in the negatives, the news had called a winter storm warning for this evening, and Grandpa was going to want to get the cattle their evening hay before the sun went down.

After that was done, the best I could hope for was Grandpa Teddy watching TV until he fell asleep. If he conked out during Wheel of Fortune again, I might be able to snake the remote off his chair.

I was sitting on the couch, about to fall asleep, when the episode of *Justified* I'd been watching was rudely interrupted by the power going out. The only light left in the house was emanating from the old fireplace on the other side of the living room.

My shoulders sagged in the darkness. "God Zammit," I muttered, repeating Great Grandpa's favorite curse, and stumbled around to the closet with the breaker panel in it, tripping over furniture and cursing every step of the way. I opened the panel up, but none of the breakers were tripped. Zammit again.

Power outages aren't uncommon when the wind picks up, but being on the end of the line, we're usually some of the last people to get it restored. On average, it can be hours or even days before the utility company gets our electricity back on—another reason to hate this place. I swear to God, once I graduate next spring, I'm going to college in Billings, Bozeman or Missoula. One of those bigger cities.

With as cold as it gets here, having no power can be dangerous—but fortunately, Dad and Grandpa keep prepared. I grabbed a battery-powered lantern off the shelf in the closet, turned it on, and woke up Grandpa.

It took him a minute, but he eventually stirred. "Whuzzat? Kristine?"

"Power's out, Grandpa," I said.

He let out a groan. "Zammit. Alright, I'll get the generator hooked up. Mind getting the fire built up again?"

"Yeah, I got it." I passed him the lantern. "Let me know if you need help."

After stoking the fire, adding a few more pieces of wood, and setting another small stack in the rack next to the hearth for later, I walked around to the kitchen window to see how Grandpa was doing. He had wheeled the portable generator out of the tool shed and was standing in ankle deep snow near the electrical meter, getting ready to hook it into the plug under the transfer switch that lets use switch between generator and commercial power, when I saw something appear in the blowing snow behind him. I didn't have time to even shout a warning before Grandpa Teddy got tagged in the back of the head with a wooden baseball bat.

Grandpa let out a cry, and dropped like a stone.

Standing over him were two bigger men. In the glow of the lantern Grandpa dropped, I could see they were bundled up in dark snow bibs, balaclavas and sherpa hats, and flannel jackets. One of them holding the Louisville Slugger I saw Grandpa get hit with.

"What the hell, Todd?" I heard the one with the bat shout, over the sound of the howling wind. "I thought you said nobody was here?!"

"I heard Mr. Camilleri saying he and the family were gonna be in Billings for the weekend!" Todd shouted in reply. "How was I supposed to know they were going to leave someone behind?!"

"Jesus Christ, dude," the bat swinger said. "Help me drag him into that tool shed so he doesn't freeze to death. With any luck, by the time he's found, they'll think he fell on accident."

Oh, Zammit.

I ducked down low, out of sight of the windows, and immediately made for the kitchen phone. I picked up the receiver, dialed 911, and put it to my ear.

Nothing. Not even a dial tone. Whatever took out the power must've taken out a phone line with it. And of course, Dad took my phone with him to Billings, to ensure I didn't use it while grounded.

God Zammit.

This was bad. This was very bad. The power and phone lines were out, the weather's rapidly turning worse, we're twenty miles outside of town, Grandpa's out cold, maybe even dead, and the two guys who hurt him were running loose on the property, presumably to rob us blind. Or do something worse.

And no one was coming to help us.

June 1565

No one was coming to help us.

Oh, the Knights in charge had sent missive after missive stating that we were badly outnumbered and in grave danger of losing Fort St. Elmo, but the Grand Master, apparently not understanding how dire the situation was, demanded that we must hold until Spanish reinforcements arrived from the mainland.

It was not made clear when exactly those reinforcements would make it, but, as it had been nearly a month of constant fighting, day and night, it seemed that even tomorrow would be too late.

The outer walls had been breached and invaded by the Ottoman's Janissaries. Knights, galley slaves, and my fellow conscripts fought like mad to stop their progress, and died for their trouble. My dear friend Vincente, who I had known since we were boys, had died after getting shot with an arquebus, after breaking his cannon ramrod over the head of a Turkish soldier charging up the battlements. I feared that I would soon shortly join him.

What keeps a man fighting, even when he knows victory is all but impossible?

My cannon now useless, I hastily picked up a sword from a fallen Knight and readied myself behind the barricaded door separating the enemy from myself and access to the rest of the fort.

My mind went to Marguerite. I had sent her missives early in the battle, to let her know I was doing fine and that I looked forward to returning to her and our sons. The last one I was able to send out of the fort was two weeks ago. It seemed unlikely I would get to send another.

Thud.

My only hope of making good on my promise was to win, or die trying.

Thud.

Another Knight ran to stand next to me, shield readied in front of the two of us.

Thud!

He looked at me and, seeing I was shieldless, said, "Try to stay behind me. Strike at anything that moves beyond my shield."

THUD.

I nodded, and steeled myself.

There was a mighty crash, and the door, alongside all hell, broke loose.

August 1940

"Bloody hell!" Sergeant Grant yelled as hell rained down around us.

It had been two months since the Italian air raids started. The initial attack had caught the Royal Air Force with their collective *qliezet ta' taht* down, and while a handful of decrepit Gloster Sea Gladiators managed to mount a hasty counter force against them in the days after, that first day, only one plane, a reconnaissance aircraft, had been shot down.

Courtesy of yours truly.

I technically didn't *shoot* him down. The only reason I was credited with the kill is the fact that the unfortunate MC.200 I had fired at had banked around to circle low over my olive trees and see what exactly was shooting at them, and the attempt to make such a tight, sharp turn in such a poorly designed plane sent the pilot into a tailspin, where the *stupratur tal-mogħoż* was sent straight to hell after crashing on my neighbor's property. There was a bullet hole found in a surviving chunk of the fuselage, which the authorities matched to my Enfield, and the rumor that some farmer shot down a modern Italian plane from an olive grove, with an obsolete bolt-action rifle, was hilarious.

And so, the "Legend of Old Grover" was born.

I did not choose the name. I personally think it's ridiculous. However, it gives the Royal Air Force lads a laugh, and considering we've been getting bombed for two months straight, any source of morale that can be found is worth its weight in gold.

The RAF did not have a permanent base here prior to the arrival of the *Regia Aeronautica*. The one at Luqa was almost complete, yet, that base, along with the two civilian airports at Ta Qali and Hal Far, were bombed into gravel, along with Valletta and a few of the bigger cities on the island. The Italians had hoped that bombing the civilians into submission would cause us Maltese to surrender and let them take over the island.

All they managed to do was piss us off instead. We swept the rubble off of Kingsway, buried our dead, and dug in *hard*.

Which is why I was currently running a bulldozer at the Luqa site. The RAF had deemed the completion of the airbase to be the number one priority for defending the island. In turn, the island was deemed to be of strategic importance for dominance of the Mediterranean, and the North African Front. Thus, Luqa became very, very important to the British Crown.

In the interest of keeping Mussolini's *ċapep ta' ħmieġ* off our island, a large portion of the local population, myself included, chipped in to help.

It was annoying to have to run for shelter every couple of hours, only to rebuild sections of damaged runway *we had just built*, but the RAF, and Sergeant Grant in particular, was pleasant to work with.

"How many does this make for today? A dozen passes alone?" I asked.

"Try thirteen," Corporal Cook muttered.

Sergeant Grant groaned, then yelped as another bomb landing on the runway sprayed asphalt and rocks all the way into the drainage ditch we were sheltering in. "Jesus, Grover, can't you shoot that guy down, too?"

"I'd love to," I said, then looked around. "Oh wait, I don't have a gun in my toolbox. Zammit!"

"Who do you hate more, the Italians, or you in-laws?" Cook asked.

"As terrible as the Italians are, they don't invade my house and ruin Christmas dinner every year." Another bomb landed nearby. More flying gravel and asphalt. "Though, at this rate, they may leave me without a house to invade."

At the far end of the unfinished runway, an Italian plane, covered in flames, hit the ground and created the biggest explosion I've seen to date. Unfortunately, our air support shot down our assailant just close enough to be counterproductive, even though the bombing had seemed to stop.

"Aw, bugger," Grant moaned. "Not more crater repair!"

"I bet the fill-in would go faster if we just left the remains of the plane in the hole and put some choke ballast around it," I suggested.

"That's not a terrible idea, Grover," Cook suggested.

Sergeant Grant waved a hand. "Do what you got to do. I need to survey the rest of the damage. Just be quick about it."

⇛⇛⇁ ⇇⇇⇇

We'd taken a quick lunch break while the paving crews were mixing asphalt for the top layer of the runway. I was sitting in the shade of my bulldozer, eating a sandwich Mary had made. Sergeant Grant had cracked open a tin of bully beef and hardtack, and sat down next to me.

"Airfield's coming along," he said, taking a bite from his improvised sandwich. "If we can keep the *Regia Aeronautica* from dispensing their arsenal upon it, we should have planes moving in a few weeks, and a fully operational permanent base set up by December."

"Mmmm." I kept my attention on my sandwich.

Grant watched me. "What will you do, Gian, once construction of Luqa is complete?"

"Go home," I said, taking another bite, "Try to keep those greasy Sicilian rats from bombing my olive groves. Defend my home to the best of my ability."

"You're going to do that all with a Pattern 1914, then?

I shrugged. "It's all I got."

Grant nodded. We briefly turned our attention back to our food for a few minutes, and then he broke the silence again. "What if you had something more to fight with?"

My eyebrows went up. "Is the Royal Air Force going to supply me with arms, Peter?"

He looked at me intently. "If you don a uniform, they will. Flight program's accepting any and all volunteers. And we need all the help we can get." He waved a hand towards the remnants of the crater we had filled to emphasize the point.

I snorted. "Peter, I have never been in a plane in my life."

"You hadn't sat in the captain's chair of a bulldozer, either, yet two months later, you're our lead civilian operator. You learn quick, Gian, and have a knack for operating machinery. I can't think of a better candidate to join."

"Where would I be flying? Italy? Germany?"

"Here," Grant said. "RAF's forming several permanent squadrons down at Hal Far. You'd be in one of them. If I put in a good word with Lieutenant Van Stry, you'd be here flying, and not in no crummy Gloster, either. You'd be in one of the newer Hawker Hurricanes."

I finished the remnants of my sandwich and dusted off my hands. "You make a tempting offer."

"Offer nothing," Grant snorted, over a mouthful of corned beef. "This little island is the lynchpin that allows the Allies to have a fighting chance in North Africa and the Mediterranean. As long as we control both of those areas, the Italians will forever be on the defensive." He set his rations aside. "Conversely, if *they* control Northern Africa, that gives their naval forces free reign to move ships to the Northern Atlantic. That gives them multiple options for moving troops, weapons and goods to Germany, as well as attacking the Home Islands. To win in North Africa is to win the war, and to win in North Africa, we need to win in Malta." Grant looked at me intently. "I'm not offering. I'm *begging*. Consider it, at the very least. It would do the boys a lot of good knowing that Old Grover is providing aerial cover."

I chuckled. Sergeant Grant made a compelling argument. And getting paid to defend my ancestral home, with weapons far superior to anything I could acquire on my own, was a big, big plus.

I contemplated it, though not for long.

I just had to do one thing before making my decision.

"I'll talk to the lieutenant about it. But first, let me make a phone call."

December, 2010

"C'mon, God Zammit, let me make a phone call," I hissed at the receiver.

This was getting me nowhere. I was holding out hope that maybe, by some miracle, the lines would come back up and I could call the police, but the lack of a dial tone coming from the phone told me that this was a pipe dream at best, and a forlorn hope at worst.

I had ran upstairs to my parent's bedroom, in part because they had a landline in there. It was also at the back corner of the house, furthest away from the stairs and the front door. To come up here from where I last saw them, the burglars would have to walk from the back door, through the kitchen to the front of the house, walk up the stairs, and then back to my parent's bedroom door. It also meant that I could keep an eye on them while they were outside, so I'd be able to see if they were coming back to the house. I carefully snuck a look through a small gap in the curtains to check.

Sure enough, they had picked up the lantern I gave Grandpa and were coming back this way from the tool shed.

Zammit.

Dad's closet door was slightly open. Taking a hint from God, I moved inside of it and shut the door, just as I heard the kitchen door slam shut downstairs. Voices, too muffled for me to make out, rose up from the floorboards underneath my feet. I tried to put my ear to the ground and listen, but my shoulder bumped something leaning against the closet wall, and fell with a dull *thump* to the ground.

The voices stopped. I barely was able to make out the words, "What was that?" below.

Double Zammit.

I heard footsteps downstairs—benefits of living in a creaky old farm-house—and in a moment of sheer panic, realized they were heading for the staircase by the front door.

My hand found the object I'd knocked over, and, recognizing the grip of the pump action I was touching, scrambled to pick it up. I think this was Dad's shotgun, a Remington 870 Wingmaster he won in a fundraising raffle a few years back. He'd let me use it, the few times he'd taken me duck hunting.

It dawned on me that if I was gonna make it out of here and save Grandpa Teddy, I was going to have to do it with violence. Fear was replaced by an oddly calm focus on what I had to do. It felt....surreal.

Great Grandpa used to tell stories about our family's ancestors, some going all the way back to the Crusades. He once told me about an ancestor of ours, one who he himself was named after, who fought and died at Fort St. Elmo during the Great Siege of Malta. Another ancestor fought alongside the British to drive invading French forces off the island, shortly before Malta became a British protectorate. And finally, Great Grandpa himself flew with the Royal Air Force, driving off the Italians and Nazis in World War II.

My family had a *long* history of defending Malta against invaders.

Now, it was my turn.

I very carefully opened the pump action a bit to check if the shotgun was loaded. I couldn't see anything, but I stuck a finger inside and felt a shell casing seating in the firing chamber, which told me what I needed to know. Just as cautiously as I had opened it, I moved the slide forward, closing the pump action with a barely audible *click*.

The footsteps drew closer.

"I think the sound came from in here, man."

My parent's bedroom door opened.

I disengaged the safety and shouldered the shotgun.

"You sure it wasn't just a cat or something?"

"I dunno, man, that was a pretty loud noise. I don't see nothing that looks like it fell."

I drew in a breath, and let it out slow.

"Nobody else is here, man. Let's just go back downstairs, get the loot and be done with it."

"Alright," said one of the voices, right before I heard a hand jostle the knob on the other side of the closet door. "I'm just gonna check in here and be done with it."

Here we go.

The door opened, and the bat swinger raised the lantern to reveal the 12 gauge being pointed right in his face.

"F'għoxx mara omm tiegħek u l-isperma li hi xorb, inti kaboċċa mingħajr bajd," I said as I squeezed the trigger.

June 1565

I found myself bound, kneeling on the floor of the courtyard, under armed guard.

The Turks were not in the least bit happy. Oh, they had won the battle and captured Fort St. Elmo, but it cost them nearly 6,000 men to do it.

Rumor had it that this total included about half their Janissaries—the most elite soldiers the Ottomans had to offer.

Of course, the survivors planned to vent their frustration over this fact by brutally executing all of us in retaliation, but it brought me a small surge of comfort, knowing that we'd dragged a large portion of their army with them. Perhaps our sacrifice here would enable the rest of the Knights to rally and repel the invaders.

I wouldn't live to see it, but the thought was nice.

The commander of the enemy's assault had let nine Knights that the Corsairs had captured go, to send a message to de Valette that the rest of the Knights of Malta were next.

The rest of us were lined up in groups of ten, and, group by group, were being put to death.

A contingent of Ottoman soldiers dragged my lot to our feet and lined us against the courtyard wall.

"Have any of you final words?' the Ottoman commander bellowed.

I thought of Marguerite, and my sons. I tried to think of something to say to them, to tell them I had not died in vain. Then I realized the Ottomans would never deliver my final words to my wife, and to be honest, I didn't want any filthy Turks to be around my family anyway.

But I did want to say something. I was going to die anyway, might as well die proudly.

"Malta is my home," I said, with no ounce of fear or trepidation in my voice. "I am proud to have lived it, to have fought for it, and to have died for it."

The Ottomans readied their swords. I felt a smile creep across my face.

"And with any luck, the lot of you will soon be joining me."

December 1942

I exited the plane landing at Luqa to the sound of fanfare. A few weeks ago, I had been in Egypt, fighting a combined force of Germans and Italians that were moving through Northern Africa. Losses among the British Army had been heavy, but we paid Rommel's *Afrikakorps* back dearly for it, in what was being called The Second Battle of El Alamein. It was there that we'd set Rommel's forces running, and with any luck, they'd run them right into the bottom of the Mediterranean.

Serves those *stupraturi tal-moghoż* right.

My squadron had been sent to assist with air support, and several of us—myself included—had become aces in just the span of a few weeks. The RAF ended up losing roughly the same amount of planes as the Axis fighters did, but that's mostly because they focused upon fighting us while ignoring the pleas for ground support from their infantry and armoured divisions. This proved to be a poor decision, because any time spent not having to avoid a dogfight with an enemy plane was spent tearing the *Afrikakorps'* ground forces to mincemeat. It was the first major successful campaign the Royal Air Force units at Malta had taken against the forces that had been bombarding us for nearly two years straight.

Hence, the fanfare upon being returned to home station.

I was eager to get back home to Mary and the kids, but I wouldn't get there right away. There was some minor inprocessing work to be done, maintenance for my Hurricane to be attended to, and then I could step away and see my wife again. Despite the delay, I was in high spirits.

"Flight Lieutenant! Flight Lieutenant!" called a voice over the cacophony. A man ran up from the crowd, a press badge identifying him a War Correspondent for the *London Gazette*, pencil and notepad at the ready. This guy had apparently been trying to get comments from all of the returning pilots. "Have you any thoughts on the success at El Alamein?"

I thought for a moment. The crowd fell silent as I contemplated my answer.

"Malta is my home," I said, the only other sound on the parking apron coming from the flashbulbs of cameras going off. "I am proud to have lived on it, to have fought and defended it, and, finally, to pay back the beggars who would dare to attack it." A cheer came up at that, and I grinned. "And with any luck, they'll have learned their lesson."

There was a mass of cheering and applause, and I took advantage of the joyous chaos to sneak away as the maintenance crews gathered around the plane to do their work.

I dropped off my flight gear at the hangar, changed into clean clothes, and made a beeline for the door.

You know what? On second thought, inprocessing could wait.

December 2010

I sat in the waiting area of the Phillips County Hospital's emergency room with a blanket around my shoulders, a warm cup of hot cider in my hands, waiting for the doctors to get Grandpa Teddy ready to be life-flighted.

Getting him to the ER had been difficult. After.....*handling*—I couldn't bring myself to admit to shooting—the bat swinger and scaring his idiot buddy Todd off, I ran downstairs, found the keys for Dad's truck, and found Grandpa Teddy where he'd been dragged into the tool shed. He was unconscious and severely cold, but breathing. I wrapped him in a blanket, dragged him up into the front seat, got the heater going, and drove the twenty miles into town as fast as the snowdrifts piled across Milk River Road and U.S. 191 would allow.

Despite how bad it looked, the doctors said Grandpa Teddy might pull through. He had head trauma, a mild case of hypothermia, and he might have broken his wrist when he fell to the ground and landed on it funny, but he was probably going to be okay, if they could get him to wake up. They were sending him down to Billings to see a head trauma specialist, just in case.

The Phillips County Sheriff's Department had been called in after I explained what had happened to the hospital staff. That led to the sheriff, a couple deputies, and an ambulance making their way out to our house, with a Department of Transportation snowplow dispatched to clear the way ahead of them. There, they found baseball bat guy dead and the one named Todd unconscious and bleeding severely, but still alive.

Dad was going to be *pissed* about the bloodstains on his carpet.

Heh. That's funny. I just killed a man, almost killed another, my grandpa was fighting for his life, Dad's shotgun got taken into evidence, I'm still suspended from school and am probably going to jail as soon as the sheriff gets back, and I'm worried about *stains on a carpet.*

276

I couldn't help it. I let out a giggle, and, like cracks appearing in a dam, the cool, calm focus and numbness that was holding me together broke apart, and I went from calm to laughing, to sobbing, quick as a switch.

The deputy who had been assigned to keep an eye on me stepped over to catch my mug of cider before I dropped it, and set it aside. He took a seat on the bench next to me, and I leaned onto him for support.

"You okay?" he asked in a slow, country drawl.

It took me a good minute, but I managed to compose myself enough to say in between sobs, "I did it. I killed him. He broke into my house, and I killed him."

"Easy, there," he said, gently. "Breathe. It's gonna be alright. Just breathe."

A couple of deep breaths later, I finally regained my composure enough to sit up straight. I looked over at the deputy. He was a shorter, stockier man, kind of like Grandpa, with black hair carefully cut in the style that Marines often do. His name tag read "J. LaForce".

He passed me my cider. "Doing better, miss?"

"I, uh, I think so," I said. "I'm sorry, I don't know what—"

He held up a placating hand. "Don't worry about it at all, miss. You've been through a highly traumatic event. You were probably all cool and calm just a minute ago, weren't you?"

I nodded lamely. "Yeah."

"What you're experiencing is the 'comedown'." He stood up, walked to the hot water dispenser right by me, and made himself a cider of his own. "You see, there are two kinds of people in this world, separated by how they react to a stressful event. Some react by locking up in sheer panic. I see it all the time. Little kids, or wives, working around their husband when he's using farm equipment, and he gets into an accident. The tractor rolls, or he gets his hand caught in a thresher. They freeze up, even if they know the right thing to do is shut off the equipment and call 911. You have to snap them out of it before they can actually do something." He sat back down next to me. "You, you're the other kind. You get that adrenaline rush and it shuts down the emotional part of your brain, and kicks the logical part into high gear. It allows you to function in a time of crisis and do what you need to do to get through it. Once the event's over though—" he made a POP! sound, and opened his hands towards me, mimicking an explosion—"....all those emotions just hit you at once, and suddenly you're either bawling your eyes out or laughing so hard you can't breathe. It'll subside, and then come back and hit you at the most random, non-sensical times. And there's not much you can do about it."

"Speaking from experience?" I asked.

Deputy LaForce took a sip from his mug of cider. "Yes, fortunately. There was once a time I would have thought the experience *un*-fortunate, until it finally sank in that I wouldn't have been alive to complain otherwise. So, I embrace it, and deal with it the best way that I can."

"Which is?"

"Rationalizing. Explaining my actions in a way that make sense. And then going out and living my best life, to show the Good Lord my appreciation for giving me the strength to get through what I got through. Your way of coping might be different than mine, Miss Camilleri, but if it is, you'll find it. It just takes time."

He hesitated for a second, like he was stopping himself from saying something, before continuing. "You know, it's really not my place to say, but those two men who came into your home tonight have been suspected of many burglaries throughout Malta and the rest of the county. Have rap sheets longer than the menu at the Hitchin' Post Café. And you not only saved yourself, you saved your grandfather, and they're not going to be harming or stealing from anyone else, because you kept it together and took action. That don't count as nothing."

We sat in silence for a bit, sipping on our hot ciders, and I took the opportunity to contemplate what he said.

"Malta is my home," I said, quietly.

"What's that?" Deputy LaForce asked.

"Malta is my home," I repeated, loud enough that he could hear this time. "And I defended it."

"That you did, Miss Camilleri." He clinked his mug against mine, and finished it off.

I smiled.

Defending Malta against invaders *was* a family tradition, after all.

Manufactured by Amazon.ca
Acheson, AB